THE ECONOMICS OF

RECESSION AND REVIVAL

An Interpretation of 1937-38

BY KENNETH D. ROOSE

D1520876

ARCHON BOOKS   1969

SBN: 208 00742 3
Library of Congress Catalog Card Number: 69-15795
Printed in the United States of America

PREFACE

THE RECESSION and revival of 1937–38 was particularly noteworthy for several reasons. It was the last major fluctuation to occur before government expenditures for defense and war came to dominate the economy. It was a sharply marked fluctuation in an economy which had not yet recovered fully from the Great Depression of 1929–33. It provided the first test of the effectiveness of the New Deal monetary, fiscal, and other measures in managing the economy. It is, finally, a fluctuation for which the statistical data are of better coverage and quality than those for any prior period. An intensive examination of this recent economic history is warranted because of these unusual features, and seems desirable as well for the light it may throw upon the causes and control of business fluctuations in general. The better empirical data for this period facilitate appraisal of the causal hypotheses of various business-cycle theories.

The study proceeds by what can best be described as the "quantitative-historical approach."[1] It employs the tools of national income analysis: private investment and consumption expenditures together with government monetary and fiscal policies uniquely determine the level of national income. Changes in other economic variables can affect the flow of income and the level of employment only through their impact on private consumption and investment and on the flow of funds to and from government accounts.[2] The national income model is clearly tautological and does not identify the causes of changes in income and employment, but it has the merit of focusing attention on those private decisions and government policies which together compose the process of expansion and contraction in the economy.

The original study, which was presented as a doctoral dissertation at Yale University, has here been expanded and completely rewritten. The acknowledgments to be made for assistance and inspiration are many. Much of the research was undertaken with the aid of a demobilization award from the Social Science Research Council. The

1. Robert A. Gordon, "Business Cycles in the Interwar Period: The 'Quantitative-Historical' Approach," *Papers and Proceedings, American Economic Review,* *39* (1949), 54.
2. These three categories could be further subdivided but are not, in the interests of simplicity and because of the limitations of the available data.

study was completed with grants from the University Research Committee and the Bureau of Business and Economic Research, Southern Section, at the University of California, Los Angeles. During the final preparation of the manuscript I have been a Faculty Research Fellow of the Social Science Research Council. Publication of the book was assisted by a generous gift from the Dorothy L. and Richard J. Bernhard Foundation.

Selected chapters benefited greatly from the criticism of Moses Abramovitz of Stanford University, Friedrich A. Lutz of the University of Zurich, Lloyd A. Metzler of the University of Chicago, John P. Miller, Ray B. Westerfield, Kent T. Healy, and William Fellner of Yale University, and Alfred Nicols, George H. Hildebrand, John C. Clendenin, and J. Fred Weston of the University of California, Los Angeles. Special thanks are due to Max F. Millikan of Massachusetts Institute of Technology who made significant contributions to the theoretical analysis and particularly to the recommendations for public policy. Finally, my greatest indebtedness is to Eugene V. Rostow of the Yale Law School who interested me in the application of empirical research to business fluctuation theory and encouraged me to go beyond the assembling and analysis of data to draw inferences about causation and to make recommendations for public policy.

I am indebted to the editors of the following journals for permission to reproduce substantial parts of my articles: "The Recession of 1937–38," *Journal of Political Economy, 56* (1948), 239–248 (Chapters 12 and 15); "Federal Reserve Policy and the Recession of 1937–1938," *Review of Economics and Statistics, 32* (1950), 177–183 (Chapter 7); "The Role of Net Government Contribution to Income in the Recession and Revival of 1937–38," *Journal of Finance, 6* (1951), 1–18 (Chapter 5); and "The Empirical Status of Business-Cycle Theory," *Journal of Political Economy, 60* (1952), 412–421 (Chapter 16).

I also want to thank Raymond P. Powell of Yale University for helpful editorial suggestions. Mrs. Margery Ratner assisted in the final processing of the manuscript and in preparation of the index.

John A. Buttrick and Robert T. Lancet were primarily responsible for drafting the figures.

KENNETH D. ROOSE

Oberlin, Ohio

CONTENTS

TABLES

FIGURES

CHAPTER 1

The Plan of Analysis

THE POINT of departure in this study of the recession and revival
of 1937–38 is the explanations of it which have previously been offered by various writers. This is followed by a detailed description
of the movements of the economic series and an analysis of the causal
significance of the different variables. Questions which must then
be asked include: What weights should be given to the many variables involved? What significance does the explanation of this fluctuation have for business cycle theory? In what respects was public
policy deficient? What would have been wise public policy under
the conditions of 1937–38? What implications does the experience
of this period have for present public policy?

Most explanations have emphasized the plural nature of the causation in the recession. Thus, as will be pointed out in Chapter 2, Alvin
H. Hansen stressed the cessation of net government contribution to
income, but also included price-cost relations, consumption, investment, and certain autonomous factors. Another prominent writer,
Sumner H. Slichter, placed heavy responsibility on the short-run expectations of businessmen, the "dangerously" low level of profits, and
commodity and inventory speculation, but also conceded that the decline in net government contribution played some part in precipitating
the decline. The results of the research of these and other writers
make it clear that the problem for causal analysis here is primarily
one of assessing the relative importance of the many contributing
factors.

A solution to this problem is vital, because, in the absence of general agreement as to primary causal factors, conflicting public policies
might be recommended. If, for example, the decline in net government contribution were to be stressed, policy makers would probably
recommend more government spending until other compensatory expenditures were in sight. But if income and employment appeared
to be falling because of a contraction in private investment expenditures, proper public policy would probably consist in removing or
overcoming obstacles to private investment expenditures, if possible,
before expanding government expenditures. Although these two poli-

1

cies are not necessarily in opposition, one is likely to be more effective than the other, thus making it advisable to obtain general agreement as to the more significant causal factors.

The variety of factors which have heretofore been treated as strategic in the 1937–38 fluctuation is evident from the several writings which are summarized in Chapter 2. In Chapter 3 the actual movements of the economic variables are examined to provide a basis for causal analysis. Chapter 4 describes the political, social, and economic environment in the thirties and its influence on the decisions which affected government operations, consumption, and private investment expenditures. Chapters 5, 6, and 7 examine the causal implications of government monetary and fiscal policies. Chapters 8 and 9 assess the impact of price-cost relationships and monopoly factors upon investment and consumption spending. Chapter 10 deals with the relationships of consumption expenditures to the recession, and finally Chapters 11–14 analyze the position of investment expenditures in the recession and revival.

The conclusions as to the nature and the causes of the recession and revival are then summarized in Chapter 15. The final chapter relates the findings of the study to business cycle theory, points up the implications of the recession for public policy, and makes some critical observations on economic developments since the end of World War II.

CHAPTER 2

Explanations Advanced for the Recession and Revival of 1937–38

EVERY WRITER, when evaluating the success of government action in promoting and sustaining business recovery in the thirties, faces the necessity for examining the recession and revival of 1937–38. Moreover, the dramatic nature of the recession and its severity make it of special interest to students of business fluctuations. Compare, for example, the speed of the decline in this recession with that in the Great Depression of 1929–33. The latter was, of course, much longer in duration, but the rapidity of the decline in income and production during the nine months, September 1937 to June 1938, was without precedent in American history. Equally abruptly the recession ended and national income and production began to rise again. These developments are emphasized in Figure 1 which shows adjusted income and industrial production, by quarters, from 1923 to 1938, based on an index of 1935–39 = 100. It is not surprising, therefore, that the business fluctuation of 1937–38 has attracted attention from a large number of writers with considerable diversity in viewpoint. Of those who have commented directly or indirectly on it, the most comprehensive studies have been made by Melvin D. Brockie,[1] Alvin H. Hansen,[2] Charles O. Hardy,[3] Douglas A. Hayes,[4] H. Gregg Lewis,[5]

1. Melvin D. Brockie, "The Rally, Crisis, and Depression, 1935–38," an unpublished doctoral dissertation, University of California, Los Angeles, June 1948; "Theories of the 1937–38 Crisis and Depression," *Economic Journal*, 60 (1950), 292–310.
2. Alvin H. Hansen, *Full Recovery or Stagnation?* (New York, 1938), "The 1937 Recession" (chap. 16) and "The Consequences of Reducing Expenditures" (chap. 17).
3. Charles O. Hardy, "An Appraisal of the Factors ('Natural' and 'Artificial') Which Stopped Short the Recovery Development in the United States," *Papers and Proceedings, American Economic Review, 29* (1939), 170–182.
4. Douglas A. Hayes, "A Study of the Recession of 1937," unpublished doctoral dissertation, University of Michigan, 1949, later revised and published as *Business Confidence and Business Activity: A Case Study of the Recession of 1937*, Michigan Business Studies, 10, No. 5 (Ann Arbor, 1951).
5. H. Gregg Lewis, *An Analysis of Changes in the Demand for Steel and in Steel Prices, 1936–1939*, United States Steel Corporation, 1939.

INDEX (1935 - 39 = 100)

Fig. 1. Total adjusted income and industrial production, by quarters, 1923–38. Total adjusted income from Harold Barger, *Outlay and Income in the United States, 1921–1938, Studies in Income and Wealth, 4* (New York, 1942), 178–183, Table 18. Data have been converted to an index base of 1935–39 = 100. This income total does not correspond to either national income or personal income as now measured by the Department of Commerce. Barger's adjusted income includes income originating in private industry, plus income distributed by government and veterans' bonus and social security benefits minus social security taxes paid by employees and inventory profits. It will be referred to hereafter as adjusted income. Industrial production from *Federal Reserve Bulletin, 27* (1941), 934. Quarterly averages were computed from monthly data. All data are seasonally adjusted.

J. E. Meade,[6] Bertil Ohlin,[7] Alexander Sachs,[8] Joseph A. Schumpeter,[9] and Sumner H. Slichter.[10] Although most of these writers be-

6. J. E. Meade, *World Economic Survey, 1937/38* and *1938/39* (Geneva, 1938 and 1939).

7. Bertil Ohlin, "Can World Prosperity Be Maintained?" *Supplement to Index* (Svenska Handelsbanken), *12,* October 1937.

8. Alexander Sachs, "The Financial Dynamics of the Recovery since 1933 and Latest Constriction Phase in Capital Flow," *Financial Management Series,* No. 53, American Management Association, 1938.

9. Joseph A. Schumpeter, *Business Cycles, 2* (New York, 1939), chap. 15.

10. Sumner H. Slichter, "The Downturn of 1937," *Review of Economics and Statistics* (before 1948 titled *Review of Economic Statistics*) *20* (1938), 97–110; "Corporate Price Policies as a Factor in the Recent Business Recession," *Proceedings of the Academy of Political Science, 18,* No. 2 (1939), 20–33; "Must We Have Another Boom?" *Atlantic Monthly, 159* (1937), 600–607.

lieved several factors rather than a single factor accounted for the recession and revival, they were not agreed as to the more important causes. The discussion below points out these disagreements.

CAUSES OF THE RECESSION OF 1937–38

The various explanations of the recession are here discussed for the most part in terms of the fundamental categories, consumption, investment, and government expenditures, which, as noted, are defined so that they uniquely determine the level of income and employment. The discussion goes beyond these broad terms only to permit a separate discussion of certain relatively autonomous private investment factors and consideration of the price-cost problem as it affected consumption and investment decisions. The explanations in the area of government expenditures and actions, the price-cost problem, and private investment are discussed first, because they received the most emphasis by scholars.

GOVERNMENT ACTION AFFECTING THE FLOW OF FUNDS

Decline of net government contribution to the income flow. The single cause given most frequently for the recession was the decline in net government contribution to income. As will be shown in Chapter 5, net government contribution declined from the peak levels of 1936 until it actually became negative in August of 1937. Hansen has emphasized this decline as an explanation of the recession.[11] According to him, the recovery from 1933–37 was consumption inspired. Since the important factor in expanding consumption expenditures was the government contribution, with its decline consumption expenditures ceased to rise. Operating through the acceleration principle, this checked additional investment expenditures. Autonomous investment was insufficient to prevent the recession.

Those who emphasized net government contribution to income pointed out that it was first swelled by the payment of the soldiers' bonus in the latter part of 1936, which gave an unusual boost to both consumer incomes and expenditures. Tax revenues were increased thereafter by the high collections from existing taxes and the new social security taxes. The result was a severe decline in net government contribution in the early months of 1937, more as the result of the increase of tax revenues than because of the reduction of government expenditures. This decline in net government contribu-

11. Hansen, *Full Recovery or Stagnation?* chap. 17, and U. S. Congress, Temporary National Economic Committee, *Hearings,* 76th Congress, 1st Session, Pt. 9 (1940), 3553.

tion was believed to have reduced the rate of increase in consumption expenditures.

In Hansen's opinion, however, the decline in the rate of increase in consumption expenditures did not make the recession inevitable: "I do not draw the conclusion that a major recession was inevitable. But I do say that either consumption had to be pushed forward or else investment had to be pried loose from the narrow limits imposed by the immediate requirements of the prevailing volume of consumption." [12]

Although Hansen gave the most elaborate statement of the relationship between net government contribution and the recession, many other writers assigned to it a more important causal position. For example, Leonard P. Ayres cited the singular importance of the reduction in the flow of income-producing expenditures of government: "It seems wholly probable that we have here the chief explanation of the exceptionally abrupt decline in business activity which took place in the autumn of 1937, and which continued with decreased violence in the early months of 1938." [13]

In addition to the considerable number of writers who stressed the causal importance of the decline in net government contribution, still others stressed the timing of its fluctuations. Angell [14] and Schumpeter both remarked upon the unfortunate timing of variations in net government contribution. Schumpeter commented: "There can be no doubt not only that income generation by government must always create problems of adaptation, but also that in this case its timing was singularly infelicitous. Its high-water mark came exactly at the time when the economic process could most easily have done without it and its cessation exactly at the time when the economic process was in its most sensitive phase." [15]

Federal reserve and monetary policy. In addition to government fiscal actions, monetary policies attracted a good deal of criticism.[16]

12. Hansen, 283.
13. Leonard P. Ayres, *Turning Points in Business Cycles* (New York, 1939), 152. For another strong position cf. Richard V. Gilbert et al., *An Economic Program for American Democracy* (New York, 1938), 26–27, 38. Less extreme statements were made by Marriner S. Eccles, *Economic Balance and a Balanced Budget,* a collection of Eccles' public papers, edited by R. L. Weissman (New York, 1940), 190; Corrington Gill, *Wasted Manpower* (New York, 1939), 221; John Philip Wernette, *The Control of Business Cycles* (New York, 1940), 178, 183, 192; John Bauer, *National Welfare and Business Stability* (New York, 1940), 70.
14. James W. Angell, *Investment and Business Cycles* (New York, 1941), 231–232.
15. Schumpeter, 1032. Cf. also Norman J. Silberling who was critical of the government spending program, *The Dynamics of Business* (New York, 1943), 438.
16. Hansen's position is described in this section. Cf. Wernette, 180–183, Ohlin,

The policies most disputed were the 100% increase in reserve requirements for member banks (August 1936 to May 1937) and the gold sterilization program begun in December 1936. The relationship between these actions and the recession is difficult to establish. Hansen suggested that the Federal Reserve Board action in raising reserve ratios contributed to the recession by weakening security prices. He argued that some of the larger banks sold large amounts of government bonds in order to meet the new reserve requirements. This led to a decline in their prices and a rise in the long-term interest rate. The selling pressure eventually affected the corporate bond and securities market and was one factor in halting the impending business boom. However, even if excess reserves had been undisturbed, bankers might have been reluctant to increase loans and investments, because of an increased emphasis on liquidity. Moreover, as will be noted in Chapter 7, the argument is weakened somewhat by the fact that the break in corporate bond prices actually preceded the fall in government bond prices.[17]

PRICE-COST RELATIONSHIPS

Price-cost developments were considered important by many writers, from the standpoint both of investment and consumption decisions. Certain prices and costs seem to have been higher than warranted by the economic situation.[18] The National Industrial Recovery Act, by encouraging monopoly prices, contributed to this end. Other contributing factors included the unwillingness of public utilities to experiment with developmental rates, the monopolistic elements of fair-trade regulations and other business practices, labor policies in the field of housing, and the exorbitant [19] cost of borrowed funds.[20]

Two very different evaluations were made of the causal significance of the increases in labor costs and in the prices of goods. On the one hand, those who stressed the role of investment expenditures in the determination of national income and output believed that the increase in wage and labor costs reduced the current profit margin. Not only this, but it created unfavorable expectations about future profits vital to investment decisions. On the other hand, those who emphasized the crucial importance of consumption expenditures in

13, H. B. Elliston, "Blaming the Money Managers," *Atlantic Monthly, 162* (1938), 103–110, and G. Griffith Johnson, *The Treasury and Monetary Policy, 1933–1938* (Cambridge, 1939), 135–136 for other statements on the significance of Federal Reserve policy in the recession.

17. Nevertheless in the same chapter it is shown that these developments, when reinterpreted, support the general causal relationship described by Professor Hansen.

18. Hansen, 286–287.

19. Exorbitant considering the quantity available.

20. Hansen, 286–287.

the determination of national income and output believed that the higher prices for finished goods and the larger share of income in the form of profits operated to restrict further expansion in consumption expenditures. From this viewpoint, a greater rise in wage and labor costs would have been a favorable development.

A strong position was taken by Brockie on the unfavorable effects of upward wage adjustments: "The basic cause of the 1937–38 crisis and depression was the encroachment of rising labor costs on profit margins." [21] While in agreement that the wage increases reduced profit margins and investment expenditures, Charles Hardy, Schumpeter, Slichter,[22] and Ohlin took less extreme positions on the causal significance of the wage increases.

The underconsumption version of the price and cost increases was given its strongest statement by various governmental representatives. In May 1937 Leon Henderson forecast a major business recession because prices were rising so rapidly that purchasing power was failing to keep pace. Too much was going into profits and savings which failed to find profitable investment outlets because of the reduced purchasing power.[23]

In an earlier speech on April 24, 1937, he expressed alarm over the failure of wages to keep pace with price increases. Much of the trouble was attributed to monopolistic and manipulative pricing.[24] He emphasized consumption expenditures as the motive power for the economic system: "When the consumer has to pay too much for what he buys, people stop buying, mills stop running; men lose their jobs, and then unemployment starts 'snowballing.' " [25]

Harry Hopkins testified that the administration believed the recession was caused primarily by unwarranted price increases and by the failure of consumer purchasing power to keep step with production.[26]

PRIVATE INVESTMENT FACTORS

The private investment factors receiving the most attention were the speculation in inventories, the short-term nature of business commitments, and the shortage of investment funds. Each of these factors will be discussed in turn.

21. Brockie, "The Rally, Crisis, and Depression, 1935–38," 295.
22. See the discussion of the points stressed by Slichter in Chapter 8 below.
23. Quoted in David Lynch, *The Concentration of Economic Power* (New York, 1946), 18–19.
24. *New York Times,* April 25, 1937.
25. *Ibid.,* July 17, 1938.
26. U. S. Congress, Senate, Special Committee to Investigate Unemployment and Relief, *Hearings,* S. Res. 36, 75th Congress, 3d Session, 1 (1938), 1338–1339, 1352–1355. Cf. Lewis B. Schwellenbach, "Depression or Recession," *Vital Speeches of the Day, 4* (1938), 465–467.

Inventory speculation. Slichter made the most detailed examination of the effects of price increases on commodity and inventory speculation.[27] He concluded that a dangerous increase in prices began about May 1936, and was influenced by four main factors: (a) the soldiers' bonus, (b) world-wide accumulation of raw materials, in response to the Spanish conflict and later to European rearmament, (c) fears of inflation, and (d) "fears of labor troubles and of higher wages."[28] Forward buying became important in December 1936 and January 1937, spurred on by anticipation of higher wages and threatened strikes. The annual statements of various New York banks contained pointed warnings against the accelerated price increases which finally reached their peak in late March and early April of 1937. Slichter suggested a number of reasons for the decline in prices at this time: (a) rumors that the United States might cut the price of gold, (b) President Roosevelt's criticism of the high prices on durable goods and his promise thereafter to direct government relief expenditures toward the consumer goods industries rather than the durable goods industries, and (c) favorable weather and promise of bumper crops which contributed to the break in agricultural prices.[29]

According to Slichter, this collapse in commodity prices dates the beginning of the 1937–38 recession. It undermined confidence in the price structure and unsettled business expectations: "The collapse of commodity speculation (1) removed the immediate fear of price advances, and (2) caught many enterprises with an uncomfortably large proportion of their working capital tied up in inventories or in orders for undelivered goods."[30]

Short-term investment commitments. Several writers pointed out that much of the business investment for 1933–37 was based upon short-term rather than long-term expectations. Hansen concluded that businessmen avoided long-term capital commitments in the recovery of the thirties. He contended that consumption expenditures led the way to recovery from the 1933 low. Thus investment, which is normally a relatively independent factor associated with long-term expectations, was instead short-term and closely geared to the level of consumption.[31] Hansen himself, however, doubted whether a full recovery would have occurred even had investment led the way out

27. Cf. also Hansen, 269.
28. Slichter, "The Downturn of 1937," 97.
29. *Ibid.*, 98.
30. *Ibid.*, 107.
31. Hansen, 278. Elmer C. Bratt also emphasized the short-run nature of the investment commitments and the dependence of investment upon consumption spending. See his *This Unbalanced World* (New York, 1940), 102, 170.

of the depression.[32] There was not enough autonomous investment.

Slichter also ascribed causal importance to the fact that businessmen were unwilling to undertake long-run major improvements: "The most important fact about the business situation in 1937 was that a high level of activity, based upon short-term expectations, failed to stimulate an expansion in demand based upon long-term plans."[33] In his opinion, the high level of business activity in 1937 was the product of short-term expectations. The increase in demand for industrial equipment arose from the attempt to get long-deferred replacements before prices went up, and was financed in large part out of working capital.[34]

Both Slichter and Hansen agreed that the investment of the thirties was limited by short-run expectations. But where Hansen attributed this to the passive response of investment to consumption expenditures, Slichter blamed the dangerously low level of profits.[35]

Professor Lewis was another writer who stressed the short-term nature of the commitments and the absence of long-term investment: "The situation was dominated by the short run outlook, and was for that reason vulnerable. All the elements of a short run boom were there, but the requirement for a sustained recovery—recovery in outlays made on the basis of the long term outlook—was lacking. Reasonable certainty as to the future was absent."[36]

Shortage of investment funds. The shortage of investment funds was a third factor which received prominent mention as a condition leading to the recession. It was attributed to the tax structure, government policies, and an immediate shortage of working capital and maintenance funds.

Tax policies and investment funds must be considered first. The real problem of investment, according to Hardy, was that funds from private investors were not made available to business concerns. Three reasons accounted for the failure of funds to flow to business concerns from that source: (a) the dissipation of corporate surplus, (b) the shrinkage of large incomes which afforded room for savings, and (c) taxation policy adverse to the functioning of the investor.[37] The tax policy largely destroyed "the incentive for wealthy individuals to invest in enterprises involving any considerable degree of risk."[38] By

---

32. Hansen, 288–289.
33. Slichter, "Corporate Price Policies," 32.
34. Slichter, "The Downturn of 1937," 107.
35. *Ibid.*, 107. Cf. also his "Corporate Price Policies," 32–33.
36. Lewis, *op. cit.*, 11. For the strongest statement blaming the recession on the failure of long-term commitments, cf. W. L. Crum, R. A. Gordon, and Dorothy Wescott, "Review of the Year," *Review of Economics and Statistics, 20* (1938), 43.
37. Hardy, "An Appraisal," 181.
38. *Ibid.* This and following quotation from 175.

heavy surtaxes the government diverted "funds from potential investment through the Treasury into the consumption stream, without providing a substitute for them in the capital goods market, except for its own investments in public works, largely of a meagerly productive character."

Despite these statements, Hardy did not believe that the tax program was an important factor in causing the recession. Surtax rates were unchanged in the period immediately preceding the recession, and the timing of the beginning and ending of the undistributed profits taxes was not coincident with the decline and the recovery.

Schumpeter also stressed the causal importance of tax policy. He believed that direct taxation of individuals was undoubtedly high enough to affect "subjective" investment opportunity. Several factors were responsible: (a) the redistribution of wealth by taxation of the higher incomes amounted to socialism,[39] (b) failure of legislation which would permit the carrying forward of business losses, (c) the new tax treatment given to personal holding companies, and (d) the capital gains tax which made the sale of new stock more difficult than it would otherwise have been.[40]

In Schumpeter's opinion, the undistributed profits tax may well have had a paralyzing influence on enterprise and investment in general. Since "accumulated reserves" strengthen business with respect to the risks of innovation, "adequate book reserves" come to be "as necessary a requisite as adequate stocks of raw materials." [41]

The shortage of investment funds was also revealed by the shortage of working capital. In the opinion of Alexander Sachs the physical shortage, not only of risk capital but of funds for current operations in established companies, was an important cause of the recession.[42] Sachs used the source and application of funds technique to trace the flow of funds through various business organizations. For the period 1933–36, 26 companies with combined assets of $6 billion were studied; in the interyear period July 1936 to June 1937 the sample was 16 companies with assets of about $2 billion.

The study showed that there was an impairment of working capital, and that in some of the larger corporations there was an actual shortage of current and long-term capital for maintenance. This was attributed to a reduction in retained profits because of the undistributed profits tax. Funds from outside investment markets and from internal savings were insufficient for plant expansion and for the in-

39. In particular, he cited the effect on "supply" of capital of the steep taxation on the thirty to forty thousand taxpayers with incomes above $30,000 per year.
40. Schumpeter, 1038–1040.
41. *Ibid.*, freely quoted from 1040–1041.
42. Sachs, "Financial Dynamics," 17.

creases in working capital which were required at the higher volume and price level. For the first time, in the year ended June 30, 1937, short-term liabilities, rather than depreciation funds or undistributed profits, became the foremost source of corporate financing.[43]

Two other calculations made by Sachs supported the claim that working capital was impaired by 1937. One was the evidence that by the middle of 1937 the velocity of trade accounts payable had slowed down so that they were no longer settled in the customary period. The percentage increase in accounts payable from June 30, 1936 to June 30, 1937 was four times as great as the increase in durable goods production. The other evidence of reduced liquidity was the decrease in the ratio of current assets to current liabilities from 4.47 to 1 on June 30, 1936, to 3.59 to 1 on June 30, 1937.[44]

The unfavorable effect of the undistributed profits tax was heightened, in Sachs' opinion, by the fact that the durable goods industries were unable to repair the depression damage to their asset position before the undistributed profits tax was enacted. However, the consumer goods industries had already repaired their position.[45]

In summary, Sachs concluded that the critical capital situation of 1937 resulted from : (a) the lag in reopening a functioning capital market; (b) the strains which the undistributed profits tax imposed upon the working capital position of American enterprise; (c) a level of activity in the summer of 1937 which was so vulnerable to the new undistributed profits taxes and social security taxes that the process of capital formation was arrested; and (d) maladjustments resulting from stagnation in new capital issues, disruption of the market for outstanding capital, and reduced corporate savings for internal capital formation as a result of increased taxation.[46]

The National Industrial Conference Board also concluded that the value of capital per wage earner reached lows in the thirties relative to the twenties. This depletion of capital limited the number of workers that could be profitably employed, and discouraged the assumption of the risks which attend any expansion policy.[47]

Finally, in the opinion of several writers, it was government policy which restricted the flow of investment expenditures. Businessmen feared antagonistic governmental policies : "worries about the federal budget, actual management of fiscal operations, and general fears

43. *Ibid.*, 17.
44. *Ibid.*, 22.
45. *Ibid.*, 23.
46. *Ibid.*, 26.
47. National Industrial Conference Board, *Studies in Enterprise and Social Progress* (New York, 1939), 224–225.

concerning governmental policies pertaining especially to taxes, labor, agriculture, profits, and industrial organization undoubtedly contributed to interrupt the advance or speed the decline." [48]

Professor Schumpeter elaborated at length on the relationship of government policies to the flow of investment. In this relationship he found not only an explanation for the recession but an answer to the charge that the recession resulted from a chronic shortage of investment outlets. Two examples make clear the type of government policies which Schumpeter believed were unfavorable to investment. One was the blanket threat of political action against the public utility industry if it accepted responsibility for new investment on a large scale. A second example was the hostility toward "monopoly power" which Schumpeter believed to be synonymous with large-scale business.[49] The combined effect of the various measures which were unfavorable to investment opportunity—increased costs, higher taxes, attacks on accepted methods of management, pricing, and financing of "big business"—accounted for the recession. In addition, it was these actions which produced the social atmosphere responsible for the chronic stagnation of the thirties: "capitalism produces by its mere working a social atmosphere—a moral code, if the reader prefer—that is hostile to it, and this atmosphere, in turn, produces policies which do not allow it to function." [50]

The explanations for the recession which emphasized developments in governmental fiscal and monetary policy, price-cost relationships, and private investment decisions have now been presented. Explanations which rested on consumption factors have already been treated in the discussion of price-cost relationships. It remains to consider the autonomous factors, construction expenditures and economic maturity, which many believed affected the course of the recession.

AUTONOMOUS FACTORS

Construction expenditures. Private construction expenditures made the poorest recovery in the thirties of all the capital formation items [51]—a failure to which the majority of writers attached importance. The recession was not attributed directly to any change in such expenditures, but their weak revival was believed to be responsible for a sharper recession than would otherwise have resulted: "Had there been launched by 1937 a full-fledged residential building

48. Crum, Gordon, and Wescott, *op. cit.,* 43.
49. Schumpeter, 1043–1044.
50. *Ibid.,* 1038.
51. The statistics supporting this statement are in Chapter 11.

boom, the cessation of federal income-stimulating expenditures, the increasing saturation in the automobile market, and the inventory crisis would in all probability still have produced a recession. But it would have been much less severe and probably of relatively short duration." [52] Professor Villard emphasized the very great importance of the housing failure: "the role of housing in the depression cannot be stressed too much." [53] He continued: "had housing alone in 1937 been as much of an outlet for savings as it was in 1925, total outlets for savings in 1937 would have been almost as high as they had been even in 1929. . . . It is obvious that the failure of housing to recover to the level attained during the twenties has been of major importance in postponing full recovery." [54]

A similar conclusion was reached by Professor Wilson: "it cannot be doubted that depressed conditions in this branch of industry were responsible, in a very large measure, for the unsatisfactory recovery of industry as a whole." [55]

Discussion of reasons for the poor showing of construction expenditures will be deferred to a later chapter. It is enough at this point to note that many believed construction bore a heavy responsibility for the low level of economic activity in the 1930's. This belief was held by analysts with widely differing theoretical approaches to the recession and business fluctuations in general. Thus the National City Bank of New York, the *Economist,* and Hansen attached importance to the weakness of the building industry. Hansen showed that plant expenditures in the 1936–39 period were $2 billion per year less than in 1923–29 ($1.9 billion against $3.9 billion). The failure of housing was even more spectacular, $1.9 billion in 1936–39 against $5.1 billion in 1923–29. He concluded: "It is in this area that one must find the explanation for the incomplete recovery of the thirties." [56]

Secular stagnation and economic maturity. The position of those who believed in the mature economy doctrine, on the relationship of secular stagnation to the recession of 1937–38, is unclear. Secular stagnation is said to arise through the operation of long-term factors such as the declining rate of population growth, the passing of the frontier, the absence of new "great industries," and so on.[57] The

52. Hansen, 298.
53. Henry H. Villard, *Deficit Spending and the National Income* (New York, 1941), 348.
54. *Ibid.,* 348–349.
55. Thomas Wilson, *Fluctuations in Income & Employment* (London, 1942), 183.
56. Hansen, *Fiscal Policy and Business Cycles* (New York, 1941), 26.
57. *Ibid.,* chap. 1; also George Terborgh, *The Bogey of Economic Maturity* (Chicago, 1945).

relevance of these forces for the 1937–38 recession is not obvious, since the latter was a short-run phenomenon. Nevertheless, there is some evidence that this thesis was advanced to explain the decline in 1929 and the low level of economic activity in 1932–38.[58]

Perhaps this belief is warranted since Hansen, the leading proponent of the secular stagnation thesis, argued that special factors accounted for the prosperous twenties. It was implied that when these factors ceased to operate the underlying stagnation forces became apparent and became causal elements in the cyclical movement.[59] However, the relationship of secular stagnation to the recession was not consistently outlined. Hansen seemed to have two interpretations. One stemmed from the view that slowly changing variables like population growth, the character of innovations, new industries, and so on, were tending to supply less impetus to investment and production. The result should have been a gradual but perceptible increase in both the number and the length of depression periods relative to expansion periods. The other view was that these stagnation factors were the ultimate explanation for the failure of a full recovery in 1936–37. The latter seems a somewhat unlikely interpretation, since Hansen concluded elsewhere that the trough of the housing cycle was sufficient to account for the weakness of the 1933–37 prosperity.

That a wide variety of explanations was offered for the 1937 recession is evident from the preceding survey. A schematic summary of these explanations is presented in Table 1.

CAUSES OF THE REVIVAL OF 1938

While the causes of the recession have received considerable attention, there has been little discussion of the factors operative in the 1938 revival. This may be due to a broad consensus that renewed government spending in the spring and summer of 1938 initiated the revival. Nevertheless, significance was attributed also to developments in the area of consumption [60] and investment decision, and to two autonomous factors, residential construction and the export surplus. Primary emphasis was upon government fiscal policy, investment factors, and residential construction.

58. Cf. Allan Sweezy, "Government Contribution," in *Economic Reconstruction,* edited by Seymour E. Harris (New York, 1945), Gilbert et al., and Angell, 266. Angell believed the economy faced secular stagnation in the thirties but denied that the factors responsible were the ones advanced by Hansen.

59. Hansen, *Fiscal Policy and Business Cycles,* "The Thirties," chap. 1, 13–47. Cf., however, his testimony before the Temporary National Economic Committee, *Hearings,* Pt. 9, 3503–3504.

60. The single consumption change cited was the reduction in consumer debt.

GOVERNMENT FISCAL POLICY

As suggested above, the majority of writers attributed the upturn to resumption of government spending on a large scale.[61] For example, Hansen concluded that the recovery was due to the positive program of public expenditures.[62] In his opinion the principal error in policy was the failure to begin expenditures much earlier and at a vastly expanded rate.[63]

Secretary of Commerce Harry L. Hopkins, representing one government agency,[64] strongly supported the argument that government policies reversed the tide. Faced with the prospect of a cumulative deflation, the Federal Government made vigorous use of the instruments which had proved so effective before: "Results were prompt and striking." [65] Government policies, directly and indirectly, resulted in outlays which reversed the downward trend in national income.

TABLE I: EXPLANATIONS ADVANCED FOR THE RECESSION OF 1937–38

   I. *Government-originated Causes*

      A. Government fiscal policy
         1. Cessation of soldiers' bonus
         2. Enactment of social security and undistributed profits taxes
         3. Timing of government expenditures
      B. Federal Reserve and monetary policy
         1. Sterilization of gold
         2. Changing of reserve ratios

  II. *Price and Cost Factors*

      A. Rise in wage and labor costs
         1. NIRA
         2. NLRA and labor disturbances
      B. Rise in prices and profits
         1. Failure of wages to keep pace with profits
         2. Increase in profit incomes which were not spent
      C. Competition and monopoly elements

61. Federal Reserve and Treasury actions received much less attention as a method of promoting the expansion than did the fiscal operations of government. For a list of monetary actions, cf. Meade, *World Economic Survey 1938/39,* 16–17. Also, many of these actions are described below, Chapters 6 and 7.

62. Hansen, *Fiscal Policy and Business Cycles,* 83.

63. *Ibid.,* 84.

64. Leon Henderson predicted a revival by September 1938, in part because of the three million checks going to WPA workmen and the new Public Works program. Henderson also viewed the reduction in consumer debt as a factor favorable to recovery. *New York Times,* July 17, 1938.

65. U. S. Secretary of Commerce, *Twenty-seventh Annual Report* (1939), viii.

      1. Assertions of government officials that prices were too high because of monopolistic action

      2. NIRA and other government price policies

      3. Increased spread between agricultural and industrial prices

      4. Intensification of antitrust action

III. *Consumption Factors*

      A. Consumer resistance to higher prices

      B. Period of underconsumption

      C. Leveling off in consumer income

      D. Too rapid expansion in short-term installment debt

IV. *Private Investment Factors*

      A. Unfavorable expectations created by price movements in securities markets

      B. Financing from corporate reserves and retained profits rather than capital markets

      C. Development of institutional financing and private placements

      D. Speculation in inventory buying

      E. Shortage of capital

      F. Investment based almost entirely on short-term expectations

      G. Optimism and pessimism in their effects on investment outlays

      H. Profitability of business enterprise

           1. Unfavorable profits expectations

           2. Dangerously low level of profits

      I. Government tax policy

           1. Higher corporate income taxes

           2. Higher individual income taxes

           3. Undistributed profits taxes

           4. Social security taxes

      J. Unfavorable government policies

           1. Unbalancing of the budget

           2. Possibility of revaluation of dollar

           3. Attacks on traditional methods of management and finance as in the SEC regulations

           4. Charge by government officials that "capital was on strike"

      K. Competition from government enterprise

           1. Uncertainties in the public utility industry

           2. Potential threat in other fields

V. *Autonomous Factors*

      A. Contraction in construction and failure of construction to revive

      B. The economic stagnation of a mature economy

      C. Negative foreign balance

      D. War scare

      E. Unprecedented drought

He concluded that the tremendous waste involved in continued deflation was unnecessary. The techniques to halt deflation and to secure recovery were available and the experience of 1938 was proof of their effectiveness.[66]

Villard conceded that the whole of government contribution may not have been income-increasing: "But there can be little or no doubt that the expansion of net expenditure in 1938 and 1939 played an important role in checking the recession and bringing about expansion."[67]

Fine gave almost full credit for the revival to the actions taken by the New Deal: "The improvement in business activity in the second half of 1938 must be attributed almost entirely to the various measures, both monetary and fiscal, adopted by the federal administration. Considered by itself, this legislation represents the most successful attempt by the New Deal to influence the course of business developments."[68]

PRIVATE INVESTMENT FACTORS

Besides government fiscal policy, several writers noted investment developments which seemed favorable to revival. Professor Angell characterized the recovery as one which was normally self-generated. Since various indices of production and employment turned up before they could possibly have been affected by increased government expenditure,[69] he concluded that the recovery was "normal" and "self-generated": "The start of this new recovery phase hence also appears to have been, in the main, a relatively 'normal' and self-generating cyclical phenomenon."[70] His conception of self-generation is that cyclical movements in business activity result from periodically revised anticipations of businessmen. If exogenous factors are assumed to be constant, these anticipations are largely based upon the previous rates of increase or decrease in national income.[71]

Improvements in the relations between businessmen and government, and inventory reductions, among other investment factors, were believed by Meade to have contributed to the recovery.[72]

66. *Ibid.,* x.

67. Villard, 341.

68. Sherwood M. Fine, *Public Spending and Postwar Economic Policy* (New York, 1944), 121.

69. This point is developed further in Chapter 5 below.

70. Angell, 232. One writer believed the "soundness of the fundamental position" accounted for the revival. Paul Einzig, *World Finance, 1938–1939* (New York, 1939), 38–39.

71. Angell, chaps. 7 and 8.

72. Meade, *World Economic Survey, 1938/39,* 19–20. Leon Henderson also regarded inventory reduction as a favorable condition for recovery, *New York Times,* July 17, 1938.

AUTONOMOUS FACTORS

Residential construction received considerable attention as a factor promoting revival. Meade attributed the increase in residential building to relaxation of mortgage terms under the Federal Housing Act, and to the fact that the rapid rise in wages and the prices of building materials in the first half of 1937 had ceased by the middle of that year and had fallen some since then.[73]

The net foreign balance, in the opinion of several, played some part in the revival. The export surplus increased in the first half of 1938 and was undoubtedly a stimulating factor in the revival.[74]

Causes which have been suggested for the revival are listed in Table 2. It should be noted that, compared with the wide range of opinion regarding causes of the recession, relatively few explanations were advanced for the revival. The primary emphasis was placed upon government fiscal policy.

TABLE 2: EXPLANATIONS ADVANCED FOR THE RECOVERY OF 1938

I. *Government-originated Causes*
   A. Resumption of government spending
   B. Favorable Federal Reserve and monetary policies

II. *Consumption Factors*

   A. Reduction in consumer debt

III. *Private Investment Factors*

   A. Normally self-generated recovery based upon revised anticipations of businessmen
   B. Improvements in the relations between businessmen and government
   C. Reductions in inventories

IV. *Autonomous Factors*

   A. Rise in residential construction
   B. Development of export surplus

73. Meade, 18–19. Lewis, too, *op. cit.*, 29, cited the rise in residential construction as a factor contributing to the recovery.

74. Meade, 14–15. It may be inferred that armament expenditures helped to sustain the level of American exports.

CHAPTER 3

Economic Developments 1935–38

(A DESCRIPTION OF THE ECONOMIC SERIES)

THE OUTSTANDING characteristic of the recovery from the depression of 1929–33 was the failure of gross national product and income to regain the levels of the 1920's in current dollars and to exceed them in constant dollars.[1] Personal income reached a peak in June 1937 of $76.6 billion, measured in current dollars, which was still approximately 12% less than the 1929 peak ($86.9 billion) and considerably less in per capita terms, but about the same in constant dollars. The gross national product in 1937 of $90.2 billion, measured in current dollars, was 13% less than in 1929 ($103.8 billion). In constant dollars, it was a little over 2% greater than in 1929. Data from another source indicate that gross national product in 1937, in current dollars, was almost 8% below the average of 1925–29.[2]

In spite of an over-all failure to attain again the levels of the 1920's, measured in current dollars, and to exceed them in constant dollars, individual components of the national product surpassed the 1929 levels in terms of either measure. Thus, among the capital formation items, increases in business inventories, in current dollars, were at a greater rate in 1937 (an increase of $1,487 million in the third quarter) than in the peak quarter of 1929 (an increase of $682 million in the fourth quarter)[3]; this means an increase of 40% in real terms if the calendar years 1929 and 1937 are compared. Government purchases of goods and services in current prices rose from $8.5 billion in 1929 to $11.6 billion, an increase of over 44% in real terms.

Thus two components of the gross national product exceeded their 1929 peaks by a wide margin in both money and real terms, even though aggregate expenditures fell considerably short of 1929 levels in current dollars and barely exceeded 1929 in real terms. The grave

1. The gross national product and income data in both current and constant prices are from U. S. Department of Commerce, Bureau of Foreign and Domestic Commerce, *Survey of Current Business, National Income Supplement, 1951.*

2. Mary S. Painter, "Estimates of Gross National Product, 1919–1928," *Federal Reserve Bulletin, 31* (1945), 872–873.

3. Barger, *Outlay and Income in the United States,* Table 11.

deficiency in the recovery of other components, particularly construction expenditures, is noted elsewhere in this chapter.[4] Because of the uneven recovery, it becomes essential to trace the behavior of series in the various fields.

Analysis of the movements of these series will serve the double purpose of presenting the diverse and sometimes unexpected movements in the economic series and of providing a basis for careful examination of the causal explanations for the recession and revival discussed in Chapter 2. It is essential to have a clear picture of developments during the period.

PLAN OF ANALYSIS

Monthly data have been employed wherever possible.[5] If monthly data are not available quarterly data are used, and, as a last resort, annual data. The recovery of the various series is measured roughly in relation to selected periods in the 1920's. In some cases the comparison is with a monthly peak, in others with a monthly average for a year. The reason for using a reference base is to establish the extent to which a full recovery was attained. It is not proposed by this method to rule on the degree to which this particular recovery and decline differs from other recoveries and declines.

The detailed description begins with the year 1935. Certain earlier political actions such as the NRA and the Revenue Acts of 1932 and 1934 will require investigation in later sections for their contribution, if any, to the recession. It is taken for granted that the general pattern of 1932–34 is known—the movements from the trough of 1932 (or 1933 for some series) to the pre-NRA boomlet terminating in June 1933, followed by a second less pronounced peak in 1934 for most series.

The series are discussed under seven headings: (a) the over-all performance of the economy, (b) financial investment, (c) the money market and banking system, (d) price-cost relationships, (e) employment and unemployment, (f) consumption factors, and (g) capital formation and expenditures.

The capital expenditures data are shown both in current and in constant prices. The income and consumption data are in current prices only. To facilitate comparison in real terms, the changes in wholesale prices and the cost-of-living index, which would be appropriate adjustments for the income and consumption figures, are discussed in the first section rather than in the fourth section. In the

---

4. Cf. below, 46–47.
5. Unless it is noted otherwise, the data wherever necessary are adjusted for seasonal variation.

general discussion below, weaknesses and inconsistencies in the data frequently will be overlooked. In later chapters, however, consideration must be given to the reliability of the data.

The Over-all Performance of the Economy

PERSONAL INCOMES

Personal incomes [6] at the beginning of 1935 ($55.5 billion, annual rate) were the highest since February 1932 ($55.5 billion also). The recovery was over 30% from the trough in March 1933 ($42.6 billion). Income rose steadily through 1935 and continued to rise in 1936. In June 1936 the big bulge in income payments occurred because of the payment of the soldiers' bonus. The adjusted service certificates payments, which were $800 million in June and $413 million in July, fell to $77 million in August and $26 million in December. The total payments for the year were over $1,400 million. The annual income rate in June 1936 rose from $65.4 billion to $76.1 billion because of these payments, and was not exceeded again until June 1937. The increase in income from May 1936 to June 1936 was approximately $900 million ($10.7 billion on an annual rate). The annual rate of income then dropped rather sharply from June ($76.1 billion) to September 1936 ($68.9 billion) although at the latter rate it was over 5% greater than before the bonus payment. At the end of the year the rate was almost 16% greater than a year before, and personal incomes were 14% greater in 1936 than in 1935. At its peak rate in 1937 of $76.6 billion in June, income was some 12% less than the average rate in 1929. In real terms the income levels were approximately the same in the two periods. Nevertheless, the real income per capita was considerably less in 1937 than in 1929.

Since the bonus payment distorts the monthly peak in 1936, a more meaningful comparison of the rates of income in 1936 and 1937 is found in the quarterly averages for the two periods. The peak flow of income occurred during the second quarter of 1937 when income rose to an annual rate of $75.9 billion compared with the $68.6 billion in the quarter ending June 1936, which includes the largest share of the bonus payments.[7]

Personal incomes, which were relatively stable through August 1937, began to decline sharply in September 1937 and by December 1937 had declined by $7 billion, or more than 9% from the year's high. Income continued to decline in 1938 until it reached a low of

6. Monthly income data are from the *Survey of Current Business, National Income Supplement 1951,* Table 48, 212–213.
    7. *Ibid.*

$67.0 billion in May 1938, a decline of over 12.5% from the previous peak in June 1937. The decline from January to May 1938 was not at a very great rate, nor was the rise from June 1938 through December 1938. By the end of the year income was almost 2% greater than the average income from 1935 to 1939. Figure 2 compares quarterly adjusted income from 1921 to 1938 with indexes of wholesale prices and industrial production.

WHOLESALE PRICES

The index of wholesale prices [8] which in 1935 ranged from 78.8 to 80.9 was only 81.5 in October 1936. But from that date until the peak in April 1937 (88.0) wholesale prices rose 8%. Even so, they were still almost 8% less than the average of prices in 1929 (95.3). They declined by less than a point to 87.2 in June 1937, and rebounded to 87.9 in July 1937. By October 1937 they had declined to

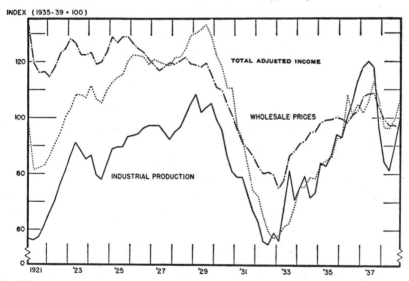

Fig. 2. Total adjusted income, wholesale prices, and industrial production, by quarters, 1921–38. Total adjusted income from Barger, 178–183, Table 18. Data have been converted to an index base of 1935–39 = 100. For a definition of adjusted income see Figure 1. Industrial production from *Federal Reserve Bulletin, 27* (1941), 934. Quarterly averages were computed from monthly data. Both series are seasonally adjusted. Original source for wholesale prices, Bureau of Labor Statistics, 1921–26 from *Wholesale Prices 1913 to 1927, Bulletin No. 473.* Secondary source: *Survey of Current Business, Supplement, 1932, 1936,* and *1940* for data 1927–38. Quarterly averages were computed from monthly data and the base was shifted from 1926 to the average of 1935–39.

8. Original source, U. S. Bureau of Labor Statistics. Secondary source, *Survey of Current Business, Supplement, 1932, 1936,* and *1940.* Base of 1926 = 100.

85.4, continued to decline in 1938 and had fallen to 77.0 in December, a lower level than in any month of 1935.

COST OF LIVING

The data on income should be compared with a cost of living index,[9] particularly if it is believed that a cause of the 1937–38 recession was a rise in prices relative to incomes. The cost of living increased by 10% from January 1935 (81.2) to October 1937 (89.2), with most of the increase from May 1936 (82.9) to May 1937 (87.8). The index then began to decline in November 1937 and had reached a low in November 1938 (84.9).

INDUSTRIAL PRODUCTION

The movements in industrial production,[10] which represents all the principal groups of industries in manufacturing and mining, are quite similar to those in adjusted income except for the degree of recovery experienced in the former series. Industrial production in January 1935 (83) was 57% greater than in the depression low of July 1932 (53). From the middle of 1935 (84) through December 1935 (95) industrial production rose by 13%. The year 1936 was notable for the recovery of industrial production by October to the average rate of production in 1929 (110). By December 1936 the index was at an all-time high of 116, 2 points greater than the peak rate in 1929.

Nondurable manufactures were primarily responsible for the high level of industrial production. They had surpassed their peak of June 1929 (95) by December 1935 (96). At the end of 1936 their production was almost 20% above the average in 1929 (111 compared with 93). They rose to a peak in April and May of 1937 (114) and then declined by approximately 25% to a low in December 1937 (87). The index had rebounded to 104 in December 1938. Production of durable goods recovered more slowly. By the end of 1935, when nondurable manufactures had surpassed their 1929 peak, durable manufactures were still 32% below their 1929 peak (96 compared with 141). At their peak in August 1937 (135) durables were 4% below their high in 1929.

The index of total industrial production reached its peak in May 1937 (121) but was virtually unchanged from March 1937 (120)

9. National Industrial Conference Board, original source. Base of 1923 = 100. Secondary source, *Survey of Current Business, Supplement, 1932, 1936* and *Survey of Current Business* (May 1941).

10. *Federal Reserve Bulletin, 27* (1941), 933–937, for all manufacturing and durable manufactures. *Survey of Current Business* (August 1940) for nondurable manufactures.

through August 1937 (119), being sustained largely by the continued increase in the production of durable goods. At its peak industrial production was 6% greater than in 1929 although, as was pointed out above, this was due primarily to the expansion in nondurable goods production.

A precipitous decline followed in the indexes of total industrial production and durable manufactures. For total industrial production the decline in the 5 months from August 1937 (119) to January 1938 (85) was almost 30%. There was a 33% fall from the peak in May 1937 (121) to the low in June 1938 (81). The decline in the durable manufactures component was even more drastic, over 50% from its high in August 1937 (135) to the low in June 1938 (65).

Production data for producers' durable and nondurable goods and for consumers' durable and nondurable goods are available from the Federal Reserve Bank of New York.[11] According to these data,[12] producers' durables reached their peak in August 1937 (92) while producers' nondurables reached theirs in December 1936 (103) and had fallen 9% by September 1937 (94). Consumers' durables reached their peak in September 1937 (96), whereas consumers' nondurables reached their peak in December 1936 (101) and had fallen 10% by September 1937 (90). These indexes indicate that production of both consumers' and producers' nondurable goods weakened after December 1936, while durable goods production continued to rise through August 1937 (producers' goods) and September 1937 (consumers' goods). These leads and lags are apparent in Figure 3, in which are plotted the production of producers' durables and nondurables, and consumers' durables and nondurables by months from 1936 to 1938.

CORPORATE PROFITS

The final measure of general industrial performance to be discussed is corporate profits. Barger's Quarterly Series [13] is compared with quarterly new corporate capital issues, in Figure 4. The low level of the recovery from 1935 to 1937 is quite apparent. There was a steady increase in net corporate profits from the first through the fourth quarter of 1936, but earnings in the latter quarter ($765 million) were less than 50% of average quarterly earnings in 1929 ($1,538 million). Moreover, corporate net profits at their peak in the fourth

11. Norris O. Johnson, "New Indexes of Production and Trade," *Journal of the American Statistical Association, 33* (1938), 341–348; "Federal Reserve Bank of New York Indexes of Production and Trade," *Journal of the American Statistical Association, 36* (1941), 423–425; Federal Reserve Bank of New York, Research Department, "Production and Trade Indexes" (June 1944).

12. These data are not comparable to the Federal Reserve Board Index.

13. Barger, Table 28.

quarter of 1936 ($1,120 million) were still 27% less than the average quarterly rate in 1929. The peak quarterly rate in the thirties was 34% less than that in 1929 ($1,696 million).

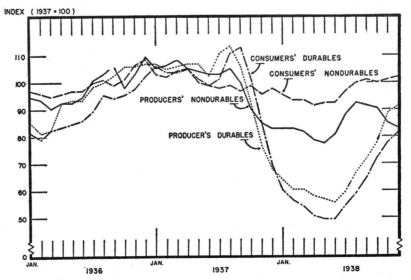

Fig. 3. Production of producers' durable and nondurable goods and consumers' durable and nondurable goods, by months, January 1936 through December 1938. Data from Federal Reserve Bank of New York, Research Department, "Production and Trade Indexes," (June 1944). Index was shifted from base of 100 = long-term trend to 1937 = 100.

Corporate profits began to decline in the first quarter of 1937 and by the third quarter had declined 20% from their peak in the fourth quarter of 1936. At the end of the year, corporate profits were less than one-half what they had been in the fourth quarter of 1936. Corporate profits fell to a low of $198 million in the second quarter of 1938, a decline of 82% from their 1936 peak. Even the maximum profit rate for four consecutive quarters [14] was 18% less than the average yearly rate from 1927 to 1929, and more than 30% less than the 1929 peak.

FINANCIAL INVESTMENT SERIES

NEW CORPORATE CAPITAL ISSUES

Extremely depressed conditions in the new corporate capital issues market were associated with this low rate of profits. (See Figure 4.)

14. Derived by adding the second half year profits in 1936 to the first half year profits of 1937.

New corporate capital issues were all but eliminated in the thirties. In 1935 monthly new corporate issues [15] (excluding refundings) were barely 5% of their average monthly rate in 1929 ($33.6 million contrasted with $666.8 million), and less than 7% of their aver-

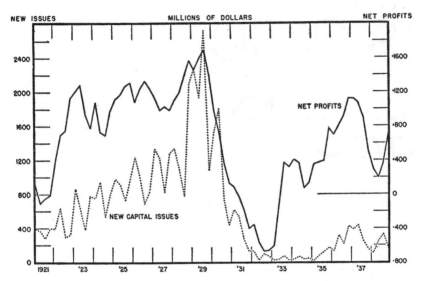

Fig. 4. Corporate new capital issues and net profits, by quarters, 1921–38. Original source for corporate new capital issues, *Commercial and Financial Chronicle*. Secondary source: Board of Governors of the Federal Reserve System, *Eighteenth Annual Report*, (1931), for 1921 and 1922; *Survey of Current Business, Supplement, 1932, 1936,* and *1940* for 1923–38. Quarterly averages have been computed from monthly data. Corporate net profits, seasonally adjusted, from Barger, *297–299*, Table 28.

age monthly rate from 1927 to 1929. New issues increased threefold from 1935 to 1936 ($33.6 million to $99.3 million), but were still only 15% of the 1929 level and 20% of their average in the 1927–29 period.

The highest monthly level of new corporate capital issues in the post-1933 years was $276.1 million in June 1937 (not shown in Figure 4). Yet this level was surpassed by 46 out of the 60 months in the years 1925–29, or in more than 75% of the months. New issues exceeded their June 1937 peak in 31 months, or 86% of the months from 1927 to 1929. The average for the 12 highest consecutive months, those from August 1936 through July 1937, was $131.5

15. These are *Commercial and Financial Chronicle* data taken from the *Survey of Current Business, Supplement, 1932, 1936, 1938* and *1940*. They include all new money issues.

million, which was less than the average monthly rate in any calendar year from 1922 to 1929.

New issues fell to a low of $11.7 million in April 1938 and then recovered to $202.3 million in June 1938. The monthly average for the year was 29% less than the year before ($72.7 million compared with $102.1 million).

CORPORATE REFUNDINGS

The picture was quite different with issues for refunding purposes.[16] However, these issues absorb no new savings and finance no new investment and therefore are much less significant as a factor affecting income and employment in the years 1935–38. In response to lower interest rates, refundings reached a monthly average of $157 million in 1935, about $41 million more per month than in 1929. The rate of refundings in July 1935 ($486.9 million) exceeded that of any month in 1927–29. Refundings continued to increase in 1936, finally reaching their peak in March 1936 ($536 million). The monthly average for the year was $282.3 million, more than twice the monthly rate in 1927–29. Refundings, which averaged $100.7 million per month during 1937, although ranging from $240 million (February) to $1.1 million (November) increased by about 5% in 1938 ($105.6 million).

This does not complete the story on business financing because, of course, private financing and financing from retained earnings also supplied some of the funds for expansion. But since no comprehensive series are available on these two sources of funds this discussion will be deferred to a later chapter.[17]

The movements of security prices were of significance for business financing in the period, and must now be examined.

CORPORATE BOND YIELDS

If the yield on bonds may be taken as an index of the cost of available investment funds, the most noteworthy development was the sharp decline in yields compared with those of the twenties. The monthly yield on bonds [18] declined almost continually from January 1935 (4.68%) to a minimum in December 1936 and January 1937 (3.67%). The latter yield compares with the minimum monthly yield in the twenties of 4.82% in March 1928. November 1934 (4.86%)

16. *Ibid.*
17. See Chapter 13.
18. Data on Moody's 120 Domestic Corporations taken from the *Survey of Current Business, Supplement, 1940,* for 1937–38 and the *Survey of Current Business* (November 1937), for earlier years. Originally compiled by Moody's Investors Service.

is the last month when the bond yield was greater than the minimum of the twenties.[19] However, as will be shown in the next section, this was due to the performance of the better grade bonds.

Bond yields reached their low in January 1937 (3.67%) and had risen almost 6% by April 1937 (3.97%). Yields declined slightly from April to August (3.88%). They then rose sharply, as income payments and industrial production declined, to 4.21% in November and to a peak of 4.50% in April 1938. By this latter date the cost of capital had increased 23% over the December and January lows in the winter of 1936–37. Bond yields then declined steadily from April through December 1938, until they were only slightly above the yields registered during the summer months of 1937.

DIFFERENCES BETWEEN YIELDS ON BAA AND AAA BONDS

There were marked differences between yields on AAA bonds and BAA bonds.[20] The 30 AAA bonds have had lower yields from July 1933 (4.36%) to the present than the minimum yield in the twenties, December 1927 to April 1928 (4.46%). But it was not until December 1935 (5.30%) that the yields on the 30 BAA bonds became lower than the minimum in the twenties (December 1927 and March 1928, 5.32%).

The yield on AAA bonds fell from August 1935 (3.60%) to their low in December 1936 and January 1937 (3.10%). The low point occurred at the same time for AAA bonds as for the average of the 120 domestic corporations. In the three months of February through April, AAA bond yields rose by 10% to 3.42% They declined again until August (3.24%) and then rose by 2% to April 1938 (3.30%), a rise of a little over 6% from the 1936–37 lows. They fell to a new low in December 1938 (3.08%).

The BAA bond yields reached a peak in March 1935 (6.20%) and then fell to a low in January 1937 (4.49%). Thereafter they rose almost without interruption until May 1938. From January 1937 to August 1937, just before the big break in prices, they rose almost 10%, compared with an increase of only 5% in AAA yields. The retreat of investors from the more risky enterprises was evidently greater even before the collapse in confidence and prices in September. The increase in BAA yields from January 1937 (4.49%) to

19. The average monthly yields in the years 1927, 1928, and 1929 for Moody's 120 Domestic Corporations were approximately 27, 27, and 33% greater respectively than the average monthly yields for the 1936–37 period.

20. AAA is the Moody rating given to the highest grade bonds, while BAA represents the lowest rating bonds which still are considered to have investment merit.

April 1938 (6.47%) was 1.98% in yield, or 44%, compared with an increase of only slightly more than 6% in AAA yields. These high yields on BAA bonds in 1938 were also considerably above those obtainable on the same grade bonds in 1927 and 1928. The average yield in 1938 (5.80%) was 6% greater than the average yield in 1927 and 1928 (5.48%). Even though bond yields tended to be lower in the thirties than during the twenties, the spread between the yields on AAA and BAA bonds increased, which suggests that lower grade issues and companies labored under a decided disadvantage.[21]

U. S. TREASURY BONDS

The trend in yields on U. S. Government bonds was also toward the extremely low rates which were characteristic of the thirties. From October 1934 (3.10%), yields were less than the minimum yields in 1927 and March 1928 (3.17%).[22] In 1935, yields on U. S. Government securities averaged 2.79% and had fallen to 2.51% by December 1936. Their low point was reached in February 1937 (2.46%), one month *after* the low for corporate bonds. The significance of this comparison is pointed out below.

Yields rose 14% by April 1937 (2.80%). They fell slightly to August 1937 (2.72%) and then rose in September 1937 (2.77%) in response to the stock market break. Thereafter they declined again to 2.48% in October 1938.

It is interesting to note that the greatest pressure on U. S. Government bonds was from February through April 1937: the yield in the latter month was not exceeded at any time during the recession. Of interest also is the lag by a month of the low in yields on these bonds behind the low in yields on corporate bonds. The break in government bond prices has been charged with responsibility for the downturn in corporate bond prices.[23] But the break in corporate bond prices occurred in February 1937, when U. S. Government bond

21. Hayes emphasized the widening spread in yield between the more "riskless" bonds (A1 ratings or better) and the lower grade bonds as evidence that the ample supply of credit in 1937 was not available on the same terms to all borrowers. "A Study of the Recession of 1937," 87–97.

22. These data are taken from the U. S. Treasury Department, *Treasury Bulletin* (March 1944), 58–59. This is the most recent revision of the index of partially tax-exempt Treasury bonds.

23. For example, Hansen describes this relationship: "There remains, however, to consider the effect of Reserve policy upon bond prices and indirectly upon the capital market. Even though the banking system as a whole unloaded very few bonds upon the outside public, it is nevertheless a fact that many of the larger banks sold bonds on a large scale. And this selling perhaps accentuated the break in the bond market, which was quickly transmitted first to corporate bonds and subsequently to corporate shares." *Full Recovery or Stagnation?* 271.

yields were still going down, so that this preliminary examination of the series seems to cast doubt upon such a theory of the relationship between government and corporate bond prices. However, in a later chapter it is shown that in the unrevised Treasury Index prices declined first in short-term U. S. Government bonds, and were followed then by corporate bonds.[24]

INDUSTRIAL STOCK PRICES

Industrial stock prices failed, by a wide margin, to regain their 1929 levels.[25] Since 1929 was an unusual year the extent of the recovery might better be measured by reference to 1928. At their peak level in March 1937 (137.4), industrial stock prices were still under their average in 1928 (139.4). By June 1937 (120.7) stock prices had retreated over 12% but they rose again through August 1937 (129.6). They tumbled 12% in September 1937 (112.4) and fell thereafter to 85.1 in December 1937, a drop of 38% from their peak, or almost 35% in five months. The decline continued to a low of 78.0 in April 1938, a retreat of 43% from the 1937 high. By December 1938, industrial stock prices had recovered to 100.0.

PUBLIC UTILITY STOCK PRICES

The movements in prices of public utility stocks [26] differ from those of the industrials in several respects. One is the wider margin by which public utility stocks failed to regain the levels of the twenties. The monthly averages for 1936 and 1937 were only 122.1 and 110.4 respectively, compared with 173.9 in 1928, 274.1 in 1929, and 250.7 in 1930.

Another important difference is that the peak was reached in January 1937, whereas the industrial peak was in March 1937. Public utility stock prices began to decline two months before industrial stock prices. The decline of 20% from January 1937 (133.0) to June 1937 (106.5) was also sharper than the decline in industrials. The recovery in the summer of 1937 was limited to one month, July. The precipitous decline began in September 1937 and by December 1937 (90.8) public utility stock prices were 32% under their year's high. At their low in April 1938 (76.6) they had declined by 42%. They then recovered to 90.7 by the end of 1938, although at a slower relative rate than did the industrials.

24. Chapter 7.

25. Standard and Poor's Corporation, *Long Term Security Price Index Record*. Taken from *Survey of Current Business* (January 1942). Base of 1935–39 = 100.

26. *Ibid.* The movements are the same if only operating utilities are used. Base is 1935–39 = 100.

Still another point of interest is that the public utility stock prices alone continued to decline after 1932 (92.1) and reached their low in March 1935 (62.1). These declines occurred as industrials rose from 59.9 in 1933 to 73.4 in 1934. The differences between the movements of the two indexes undoubtedly reflect in part the uncertainty as to the ultimate effects of government legislation on the public utility holding companies, and public competition and hostility generally.

RAILROAD STOCK PRICES

The movements in railroad stock prices [27] roughly paralleled those of the industrials, although the secular decline in railroad earnings limited the recovery of railroad stock prices compared with that of industrial stock prices. Railroad stock prices advanced 80% from 1935 (90.2) to their peak in March 1937 (165.8). At their peak, however, railroad stock prices were a little over 50% of the 1927–28 average (328.4) and were only approximately 42% of the 1929 average (390.7).

Unlike the industrial average, railroad stock prices declined steadily from April 1937 through the rest of that year. They were less than one-half of their March peak in December 1937 (81.1) and reached their low in April 1938 (56.7), roughly 35% of the 1937 high. Prices were still depressed at the end of the year (76.4) but were 20 points above the year's low.

THE MONEY MARKET AND THE BANKING SYSTEM

SHORT-TERM INTEREST RATES

Rates on short-term prime commercial paper give striking evidence of the extent to which monetary policy was directed toward lowering interest rates. Rates on four to six months' paper [28] fluctuated from .75% to 1.00% during the years 1935, 1936, and the early part of 1937. They ranged from .625% to 1.00% during the decline and recovery of 1937–38. Comparable monthly rates in 1927 were from 4 to 4.5%, in 1928, 4 to 5.75%, and in 1929, 5.25 to 6.25%. It seems unlikely that short-term interest rates could have been of major causal importance in the recession unless it is argued that the recession might not have occurred if interest rates had declined to zero or lower.[29] Compared with other factors, short-term interest rates seem to have been distinctly favorable to continued expansion.

27. *Ibid.* Base is 1935–39 = 100.
28. U. S. Board of Governors of the Federal Reserve System, *Banking and Monetary Statistics* (1943), 450–459. Rates are for New York City.
29. Yields actually became negative on the shortest term Treasury bills because of the favorable tax treatment accorded them in certain states.

RESERVE BANK CREDIT

Total Reserve bank credit [30] was virtually constant from 1935 through March 1937. From March 1937 ($2,472 million) to May 1937 ($2,577 million) there was an increase of $105 million, largely because the Reserve authorities attempted to support the government bond market. As a consequence, United States securities held increased by $96 million from March 1937 ($2,430 million) to May 1937 ($2,526 million). Bills discounted and bills bought were of negligible quantity during the period and changes in the amounts held were very small. Bills discounted increased from $3 million in February 1937 to $16 million in May 1937, and to a peak of $24 million in September 1937. Bills bought increased from $3 million in March 1937 to $5 million in May 1937. These two classes of Reserve credit could not have been of causal importance in the recession.

MEMBER BANK LOANS AND INVESTMENTS

Member bank loans and investments should be studied for some indication as to whether Reserve bank credit was a factor in facilitating or preventing loans and advances from being made to business. Loans of reporting member banks in 101 leading cities rose by over $500 million from August 1935 ($7,847 million) to August 1936 ($8,365 million). They then increased substantially, by $1,661 million, to $10,026 million in September 1937. Thereafter loans declined to a low in July 1938 ($8,213 million) and were but slightly above this by December 1938 ($8,465 million).

There was a steady increase in government bonds held by member banks. In the 18 months from January 1935 ($8,452 million) to July 1936 ($10,762 million) they increased by over $2.3 billion.[31] In the next 15 months government bonds held declined by $1,716 million. The pronounced decline began in March 1937 when holdings were reduced to $10,008 million, a decline of $322 million over February 1937. From March ($10,008 million) to April ($9,628 million) the amount held was reduced by $380 million, the maximum monthly decline. The low in October 1937 ($9,046 million) was followed by an increase to $9,899 million in December 1938.

All other investments of member banks [32] increased only moderately from January 1935 ($2,976 million) to their peak in July 1936

30. Bills discounted, bills bought, U. S. Government securities, and all other credit, taken from *Banking and Monetary Statistics*, 369–372.

31. *Ibid.*, 132–157. Approximately the same increase occurred in 1934, from $5,692 million to $8,163 million.

32. *Ibid.*, 132–157.

($3,348 million). They declined 101 million by December 1936 and then increased to their March peak ($3,316 million). The decline, beginning in April 1937, was uninterrupted through December 1937 ($2,874 million). By December 1938 other investments had increased to $3,222 million. The effect on total investments of member banks [33] of the decline in these two series was a decrease of over $2.1 billion from July 1936 ($14,110 million) to November 1937 ($11,997 million). The pressure was greater in the U. S. Government bonds held, although they declined only 16% compared with a 14% decline in all other investments. However, the decline in government bonds held from July 1936 to April 1937 was over 10%, compared with a decline of only 2.8% in all other investments.

EXCESS RESERVES OF MEMBER BANKS

Excess reserves of member banks increased from an average of $528 million in 1933 [34] to $3,105 million in the two-week period August 1 to 15, 1936,[35] largely as a result of the steady inflow of gold from abroad. It was at this time that the Federal Reserve Board increased reserve requirements by 50% in an attempt to reduce the expansion which was possible on the basis of the existing member bank reserves. This action reduced excess reserves to $1,950 million in the latter part of August. On December 21, 1936, the secretary of the Treasury announced the beginning of a gold sterilization program to prevent inflowing gold from becoming a part of the monetary reserves of the banking system. This policy remained in force until April 16, 1938, when the accumulated gold, amounting to $1,392 million, was transferred to the Treasury's balance with the Federal Reserve System.

The Board of Governors on January 30, 1937 announced a second increase in reserve requirements of $33\frac{1}{3}\%$ to take effect in two equal increases, one on March 1, 1937, and the other on May 1, 1937. The increase in the reserve requirement reduced excess reserves from $2,078 million in February 1937, to $1,398 million in March 1937, and from $1,594 million in April 1937, to $918 million in May 1937. The effects of these increases on the various types of member banks will be discussed in Chapter 7.

The low in excess reserves was reached by August 1937 ($773 million). They then began to increase and following the desterilization of gold in April 1938 were $2,548 million. They reached a new high in October 1938 ($3,227 million) and were $3,205 million at the end of the year. The quarterly changes of excess reserves in mem-

33. *Ibid.*
34. *Ibid.,* 368.
35. *Federal Reserve Bulletin, 23* (1937), 4.

ber banks from 1929 through 1938 are graphed in Figure 9, Chapter 6. The monthly data from July 1936 through June 1937 are also shown in Figure 10, in the same chapter.

CHANGES IN OUTSIDE DEBITS AND TOTAL DEMAND DEPOSITS

Outside debits [36] rose steadily from the first quarter of 1935 ($44,550 million) to a peak in the first quarter of 1937 ($60,590 million). However, this peak was less than any quarterly average from 1925 to 1930. In the second and third quarters of 1937, outside debits declined approximately $1 billion to $59.3 and $59.4 billion respectively (quarterly averages at annual rates). By the fourth quarter of 1937 ($56.6 billion) they had declined roughly $3 billion, and an additional $7 billion by the second quarter of 1938. By the end of the year they had risen to $53.9 billion.

Total demand deposits [37] rose $4.8 billion from 1935 ($22.4 billion) to 1936 ($27.2 billion), and an additional half billion in 1937 despite the decline in activity during the latter part of that year. There was then a decline of four-tenths of a billion in 1938.

PRICE-COST RELATIONSHIPS

Changes in price-cost relationships, as has been remarked, were assigned significance in the 1937–38 period by several authors, though for different reasons. In the opinion of some, it was the failure of wages to rise as fast as the prices of finished products [38] which was largely responsible for the recession. To other writers it was the encroachment of wages upon profits and profit expectations which led to the recession. These series deserve careful review and description because of the importance attached to them.

AVERAGE HOURLY WAGE RATES IN MANUFACTURING

The change in average hourly wage rates in manufacturing is of major interest as a cost development. By January 1935, they were once again at the peak rate ($.594) which they had reached in September 1929.[39] The average for the year 1935 was 60 cents per hour, 1 cent per hour more than in 1929. From February 1936 the rate ($.609) increased to $.638 in December 1936, with the largest monthly change of 1.2 cents per hour occurring from November to

36. Barger, Table 20. Figures are for 140 cities outside New York City.
37. Villard, *Deficit Spending and National Income*, Table 19, 313.
38. And consequently a failure of consumption expenditures to keep pace with prices.
39. National Industrial Conference Board, *Wages, Hours, and Employment in the United States, 1914–1936* (New York, 1936), and *Survey of Current Business, Supplement, 1940*. Figures are for 25 manufacturing industries.

December. The most marked increase was from $.639 in January
1937 to $.718 in October 1937, a rise of almost 8 cents per hour or
12.4% in the 10-month period. The increase from January 1937 to
July 1937 ($.712) was 11%. It was during this same period that
Leon Henderson forecast an impending recession because he believed
consumer purchasing power was failing to keep up with prices.[40] The
hourly wage rate in manufacturing increased by 21% from September 1929 ($.594) to October 1937 ($.718). From this peak it declined to $.714 in January and February 1938, and then rose to a new
peak of $.720 in March 1938. It had declined slightly by the end of
the year. These quarterly changes are graphed in Figure 5 along with

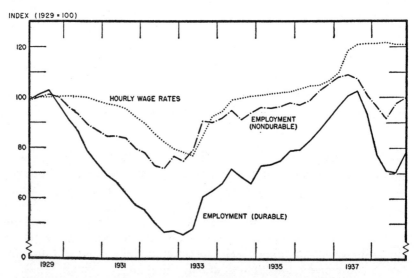

Fig. 5. Average hourly wage rates and employment in the manufacture of
durable and nondurable goods, by quarters, 1929–38. Original source for
average hourly wage rates in manufacturing, National Industrial Conference
Board, *Wages, Hours, and Employment in the United States, 1914–1936.*
Secondary source: *Survey of Current Business* (October 1936), for 1929–31;
Survey of Current Business, Supplement, 1936, for 1932–33; and *Survey of
Current Business* (January 1940), for 1934–38. Quarterly averages were com-
puted from monthly data and converted to index numbers based on 1929 = 100.
Original source for employment in manufacture of durable and nondurable
goods, Bureau of Labor Statistics. Secondary source: Revised seasonally
adjusted indexes of employment through June 1937 from the *Federal Reserve
Bulletin, 24* (1938), 842–845.; July 1937–December 1938 data from *Survey of
Current Business* (March 1941). Quarterly averages were computed from
monthly data and the index base was shifted from 1923–25 = 100 to 1929 = 100.

40. See Chapter 2.

employment in the manufacture of both durable and nondurable goods.

AVERAGE WEEKLY EARNINGS AND HOURS WORKED

In January 1935 average weekly earnings [41] were only $21.47 compared with an average of $27.53 in 1927, $27.80 in 1928, and $28.55 in 1929. The explanation of the lower weekly take-home pay must lie in the reduction in number of hours worked over the period, because average hourly wage rates on this date were equal to the peak rate in 1929. The hours reported worked declined by 12 hours from an average of 48.3 per week in 1929 to 36.3 in January 1935. With hourly wages at $.594, weekly wages declined over $7 per week because of the reduced number of hours worked.

By the end of 1935, weekly earnings had risen to $23.16.[42] A 10% increase in six months followed from July 1936 ($23.95) to December 1936 ($26.36). In the next five months there was another large increase of $1.74 per week, or almost 7%. This, it must be noted, was on top of the 10% increase which immediately preceded it. Hours worked per week by this time had risen to 40.9.

There was a gradual decline from the peak average earnings of $28.10 per week in May 1937 to $27.10 per week in September 1937, primarily because overtime was reduced. The low was reached in January 1938 ($22.85) and average weekly earnings had risen to $26.20 in November 1938. The average level for the year ($24.43) was about the same as in 1936 ($24.39).

It is revealing to compare real weekly earnings at their peak in 1937 with their peak in 1929. Although weekly earnings were still under their 1929 peak ($28.10 compared with $29.22), real weekly earnings were more than 10% greater than in 1929. The difference is accounted for by the change in the cost of living between the two periods, 101.2 in October 1929 compared with 87.8 in May 1937. The comparison would be even more striking if average hourly wages were reduced to real terms.

PAYROLLS IN MANUFACTURING

Payrolls in manufacturing are another important barometer of developments in cost relations. The recovery for payrolls in all industries [43] was 21% from July 1935 (69.1) to July 1936 (83.5). There

41. National Industrial Conference Board, *op. cit.* and *Survey of Current Business, Supplement, 1940.* Figures are for 25 manufacturing industries.
42. *Ibid.*
43. Original source: Bureau of Labor Statistics. Secondary source: *Survey of Current Business* (December 1938), for 1927–33; (October 1939), for 1934–37; and (March 1941), for 1938. Data are seasonally unadjusted. Base is 1923–25 = 100.

was another sharp increase of 19% through December 1936 (99.2). This was followed by a 10% increase from February (100.1) to the peak in May 1937 (110.1), at which level payrolls were approximately equal to their average in 1929 (110.4) but were still 4 per cent below their peak in 1929.

Payrolls sagged to 105.2 in June and July 1937. The secondary peak in August 1937 (108.7) was followed by a decline to 104.9 in October 1937. There was a precipitous decline of 20% to December (84.6). The decline was extended through June 1938 (71.6), in all a 35% decline from the peak in 1937. By the end of the year payrolls had risen to 88.1.

The greater fluctuations in durable goods than in nondurable goods are clearly evident when payrolls in manufacturing are broken down into these two categories. From January 1935 (55.1) to September 1936 (80.1), durable goods payrolls increased by 25 points or 45%. In the next 9 months the index rose by another 33 points, or 41%, to 113.3. The rise in nondurable payrolls was much less pronounced, just under 10% from January 1935 (81.3) to July 1936 (89.0). There was a sharp rise then of 20% from July to the March-April level of 107.0.

Nondurable payrolls reached a peak of 108.1 in August 1937, and durable payrolls firmed to a secondary peak of 109.2 in the same month. The decline from August to September in durable payrolls was reversed in October. But the decline which began for nondurables in September 1937 was uninterrupted, with a single exception, until the low of 83.0 in June 1938, a decline of 23% from the peak in 1937. Durable goods payrolls declined by 48% from their May 1937 peak to their low in July 1938 (58.5), a lag of one month behind the nondurable payrolls. By the end of the year both had recovered to approximately their average in 1936.

COMPONENTS OF WHOLESALE PRICES

The movements in the general index of wholesale prices have already been described.[44] A breakdown of this index into finished products, semimanufactures, and raw materials [45] reveals differences in movements within the components.

Prices of finished products. The prices of finished products showed little increase from January 1935 (80.8) to October 1936 (82.0). There was an increase of less than 8% from November 1936 to the

---

44. See earlier section of this chapter under heading, "The Over-all Performance of the Economy."

45. Original source: Bureau of Labor Statistics. Secondary source: *Survey of Current Business, Supplement, 1932, 1936,* and *1940.* Base is 1926 = 100.

peak in September 1937 (89.1). It should be noted that this peak occurred five months after the peak for general wholesale prices. A steady decline followed to the end of 1938 (80.2), when the index was slightly less than in any month during 1935.

Prices of semimanufactured goods. The price rises in semimanufactured goods were more substantial. From January 1935 (71.2) they increased 7% to October 1935 (76.3). A year later prices were unchanged. However, by March 1937 (89.6) there had been a 13.4 point increase, a rise of 17.6% compared with a rise of 8% in general wholesale prices. In April wholesale prices of semimanufactured goods began a decline which ended with a low of 74.1 in June 1938. By the end of the year semimanufactured goods prices were 75.2, slightly under the average in 1936 of 75.9.

Prices of raw materials. Raw material wholesale prices were the most volatile series. After little change in 1935, they rose by approximately 20% from May 1936 (75.8) to their peak in March 1937 (90.1). The qualification should be added, however, that in perhaps the most critical period (September 1936 to March 1937) the relative increase was only 10% (from 81.8 to 90.1). A steady decline then followed to a low in May 1938 (70.7). By the end of the year the index was still only 70.9.

Prices of farm products. From July 1935 (77.1) farm prices advanced irregularly by 5% to 81.3 in July 1936.[46] There was an advance of 12.8 points from August 1936 to the peak in March 1937 (94.1), a gain of slightly under 16% compared with a gain of 20% in raw material prices for the same period. One of the components of the index, grains, advanced spectacularly from 73.0 (June 1936) to 119.2 (April 1937), an increase of 63%, and then fell spectacularly by 50 points, a decrease of 42%, during the following seven months through November 1937.

WORLD PRICE OF FOODSTUFFS AND RAW MATERIALS

This series includes the components cotton, rubber, silk, sugar, tea, tin, and wheat.[47] From a low in March 1935 (39.4) there was a rise in January 1936 (44.8), and a subsequent decline to 42.1 in June 1936. The sharp rise commenced in July 1936 and the peak was reached at 59.4 in April 1937, an increase of 41%. However, in the 1920's there were comparable rates of increase, notably from 77.8 in June 1922 to 112.8 in April 1923, an increase of 45%. The decline began in May 1937 and continued through December 1938 (36.5).

46. Prices were slightly under this July 1935 level from March through May 1936.
47. *Survey of Current Business* (January 1939), and *Supplement, 1940.* The base for the series is 1923–25 = 100.

CONSTRUCTION COSTS

Finally, the movements in construction costs must be described. Probably the major single reason given for the limited extent of the recovery is the failure of housing expenditures to regain the levels of the 20's. Therefore the movements in the building costs series may provide a partial explanation for the inadequate revival of housing expenditure.

Wholesale building costs. Wholesale building material costs were relatively stable from January 1935 (84.9) to June 1936 (85.8).[48] From June 1936 to the peak in May 1937 (97.2) prices advanced by over 13%. At this level building costs were above those in any month during 1928 and 1929, but were 8% less than in February 1925 (105.2) when housing construction was at the highest level reached prior to the construction boom of post-World War II.

Beginning in June 1937 building costs declined, and reached their low in July 1938 (89.2). They had advanced only to 89.4 by December 1938. Thus building costs increased substantially from 1936 to 1937, but it is not immediately evident that these increases were excessive as compared with those in other fields. However, the very weak nature of the revival in housing suggests that any increases in building costs were particularly unfavorable to an increased volume of construction.

Skilled labor rates in construction. For the years 1935 and 1936 the changes in skilled labor rates were much the same as in the prices of building materials.[49] Wage rates were relatively stable from January 1935 ($1.11 per hour) through June 1936 ($1.14 per hour). Skilled labor rates are somewhat unique, however, among the series studied for they continued to increase throughout 1937 and 1938 and were at their peak rate in December 1938 ($1.43 per hour). They increased by 20% from June 1936 ($1.14 per hour) to August 1937 ($1.37 per hour). At the latter rate wages had increased to the peak of $1.37 in August 1929.[50]

Rates for unskilled labor in construction. Labor rates for common

48. Original source: Bureau of Labor Statistics. Secondary source: *Survey of Current Business, Supplement, 1932, 1936,* and *1940.* Data before 1927 from the U. S. Department of Labor, Bureau of Labor Statistics, *Wholesale Prices 1913 to 1927, Bulletin No. 473.* The base for the index is 1926 = 100.

49. Original source: *Engineering News Record.* Secondary source: *Survey of Current Business* (September 1933), for 1922 to 1932; *Supplement, 1936* and *1940,* for 1933-38.

50. A lag in skilled labor rates in construction may be characteristic of the downside in economic activity, because the same sort of lag was also experienced in 1929 and 1930. Skilled labor rates increased through 1930 and reached their peak in December 1930.

construction displayed much the same pattern as did skilled labor rates.[51] From a low in May 1935 ($.523) these rates increased by 4 cents per hour to July 1936 ($.563). There was over a 10 cent per hour or approximately a 19% increase from July 1936 through August 1937 ($.668 per hour). As with those for skilled labor, rates for common construction labor continued to rise after the general decline in business activity in September 1937. Their peak was reached in January 1938 ($.680 per hour). At this level they exceeded the previous average monthly peak in 1930 ($.561) by over 21%.[52] Wage rates in August 1937 ($.668) were 18% above their peak in December 1929 ($.565).

EMPLOYMENT AND UNEMPLOYMENT

EMPLOYMENT IN ALL MANUFACTURING INDUSTRIES

The inherent difficulty in collecting data on unemployment and the rather large differences in the principal estimates of unemployment make the indexes of employment a more reliable indication of the degree of resource use than unemployment statistics. The seasonally adjusted estimates of the Federal Reserve Board [53] show employment in all manufacturing industries at 88.9 in January 1935. By December 1935 (94.7) employment had increased over 6%. The increase from April 1936 (95.1) to July 1937 (112.2) was 17 points or approximately 18%. At this peak employment was 4% greater than in August 1929 (108.4).

There was a 12% decline from August 1937 to December 1937 (98.2). The low for employment, in June 1938 (86.3), was 23% under the peak employment of July 1937. Employment had recovered to 96.7 by the end of the year.

Some differences can be observed between the behavior of employment in the durable goods industries and that in the nondurable goods industries. The fluctuations were larger in the former than in the latter. Employment in the durable goods industries increased 12% from January 1935 (75.3) through March 1936 (84.3). The rate of increase was considerably greater from March 1936 through De-

51. Original source: *Engineering News Record*. Secondary source: *Survey of Current Business* (September 1933), for 1922 to 1932, *Supplement, 1936* and *1940* for 1933–38.

52. The average monthly rate in 1930 was surpassed, however, by 1936 when rates averaged $.564.

53. Original source for all employment data: Seasonally unadjusted—Bureau of Labor Statistics. Seasonally adjusted—*Federal Reserve Bulletin, 24* (1938), 838–845, for data prior to 1933; *25* (1939), 880, for data 1934 through June 1937; *Survey of Current Business* (March 1941) for July 1937 through December 1938. The index is based on 1923–25 = 100.

cember 1936 (100.2), roughly a 19% increase. The peak in July 1937 (109.2) was only slightly less than the August 1929 peak (109.7). Employment had fallen to 92.3 by December 1937 and the low of 72.8 was reached in July 1938, a decline of 33% from the peak of 1937.

Employment in nondurable goods industries in January 1935 (101.8) was slightly above the average monthly employment in 1928 (101.6). The index was virtually unchanged by March 1936 (102.4). Beginning in March 1936 there was an accelerated increase to the peak in May 1937 (115.7), a rise of 13%. The peak in durable employment, however, was in July 1937. The major decline began in September 1937, and employment in nondurable goods industries had fallen by 12% at its low in June 1938 (98.6). It should be observed again that the trough for nondurable employment (occurring in June 1938) preceded that for durable employment, by one month. Data on a quarterly basis for these series have been compared with average hourly wages in Figure 5.

UNEMPLOYMENT

The margin of error in the data is extremely large, yet it is useful to get some idea of the general level of unemployment from 1935 to 1938. The National Industrial Conference Board [54] estimated unemployment at 11.2 million in January 1935. This fell to 6.3 million in September 1936 and rose to a new high of 7.6 million in January 1937. It then fell to a low of 5.1 million in both August and September 1937 and rose rapidly thereafter to 10.8 million in May 1938, an increase of over 100%. By the end of the year unemployment had decreased to 9.3 million. [55]

Estimates provided by the American Federation of Labor [56] also indicate that the low in unemployment was reached in September 1937, but at an absolute level 2.4 million higher than that reported by the National Industrial Conference Board. Similarly, the first source put the peak of unemployment in May 1938 at 11.4 million, which is 0.6 million greater than the estimate of the National Industrial Conference Board.

---

54. National Industrial Conference Board, "Employment and Unemployment of the Labor Force 1900–1940," *Conference Board Economic Record, 2* (1940), 86.

55. Samuelson and Nixon indicate that the National Industrial Conference Board estimates were consistently too low throughout the period because of an understatement in the base census year of 1930. Russell A. Nixon and Paul A. Samuelson, "Estimates of Unemployment in the United States," *Review of Economics and Statistics, 22* (1940), 101–111.

56. *American Federationist*, "The Federation's Revised Unemployment Estimate," *43* (1936), 64–73; and Nixon and Samuelson.

On the basis of either series, unemployment appears to have been at its minimum level in September 1937, the month when most of the major economic series declined sharply. It reached its maximum in May 1938, the month before the revival in most of the important series.

CONSUMPTION FACTORS

TOTAL CONSUMPTION EXPENDITURES

The next series to be reviewed relate to consumption expenditures. Many analysts have argued that the recovery in the thirties was inspired primarily by consumption expenditures, so these series deserve careful description.

Total consumption by quarters increased continuously from the first quarter of 1935 ($13,667 million) to the fourth quarter of 1936 ($16,430 million), an increase of almost $3 billion or over 20%.[57] Consumption expenditures declined in the first quarter of 1937 ($15,952 million) but rose again to their peak in the third quarter of 1937 ($17,264 million). Consumption may have been important in the 1936–37 recovery, but this peak rate of expenditure was over $2.5 billion less than the peak rate in the third quarter of 1929 ($19,785 million). Total consumption expenditures at their peak in the third quarter of 1937 were more than 10% less than in their peak in 1929.

Consumption expenditures then declined from the third quarter of 1937 ($17,264 million) to their low in the second quarter of 1938 ($14,749 million), a drop of $2,515 million or 14.6%. By the fourth quarter of 1938 ($16,728 million) consumption expenditures were above their average quarterly rate in 1937 ($16,602 million).

Emphasis has been placed upon the induced effects of changes in consumption upon investment expenditures. Some who believe that the 1933–37 recovery was largely consumption inspired attribute large significance to the decrease in the rate of increase of consumption expenditures as the cause for the recession. The data on consumption expenditures reveal that they not only failed to increase but actually declined from the fourth quarter of 1936 through the second quarter of 1937. However, the rate of increase was $1,100 million during the third quarter (the crucial period immediately preceding the break in most economic series), which was a greater increase absolutely and relatively than that of any earlier quarter from 1935 to 1937.

57. Barger, Table 9. These estimates are seasonally adjusted but the components are seasonally unadjusted.

CONSUMER INSTALLMENT CREDIT

Changes in short-term consumer debt have often been used as an extremely sensitive index of changes in consumer behavior. Monthly data show that consumer installment credit increased by over $2,300 million, or more than 58%, from January 1935 ($4,037 million) to December 1936 ($6,396 million).[58] This peak was not exceeded until April 1937 ($6,481 million). Consumer short-term debt rose from April to its peak in December 1937 ($7,054 million). However, the increase was at a decelerated rate, which lends some support to the argument that a decreasing rate of increase in consumption expenditures was prominent in explaining the downturn of September 1937. There was a steady decline in 1938 to a low in August 1938 ($6,245 million). By December 1938 short-term consumer debt had increased to $6,618 million.

DEPARTMENT STORE SALES

Department store sales, another important measure of consumption expenditures, increased by almost 10% from January 1935 (84) to February 1936 (92).[59] From February 1936 to November 1936 (105) they increased by 14%. There was a period of relative stability from February 1937 (108) through October 1937 (108), although the peak was attained in May 1937 (111).

The failure of department store sales to expand after May 1937 adds additional support to the argument that the decline in rate of increase of consumption expenditures was a cause of the recession. By May 1938 (95) these sales had declined 14%. In December 1938 they had recovered to slightly above the average monthly level of sales in 1936 (100).

Capital Formation and Expenditures

Important features of the recovery and decline are revealed by consideration of the major series on capital formation. Quarterly series on gross private capital formation, net private capital formation, producer equipment expenditures, private construction, changes in business inventories, and net foreign balance are available.[60] Data are also presented on annual totals of various capital formation items and gross and net savings.

58. Duncan McC. Holthausen, "Monthly Estimates of Short-Term Consumer Debt, 1929–42," *Survey of Current Business* (November 1942), 9–25.
59. *Federal Reserve Bulletin, 30* (1944), 549. The index is based upon 1935–39 = 100.
60. All the quarterly capital formation series are taken from Barger, Table 11.

GROSS PRIVATE INVESTMENT

Gross private investment [61] had recovered from depression lows by the first quarter of 1935 ($1,093 million). There was an increase of 58% to the fourth quarter of 1935 ($1,732 million), followed by a substantial increase, of 82%, from the first quarter of 1936 ($1,699 million) to the fourth quarter ($3,092 million). The latter rate was approximately equal to the quarterly average in 1924 ($3,243 million).

Gross private investment fell in the first quarter of 1937 ($2,882 million) but increased rapidly in the second quarter ($3,721 million), to a level only slightly below the average quarterly rate in 1929 ($4,043 million). The peak in the third quarter of 1937 ($4,246 million) was exceeded by only three quarterly periods in the twenties, the third quarter of 1923 ($4,263 million), the first quarter of 1926 ($4,460 million), and the fourth quarter of 1928 ($4,430 million).[62] A peculiarity of the peaks in the third quarters of both 1923 and 1937 was the large portion contributed by changes in business inventories, $1,113 million in the former period and $1,487 million in the latter period. This may be seen directly by referring to Figure 6, in which net private investment and the change in business inventories have been compared by quarters from 1921 to 1938. It will be argued later that a considerable part of these accumulations was unintended. This makes comparisons between such peaks and others with more normal investment compositions somewhat unreal.[63]

Following this peak, there was a drastic decline of almost 50% to the fourth quarter of 1937 ($2,197 million). Gross private investment rose from its low in the second quarter of 1938 ($1,310 million) to the still low level of $1,857 million in the fourth quarter of 1938.

NET PRIVATE INVESTMENT

The differences between the series on gross private investment and net private investment are the estimates of capital consumption. The striking thing about net private investment is that, with due allowance for capital consumption, it remained negative until the second quarter of 1936 ($335 million). This fact is pointed up by Figure 6. There was a large increase to the fourth quarter of 1936 ($1,094 million), followed by a decline in the first quarter of 1937 ($829

61. This series includes gross producer durable goods, gross private construction, change in business inventories, and the foreign balance.

62. It was equal to the third quarter of 1929 and only slightly above the fourth quarter of 1929.

63. See Chapter 12 on the role of inventory expenditures in the recession.

million). The second quarter of 1937 witnessed an increase to $1,617 million, of which almost one-half was in business inventories. At its peak in the third quarter of 1937 ($2,109 million), over two-thirds of net investment was in business inventories. This level was ex-

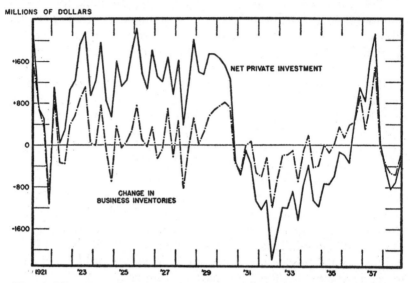

Fig. 6. Net private investment and change in business inventories, seasonally adjusted, by quarters, 1921–38. From Barger, 114–119, Table 11.

ceeded in only two quarters in the twenties, the third quarter of 1923 ($2,160 million) and the first quarter of 1926 ($2,227 million). Thus first comparison of both gross and net private investment suggests that the recovery was reasonably close to the level of the twenties, contrary to established opinion. However, as will be evident in the consideration of inventories below, some of the recovery in the thirties is more apparent than real. There was only a slight recovery in some of the series. For example, construction, one of the relatively autonomous components of capital formation, was particularly notable for its failure to regain the levels of the twenties.

CONSTRUCTION EXPENDITURES

This failure is quite noticeable when construction expenditures are compared with producer durable equipment expenditures, as has been done in Figure 7. Barger's quarterly series on gross private construction [64] rose from its low in the first quarter of 1935 ($293 million) to more than twice that figure in the fourth quarter of 1936

64. This series includes gross residential and gross business construction.

($692 million). However, at this date, it was only slightly over one-fourth of the quarterly peak in the twenties (the first quarter of 1926, $2,505 million).[65] Construction expenditures rose by 25% in the first quarter of 1937 ($862 million), to a level still only about one-third of the peak quarterly rate in the twenties. The decline which followed reduced construction expenditures by one-fourth to their low in the

INDEX (1925-29 = 100)

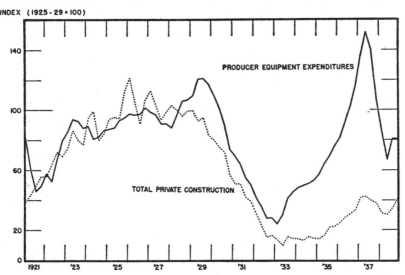

Fig. 7. Total private construction expenditures and producer durable equipment expenditures, seasonally adjusted, by quarters, 1921–38. From Barger, 114–119, Table 11. Data for both series were converted to index numbers with a base of 1925–29 = 100.

second quarter of 1938 ($628 million), a moderate decline compared with other capital formation components. By the fourth quarter of 1938 construction expenditures had recovered almost to the 1937 peak.[66]

PRODUCER DURABLE EQUIPMENT EXPENDITURES

While construction expenditures remained depressed in the mid-thirties, the picture was much different with respect to producer durable equipment expenditures. (See Figure 7.) The latter rose sharply from the first quarter of 1935 ($788 million) to the first quarter of 1936 ($1,129 million). In the next three quarters there was a $473 million increase. An idea of the height of equipment expenditures in the mid-thirties can be gained if it is realized that this

65. The annual total would place the peak in 1925.
66. According to the Federal Reserve Board index based on F. W. Dodge Corporation data, residential construction was considerably above the 1937 peak—57 in December 1938 compared with 47 in February 1937 (1923–25 average = 100).

peak in 1936 was exceeded only during the second, third, and fourth quarters of 1929.

In the first quarter of 1937 ($1,878 million) durable equipment expenditures were more than $200 million above their peak rate in the third quarter of 1929 ($1,672 million). Even this peak was exceeded in the second quarter of 1937 when expenditures rose to $2,098 million, 25% above the peak in 1929. A slight decline in the third quarter of 1937 was followed by a rather large decline to $1,472 million in the fourth quarter. However, the average quarterly rate in 1937 ($1,847 million) was more than 14% higher than the average in 1929 ($1,617 million).[67]

An explanation of this high level of expenditures on producer equipment at a time when producer plant expenditures failed to expand should provide some insight into the causes which operated in the 1937 decline.

CHANGE IN BUSINESS INVENTORIES

The change in business inventories was the other major component of capital formation which recovered to levels above those of the twenties. The extent to which the high levels of business inventories were composed of intended or unintended investment will be discussed in Chapter 12. For the present only the movements in the series will be outlined.

Two sources of data give a finer breakdown than annual totals, Barger's Quarterly Series [68] and the National Industrial Conference Board Monthly Index of Inventories in Manufactures.[69] Barger's estimates are based upon manufacturing and distribution, although the manufacturing component is derived from the National Industrial Conference Board Index. At best, either of these series is only a rough approximation to the actual inventory change because of the great difficulty in securing adequate coverage and in making allowance for price changes.

In Barger's estimates (see Figure 6) inventory change was negligible ($2 million) in the first quarter of 1935, was negative ($141 million) in the second quarter, and was negligible again ($15 million) in the third quarter. In the next four quarters, it varied from $139 million in the first quarter to $433 million in the third quarter of 1936. A large increase of $937 million took place in the fourth quarter

67. There was a substantial recovery shown in the data on producer equipment expenditures of the Department of Commerce, but the peak rates fell below the peak rate in 1929.

68. Barger, Table 11.

69. National Industrial Conference Board, "Inventories, Shipments, Orders, 1929–1940," *Supplement to Conference Board Economic Record, 2* (1940), 3.

of 1936, a greater increase than occurred in any quarter of the boom years, 1924–29.

In the first two quarters of 1937 business inventories rose $306 million and $787 million respectively. The increase of $1,487 million in the third quarter of 1937 exceeded that of any quarter in the 1920's except for the first quarter of 1921 ($1,548 million). When the general decline in business began in the fourth quarter of 1937 inventories also declined, and continued to decline for each quarter through 1938 although not at as great a rate in the last two quarters.

A monthly index of the National Industrial Conference Board shows a very great expansion in business inventories. From January 1935 (79.3) they increased by 9% to December 1935 (86.4).[70] They rose only moderately through July 1936. A very sharp rise then occurred from July 1936 (89.4) to October 1937 (126.7), an increase of over 40%. Inventories then declined to a low in December 1938 (101.9).

It is necessary to employ annual figures for breakdowns of other components of capital formation, such as gross and net total capital formation, gross and net public capital formation, business capital formation, business construction, and residential construction. The principal source is Kuznets.[71] Terborgh's estimates are a useful check.[72]

GROSS AND NET TOTAL ANNUAL CAPITAL
FORMATION

All of the annual totals of capital formation, both gross and net, were considerably below the 1929 levels. Gross capital formation [73] advanced from $9,355 million in 1935 to $13,817 million in 1936, an increase of 48%. The peak in 1937 ($17,497 million) was 12.5% less than in 1929 ($19,986 million). In constant prices it was 10.5% less than in 1929, and in per capita terms gross capital formation was 15.9% under that in 1929. Gross capital formation declined by $4,753 million to $12,744 million in 1938.

For the first time since 1930, net capital formation was positive

70. The base for this index is 1935–39 = 100.

71. Simon Kuznets, "Commodity Flow and Capital Formation in the Recent Recovery and Decline, 1932–1938," Bulletin No. 74 (New York, 1939), 2, 11; and *Commodity Flow and Capital Formation, 1* (New York, 1938), for earlier data. The annual totals on the capital formation items below are all taken from this source.

72. George Terborgh, "Estimated Expenditures for New Durable Goods 1919–1938," *Federal Reserve Bulletin*, 25 (1939), 731–736.

73. Residential construction, producers' durable commodities, business construction, net flow to inventories, public construction, and net foreign balance. Data on all these capital items are presented below except for net flow to inventories, which is included in the discussion of quarterly data.

in 1935 ($1,517 million). By 1937 ($8,182 million) it was only 19% less than in 1929 ($10,082 million); in constant prices it was 17% less, and in per capita terms 22% less.

Gross and net public capital formation. Gross public capital formation ranged from $1,995 million in 1935 to a peak of $3,455 million in 1938. In 1937 ($2,889 million) it was 6% less than in 1929 ($3,073 million), although in 1929 prices it was 1% greater than in 1929.

Net public capital formation ranged from $1,809 million in 1935 to a peak of $2,483 million in 1936. In 1937 ($1,967 million) it was 20.4% less than in 1929 ($2,471 million). In constant prices it was 13.8% under the 1929 level, and on the per capita basis it was 18.8% under the 1929 level.

Gross and net capital formation for business use. Gross capital formation for business use increased from $6,590 million in 1935 to $12,270 million in 1937. At this peak it was approximately 12% less than in 1929 ($13,903 million). In constant prices it was 6% less than in 1929 and on a per capita basis 11.5% less.

Net business capital formation was negative until 1935 ($1,291 million). At its peak in 1937 ($6,485 million) it was 4.2% less than in 1929 ($6,769 million). In constant prices the percentage difference was slightly less, only 2%, although on a per capita basis it was 7.9%.

Gross business construction. Gross business construction increased from $1,463 million in 1935 to $2,555 million in 1937, when it was still more than 44% under 1929, the peak year of the twenties.

Net business construction and net producers' durable expenditures. Net business construction is not separated from net producers' durables. The two rose from $121 million in 1935 to their peak of $3,148 million in 1937. In constant prices, expenditures at this peak were 35.1% less than in 1929. It is obvious, therefore, that a substantial deficit in the 1937 total net private capital formation was in business construction, because the quarterly series show that business durable expenditures were at record highs.

Gross and net residential construction. Gross residential construction experienced an extremely weak recovery. From $923 million in 1935 it increased to $1,956 million in 1937, and then fell to $1,746 million in 1938. In current prices, the peak in 1937 was 35% less than in 1929 ($3,010 million). This latter total was 42% less than the peak in gross construction in 1925 ($5,202 million). Residential construction in 1937 was 62% less than in 1925. Net residential construction was negative throughout the period.

Net claims against foreign countries. The final capital formation item, net claims against foreign countries, fell from minus $153 million in 1935 to minus $305 million in 1936. It was still negative in 1937 (minus $68 million) but rose to plus $741 million in 1938.

THE PRINCIPAL ESTIMATES OF GROSS AND NET SAVINGS

To summarize the capital formation relationships, comparisons of selected estimates of gross and net savings are presented in Tables 3 and 4. The gross savings estimates include those of Goldsmith,[74] Kuznets,[75] and Terborgh.[76] The net savings estimates are those of Kuznets and Goldsmith only.[77]

TABLE 3: GROSS SAVINGS ESTIMATES, 1933–37
(To the nearest half billion dollars)

Year	Goldsmith	Kuznets [a]	Terborgh [b]
1933	5.5	7.5	6.5
1934	7.5	10	9
1935	10	15	14
1936	17.5	21	19.5
1937	18.5	25	23

a. Includes Kuznets' consumer durable series.

b. Kuznets' net change in business inventories and net claims against foreign countries included.

Source: Adapted from Goldsmith.

TABLE 4: NET SAVINGS ESTIMATES, 1933–37
(To the nearest half billion dollars)

Year	Goldsmith	Kuznets
1933	−6.0	−3.5
1934	−4.5	−2.0
1935	−2.0	1.5
1936	4.5	5.5
1937	5.5	8.0
1933–37 Total	−2.5	9.5

Source: Kuznets, Bulletin No. 74; Goldsmith.

The increase in gross savings or capital formation from 1935 to 1937 varies from 65% for Terborgh to 85% for Goldsmith. Kuznets'

74. R. W. Goldsmith and Walter Salant, "The Volume and Components of Saving in the United States, 1933–1937," *Studies in Income and Wealth, 3*, Pt. 4 (New York, 1939), 241.

75. Kuznets, Bulletin No. 74, 2.

76. Terborgh, 731.

77. Goldsmith, 236.

increase was 67%. Kuznets' estimates of net savings for 1935–37 were much larger than those of Goldsmith. (See Table 4). This has been pointed out by Barger,[78] and is not surprising because the approaches differ markedly. Barger makes no attempt to reconcile the two approaches, but suggests that the Goldsmith method, which relies upon the financial or cash balance approach rather than upon measures of physical commodities, is probably susceptible to the greater error. Goldsmith believes that differences between the two series may arise because of inventory price changes and because of the exclusion of certain inventories from his series. However, Harris expressed doubt that these factors are sufficient to explain differences of this magnitude. Thus he commented:

It is not easy to reconcile these differences though Dr. Goldsmith makes an attempt to do so. He does not seem to us to be entirely successful. . . . In general, this may be said. The concept of saving used by Dr. Goldsmith is a monetary or financial concept. Industry may encounter losses, thus consuming part of its capital. Then the net result given by his study would probably be a reduction of capital (dissaving). But the real capital plant may increase, nevertheless, because new capital may be obtained via the security markets or through additional help from the banks.[79] Dr. Kuznets would then properly conclude that there had been a *net* capital formation. Furthermore, the two writers do not consider exactly the same categories of capital; and various problems of evaluation arise, which may account for differences.[80]

Goldsmith's breakdown of savings is of interest because it shows that much of the savings was being done by individuals. Business and government savings were negative from 1935 to 1937 except for government savings in 1937. Cash and deposits of individuals (a very rough measure of cash balances and capital balances held) increased by $2.6 billion in 1935 and by $3.9 billion in 1936. The increment in cash and deposits then fell abruptly to $0.5 billion in 1937, partly as a result of an increase in savings in insurance and pension reserves, and partly because of the increase in purchases of consumer durable goods. Goldsmith points out that there was an extraordinarily large increase in cash and bank deposits of individuals as well as in business inventories. Also, the higher ratio of gross to net investment tended to have a greater effect on the economy through the larger flow of producers' goods: "Cash and bank deposits among the increase in assets of individuals, and inventories of raw materials and

78. Barger, 359–361.

79. Only this latter reason would appear to be valid. New securities would result in savings which would also be reflected in the Goldsmith estimates.

80. Seymour E. Harris, *Economics of Social Security* (New York, 1941), 85 n.

finished goods among the increase in assets of business enterprises, were apparently much more important, both absolutely and relatively, than in the late 'twenties. On the other hand, the much higher ratio of gross to net saving in 1936–37 meant that the same amount of net saving reflected larger expenditures on durable goods, and thus a larger effect on the economic system than a decade earlier." [81] These developments will be given detailed consideration in the sections on inventories and the sources of business funds for investment.

The final series to be described are indexes of imports and exports and net income-increasing expenditure of government.

IMPORTS

There was a somewhat greater recovery in imports than in exports.[82] In 1935 the index fluctuated between 48 (February) and 59 (July), and was 58 at the end of the year. From May 1936 (58) there was a substantial increase to December 1936 (77). From January 1937 (74) there was a rise of 25% to the peak in June 1937 (93). At this level, imports were almost 25% under their peak in May 1929 (122). Thereafter imports declined sharply, by 30%, to the end of the year (65). The low was reached in May 1938 (45), and a slight increase followed to December 1938 (54).

EXPORTS

The index of exports followed an erratic course in 1935, fluctuating between 45 (January) and 62 (November), and completing the year at 56. The fluctuations were much milder in 1936, from 51 (January) to 57 (December). There was then a sharp increase of more than 40% from January 1937 (57) to May 1937 (81). Exports at this peak were almost 37% below their peak in March 1929 (128). Thus, while imports were one-quarter under their 1929 level, exports were more than one-third below it.

The decline in the index for exports was extremely moderate from May 1937 (81) to December 1937 (80). Exports no doubt were stabilized by the rapidly expanding world armaments race. However, contrary to the behavior of most other series, there was no expansion in exports in 1938. From a low of 58 (November 1938) exports recovered to 67 (December 1938). Nevertheless, the relatively greater stability in exports from the third quarter of 1937 throughout 1938 resulted in a positive net foreign balance.

81. Goldsmith, 238 n.
82. *Survey of Current Business, Supplement, 1932, 1936, 1940.* The indexes are based on 1923–25 = 100.

NET INCOME-INCREASING EXPENDITURES OF
GOVERNMENT

The final series, net income-increasing expenditures of all governmental units, is an exceedingly important one because many writers believe that the virtual cessation of such expenditures in 1937 was primarily responsible for the recession.

Professor Villard's series includes expenditures of all governmental units (federal, state, and local) and has been computed with extreme care in determining the income-increasing or -decreasing nature of the various types of governmental expenditures and receipts. Income-decreasing receipts are defined to be those tax receipts which reduce consumption expenditures, while income-decreasing expenditures are the disbursements which flow into capital balances.[83]

The average net income-increasing expenditures by governmental units during 1935 was $266 million. During that year these expenditures ranged from a peak of $353 million in June to a low of $158 million in November. From February 1936 ($126 million) they rose to their peak in June 1936 ($548 million), largely as the result of the prepayment of the adjusted Veterans' Service Certificates. During the remainder of the year, they ranged from $445.5 million in July to $266.3 million in November. In December 1936 they were $365.7 million.

These expenditures remained high through the first two months of 1937 at $264 million and $196 million respectively. The drastic decline began in March ($36.7 million) and continued to August 1937 when they actually became negative ($66.8 million). The net contribution was also negative ($46.2 million) in November 1937. The average monthly contribution for 1937 was $66.8 million as compared with the average in 1936 of $338.2 million. The decline was less pronounced if fiscal years are compared. The monthly average for fiscal year 1936 was $294.4 million compared with $228.6 million for fiscal year 1937.

There were substantial increases in such expenditures in January 1938 ($267.5 million) and March 1938 ($279.7 million) with little apparent effect on economic activity. Net income-increasing expenditures were resumed at a higher level of around $300 million per month beginning in June 1938.

A study of this series suggests that the decline in expenditures as

83. Villard, 323, Table 21. He examines all governmental expenditures and receipts and classifies each according to its effect on income. The sum of all the income-increasing expenditures minus the sum of all income-decreasing receipts is equal to net income-increasing expenditures.

measured month by month or in average monthly expenditures per fiscal year was not as drastic in the crucial period of July 1936 to June 1937 as monthly averages on a calendar year basis would indicate. Expenditures from January 1937 through June 1937 averaged $115 million per month, while in the first three months the average was $165.6 million. If there was any lag in the effect of government net income-increasing expenditures on income this latter rate is likely to have been effective in the spring months of 1937. The causal relationship of the decrease in net income-increasing expenditures by government to the recession will require more detailed discussion in a later chapter.[84]

Summary

The outstanding characteristics of the recovery were the achievement of new highs in industrial production, accompanied, however, by a large volume of unemployment and a failure of national income to exceed its levels of the 20's. Among the capital formation items, producer durable equipment expenditures were at high levels while producer plant expenditures were at extremely low levels. Among the cost items, hourly wages and real weekly wages reached new peak levels. Prices of finished and semifinished goods and of raw materials rose substantially immediately before the recession. Monetary and credit conditions were unusually easy. The budget was almost balanced as tax revenues increased and government expenditures were held relatively constant.

The nine-month recession itself was without parallel for its severity in American history: industrial production declined by 33% and durable goods production by over 50%; national income declined by 13% and payrolls by 35%; industrial stock averages declined by over 50%, a 35% decline in five months; and manufacturing employment declined by 23%. At the same time most prices and costs tended to be resistant, although prices of raw materials declined by 21%. Table 5 presents a convenient summary of the upper and lower turning points, dated by monthly occurrence, in the various important economic series.[85]

Examination of the various economic series has suggested that there is evidence to support a variety of explanations of the recession, including the failure of consumption expenditures to expand, de-

84. Cf. Chapter 5.
85. Adapted from Arthur F. Burns and Wesley C. Mitchell, *Measuring Business Cycles* (New York, 1946), 88–89. On the basis of other data not presented in the table, for three series, Burns and Mitchell selected some other month than that in which the maximum or minimum value actually was reached. Cf. their footnotes E, H, and I.

TABLE 5: SEQUENCE OF CYCLICAL TURNS IN THE
1937 RECESSION AND THE 1938 REVIVAL

40 American Series

Year	Month	Specific-cycle peak
1936	Dec.	Production of producers' nondurable goods
		Production of consumers' nondurable goods
		Orders for manufactured goods
1937	Jan.	Man-hours worked, nondurable manufactures
		Corporate bond prices [a]
		Number of business failures, *inverted* [b]
		Net demand deposits of member banks
	Feb.	Private construction contracts
		New corporate capital issues
	March	Bank debits outside New York City
		Total industrial production, Standard Statistics Co.
		Industrial common stock prices
	April	Index of wholesale prices
		Freight car loadings [a]
		Man-hours worked in manufacturing
	May	Retail sales [c]
		Total industrial production, F.R. Board
		Production nondurable manufactures [a]
		Payrolls in manufacturing
		Payrolls, nondurable manufactures
		Total exports
	June	Total income payments [d]
		Total imports
	July	Total civil nonagricultural employment
		Electric power production
		Man-hours worked, durable manufactures
		Total construction contracts
	Aug.	Production of durable manufactures
		Production of producers' durable goods
		Payrolls, durable manufactures
		Loans of reporting member banks
	Sept.	Production of minerals [e]
		Production of consumers' durable goods
	Oct.	Index of cost of living [a]
		Department store sales [f]
		Chain store sales [g]
		Average hourly earnings in manufacturing
		Inventories held by manufacturers
1938	Feb.	Commercial paper rates
	April	Yield of corporate bonds

TABLE 5: SEQUENCE OF CYCLICAL TURNS IN THE
1937 RECESSION AND THE 1938 REVIVAL (*continued*)

Year	Month	Specific-cycle trough
1937	Dec.	Production of nondurable manufactures
1938	Feb.	Total construction contracts
		Private construction contracts
	April	Freight car loadings
		Total industrial production, Standard Statistics Co.
		Production consumers' nondurable goods
		Industrial common stock prices
		Corporate bonds prices
		Net demand deposits member banks
	May	Bank debits outside New York City
		Retail sales
		Department store sales
		Chain store sales [c]
		Electric power production [h]
		Production of minerals
		Production of producers' nondurable goods
		Man-hours worked, nondurable manufactures
		Total imports
		Orders for manufactured goods
	June	Total income payments
		Total civil nonagricultural employment
		Total industrial production, F.R.Bd.[a]
		Production of durable manufactures
		Production of producers' durable goods
		Production of consumers' durable goods [a]
		Payrolls in manufacturing
		Payrolls, durable manufacturing
		Payrolls, nondurable manufacturing
		Man-hours worked in manufacturing
		Man-hours worked in durable manufactures
	July	Number of business failures, *inverted*
	Aug.	Average hourly earnings in manufactures
1939	Jan.	Total exports
	April	Loans of reporting member banks
	June	Index of cost of living
		Inventories held by manufacturers
	Aug.	Index of wholesale prices
	Sept.	New corporate capital [1]

In this table the series on corporate bond prices is the same as corporate bond
yields, except that it is inverted. There is no entry for commercial paper rates
and bond yields at the trough; . . .

a. The same value in the preceding month.
b. Slightly higher value in Oct. 1936.
c. The same value two months earlier.
d. A higher value in June 1936 (payments to veterans).
e. A higher value in March 1937.
f. The same value in Feb. 1937.
g. The same value in May and Sept. 1937.
h. A slightly lower value in Jan. 1938.
i. A lower value in April 1938, Jan. and May 1939, and June 1940.

Source: Burns and Mitchell, 88–89, Table 19.

creased investment outlays, piling up of inventories, the cessation of net government contribution to income, Federal Reserve policy, the pressure of increased wage costs on prices and profits, and the reduced consumption expenditures because of the relative expansion in the profit share in income. Chapter 2 has summarized the various causal explanations which have been suggested for the recession and revival and Chapter 4 will present the political, social, and economic framework in which these factors operated. Succeeding chapters will then assess the relative validity of the various explanations.

The Political, Social, and Economic Environment in the Thirties

THE EVENTS of 1937–38 cannot be evaluated adequately without an appreciation of the political, social, and economic forces which shaped public opinion and conditioned government and business decisions. Many of the determinants of business and consumer decisions lie outside the purely economic realm. Thus, while decisions to invest may be based upon economic calculus,[1] the timing of investments may be affected by uncertainties arising from noneconomic sources.

It is probable, moreover, that the influence of the active political, social, and economic forces upon economic decisions not only is direct but is exerted also through changes in the realm of moral values. By affecting the operative system of values, these forces may significantly alter the goals of business, government, or society as a whole. The observation of the economist that needs or desires are not synonymous with effective demand must then be qualified further by the fact that these changes in the political, social, or economic environment may even restrict the areas within which effective demand may be satisfied.

For these reasons, a description of the national environment in the 1930's is most desirable. First a chronology of the outstanding events in the period will survey some of the more important legislation which affected the national environment. Then consideration must be given to the political, social, and economic attitudes which promoted sharp conflict over this legislation.

LEGISLATION AFFECTING RECOVERY, REFORM, AND REGULATION

In retrospect it appears that the Hoover administration was slow to take positive steps against the 1929 depression, relying rather

1. In this connection it is interesting to note that the late John M. Keynes believed that even here decisions were made largely on irrational rather than rational grounds. Most of our decisions, he said, "can only be taken as the result of animal spirits—of a spontaneous urge to action rather than inaction, and not as the outcome of a weighted average of quantitative benefits multiplied by quantitative probabilities." Cf. *The General Theory of Employment, Interest and Money* (New York, 1936), 161.

upon the emergence of natural factors to limit the depression and initiate a revival. The result was that President Roosevelt received an election mandate for a policy of action. The "New Deal," born after Roosevelt's election, evolved largely in a piecemeal fashion rather than as a comprehensive program of recovery and reform.

RECOVERY MEASURES

The first series of measures, the Emergency Banking Act of March 9, 1933, and later, the Banking Act of June 16, 1933, was designed to restore confidence in the banking system. The next problem was agricultural prices and expansion of farmers' purchasing power. The Agricultural Adjustment Act of May 13, 1933, proposed to deal with these problems through subsidies and crop controls. The passage of the National Industrial Recovery Act followed on June 16, 1933. It aimed to alleviate business distress by putting a floor under prices, and, with the relaxation of antitrust legislation, by allowing industry to eliminate "unfair" competitive practices by agreement. Labor was safeguarded against this cartelization of industry by provisions which abolished child labor and established minimum wage standards, maximum hours, and collective bargaining procedures.

By the middle of 1933, therefore, reforms had been effected in the banking system and measures had been taken to improve the lot of the farmer, businessman, and laborer. Then, in January 1934, the dollar was devalued. It was hoped by this means to raise domestic prices, restore the farmer's purchasing power, and increase American exports.

The direct attack on unemployment was made through the Public Works Administration in 1933, the Civilian Conservation Corps in November 1933, and the Works Progress Administration in 1935.

MEASURES OF REFORM AND REGULATION

The next series of measures was enacted to regulate or alter certain practices in the sphere of business operation. From one viewpoint they were designed to eliminate unethical, unsound business practices; from another, they were an attack on traditional, established ways of conducting "legitimate" business operations. The measures included the Securities Exchange Acts of 1933 and 1934, the Public Utility Holding Company Act of 1935, establishment of the Tennessee Valley Authority in 1933, and the Banking Act of 1933 which divorced investment banking from commercial banking. The congressional investigation of investment banking, stock exchanges, and financial practices was undoubtedly an important contributory factor in producing this legislation. Accompanying these measures were the tax laws of 1932 and 1934 which increased corporate and individual income taxes, and that of 1936 which taxed undistributed corporate profits for the first time.

It is worth noting that when the NIRA and the AAA were declared unconstitutional many of the reform aspects of each were re-enacted in the National Labor Relations Act and in the expansion of the Soil Conservation programs.

THE ECONOMIC AND POLITICAL CONTROVERSIES OF 1936–37

These legislative actions supplied the background for the serious economic and political controversies of the period 1936–37. A particularly violent dispute stemmed from the aggressive organization of the Congress of Industrial Organization, encouraged by the NLRA. A related issue was the use of the "sit-down" strike to enforce labor demands. A third, highly inflammable issue was the fight over reorganization of the Supreme Court. The bonus payments were a fourth controversial issue. A fifth issue concerned the shift in public policy from support for business combinations (NIRA, for example) to attacks on monopoly and "economic royalists." Finally, there was the bitterness engendered by the unbalanced national budget and the expansion of the national debt.

These economic events occurred in the midst of a highly emotional controversy as to desirable methods and goals for the political, social, and economic life, and were accompanied by bitter division of opinion over the New Deal, its measures and philosophy. The sharp exchanges between public and business officials, the bitter denunciation of government in business and financial circles, and the strong convictions which supported these opinions must be recognized and appreciated before a just appraisal of the times is possible.

THE CONTROVERSY OF THE THIRTIES AS SEEN FROM THE "LEFT" AND FROM THE "RIGHT"

A complete survey of the trends in political, social, and economic opinions will not be attempted here.[2] However, examination of the positions of the more ardent "New Dealers" and reactionary "right-wingers" gives some insight into the "feelings of the times." In the main, the statements which follow were taken from works actually published in the period 1933–38. They are, therefore, less reflective in content and less influenced by hindsight than are the evaluations of "New Deal" economics published in the late thirties and early

2. Such as appears, for example, in Charles and Mary A. Beard, *America in Midpassage, I* (New York, 1939).

forties. Nevertheless, decisions of businessmen, consumers, and government representatives, from 1933 to 1938, were affected by what they thought of the New Deal measures as they were being put into operation, rather than by what they said about the Roosevelt program years later.

THE ARDENT NEW DEALERS

It was not until after the first few months of the New Deal that the initial spirit of widespread good will and cooperation was replaced by a bitter contest between the left and right wings of American political life. The writings of the ardent New Dealers reveal some of the emotion which prompted portions of the legislative program. The more extreme spokesmen were unreserved in attacking "rugged" individualism and numerous business policies and practices. Secretary of Interior Harold L. Ickes expressed very clearly the deep-seated antagonism of some members of the administration toward the titans of the business world in the following manner:

The strangest procession to come to Washington after March 4, 1933, was composed of those who had been among the great and the powerful under the old régime. Rugged individualists who had been loudly asserting their own self-sufficiency, their ability to stand on their own feet, to conduct their own affairs without any suggeston from Government, came, a broken and humble crowd. . . . Nothing proud or haughty or overbearing about these men now. They knew that they had failed to meet the test, . . . They had been naughty but they would never be naughty again, if only their past transgressions might be forgiven; if only dear, kind, nice Government would drive away the big, bad wolf that was frightening them.[3]

Mr. Ickes went so far as to attack these men personally:

This panicky turning to Washington demonstrated that frequently the bigger the man when things are going well, the greater the coward when adversity comes. In their extremity, these boastful, aggressive supermen, these rugged individualists, came fearfully to Washington to beg the President to help them save some little from the disaster that by their arrogance and pride and lack of understanding of economic laws and social forces they had themselves precipitated.[4]

He then proceeded to reproach these men of power and prestige for being antidemocratic:

Strangely enough, there are men who will fight, as there have ever been men who have fought, to prevent a desirable social advance and a broad

3. Harold L. Ickes, *The New Democracy* (New York, 1934), 26–27.
4. *Ibid.*, 30.

economic improvement that will raise the general average of life. These men would not avow it, at least publicly, but they believe in wealth and political power concentrated in the hands of a powerful oligarchy, so long as they can be members of that oligarchy. They sneer at democracy and do not hesitate to corrupt it to serve their own ends. . . . These men are strongly entrenched. While they constitute only a small minority, they are no mean foe. Possessed of great wealth, able to muster powerful political support, buttressed by special privilege, and boasting social prestige, they are prepared to fight to the last to retain the advantages that they have unjustly seized for themselves.[5]

Not only were these individuals antidemocratic, but Ickes charged them with appealing to constitutional principles merely to protect their own special interests.[6] Attorney General Homer S. Cummings, another member of the President's cabinet, attacked the minority for using its power to private advantage rather than to meet the "needs of the country as a whole." [7]

While these minority business groups were harshly criticized, administration policies were given highly favored treatment. Thus, for example, in describing the National Industrial Recovery Act, one writer said: "The huge N.R.A., controlled by the outspoken General Johnson, is picturesque and striking. . . . The N.R.A. is a tremendous effort to instill into the country the idea and the sense that business should be a national game—not necessarily a communistic one, but one in which the individual should never forget the interests of the nation." [8] In Faÿ's opinion, if good were to be obtained as a result the NRA had to "spread and permeate the country" and become a "national passion and obsession . . ." [9]

In addition to directing a favorable light toward administration actions, the ardent New Dealers gave vigorous support to national planning of economic life. Thus, Ickes asserted the willingness of the administration to act for the general welfare if private capital was unwilling to do the job of providing production and employment.[10]

Secretary of Agriculture Henry A. Wallace emphasized a need, also, for cooperative planning:

Reactionaries have fought every step of the way against the more enlightened practices of business, such as shortening hours, eliminating child labor, raising wages, reducing sales prices, and granting labor the right to

5. *Ibid.*, 144.
6. *Ibid.*, 155.
7. Homer S. Cummings, "Preserving Democracy," Jackson Day Banquet Address, Stevens Hotel, Chicago, January 8, 1938.
8. Bernard Faÿ, *Roosevelt and His America* (Boston, 1933), 340–341.
9. *Ibid.*, 343–344.
10. Harold L. Ickes, *Back to Work* (New York, 1935), 233.

collective bargaining. . . . Undoubtedly business in the future must move deliberately in this direction, and to do so under modern conditions will mean some method of co-operative effort and co-operative planning. . . . The leaders of the present and future must display imagination as daring as that of the early industrialists, but this imagination must deal with the co-operative machinery which can balance consumption with production on an ever-broadening scale.[11]

At the same time Harry Hopkins, as administrator of the Works Progress Administration, pointed out certain social consequences that result from an economic society in which some people have much and other people have nothing: "We are beginning to wonder if it is not presumptuous to take for granted that some people should have much, and some should have nothing; that some people are less important than others and should die earlier; that the children of the comfortable should be taller and fatter, as a matter of right, than the children of the poor." [12] He denied that such conditions needed to exist in America: "there is no need for any American to be destitute, to be illiterate, to be reduced by the bondages of these things into either political or economic impotence." [13]

It can be seen, then, that the ardent New Dealer opposed "rugged" individualism. He supported enthusiastically specific administration measures, and believed that government intervention was necessary to achieve certain social and economic ends. In addition, he felt a great sense of loyalty to the President. Thus, Homer Cummings asserted: "The rich and powerful may have forgotten what he did for them, but the lowly and the dispossessed have not abated one iota of their faith. The people have not forgotten. They could not forget. No one can make them forget. They know what they have been through with him, and they propose to go with him to the end of the road." [14]

Similarly, a biographer could say of him: "So Roosevelt stands in the midst of confusion, more obstinately determined than ever to carry out the enterprise in social justice which destiny has entrusted to him. . . . Those rights which he was the first to insure to the overwhelming majority of his fellow-citizens can never again be taken from them; . . ." [15]

This characteristic tribute came from one of his warmest supporters:

11. Henry A. Wallace, *Whose Constitution: An Injury into the General Welfare* (New York, 1936), 171–172.
12. Harry Hopkins, *Spending to Save* (New York, 1936), 184.
13. *Ibid.*, 179.
14. Cummings, 12.
15. Emil Ludwig, *Roosevelt: A Study in Fortune and Power* (New York, 1938), 344.

As the one entrusted by the President with the grave responsibility of administering this huge total sum of 3 billion 700 million dollars, I want to say that whatever success has attended that administration has been due to the guidance and inspiration of the President. His has been the vision that has never dimmed. Franklin D. Roosevelt will be written down in history not only as the world's greatest builder; he will likewise be known for all time to come as the greatest planner.[16]

Let the President himself be the final spokesman for the administration's attitude toward its opposition:

For twelve years our nation was afflicted with hear-nothing, see-nothing, do-nothing government. The nation looked to that government but that government looked away. Nine mocking years with the golden calf and three long years of the scourge! Nine crazy years at the ticker and three long years in the bread lines! Nine mad years of mirage and three long years of despair! Powerful influences strive today to restore that kind of government, with its doctrine that that government is best which is most indifferent to mankind.

For nearly four years now you have had an administration which instead of twirling its thumbs has rolled up its sleeves. And I can assure you that we will keep our sleeves rolled up.

We had to struggle with the old enemies of peace—business and financial monopoly, speculation, reckless banking, class antagonism, sectionalism, war profiteering. They had begun to consider the government of the United States as a mere appendage to their own affairs. We know now that government by organized money is just as dangerous as government by organized mob.

Never before in all our history have these forces been so united against one candidate as they stand today. They are unanimous in their hate for me—and I welcome their hatred.[17]

The President, after reviewing the various measures and actions of the New Deal continued: "For these things, too, and for a multitude of things like them, we have only just begun to fight." [18]

THE ADMINISTRATION'S CRITICS

The "rugged" individualists, the "privileged" few, and the "economic royalists" were not without their spokesmen. It was not long before the " 'spontaneous spiritual uprising of March, 1933, dissolved.' " [19] So much was this so that by the beginning of 1935, "the immense strain thrown upon the nerves, sentiments, and acquisitive

16. Ickes, *Back to Work*, Preface, viii.
17. Madison Square Garden Campaign Address of October 31, 1936, *New York Times,* November 1, 1936.
18. *Ibid.*
19. Charles and Mary Beard, 255.

instincts of individuals had begun to snap the bonds of cooperation imposed by fear, law, and administration." [20]

Soon representatives of business were hurling countercharges against the administration. Since the principal cleavage appears to have been between government and business, it is the beliefs of the latter which must be contrasted with the ardent New Dealer opinion if the sharp conflict of the times is to be pointed up.

The business attack took the form of defense of individual liberty and freedom and opposition to the New Deal, which was charged with being bureaucratic and socialistic. In addition, ridicule and scorn were directed toward the New Dealers.

If the New Dealers made a plea for social planning as an aid to the "good" national political and economic life, the business spokesmen were equally vocal in rejecting planning and supporting instead the values of individualism and human liberty. In the opinion of Robert L. Lund, executive vice-president and general manager of the Lambert Pharmacal Company, the day when individual liberty would vanish was fast approaching:

We are approaching a day when individual liberty will vanish, in which citizens will be at the beck and call of government bureau autocrats. These, we would find, would order our lives and take a substantial part of our earnings; for the support, after gigantic deductions for costs, of the less industrious.

Individual liberty and complete economic security are not compatible. Our people have had the courage and enterprise to carve their own fortunes. It would be a tragedy to make of them bureaucratic serfs.

The little-understood, Socialistic experimentation which is called the "New Deal" leads toward just that. [21]

The president and general manager of the Detroit Steel Casting Company, and vice-president of the National Association of Manufacturers, S. Wells Utley, believed that the expansion of government functions was at the expense of individual freedom:

No man can freely and impartially discharge his duties as a citizen so long as he is supported through the payroll of political government; so long as his daily bread comes as a hand-out from that government; so long as the amount and character of the crops he plants, or the business he does, is subject to political control; so long as his operations are dependent on contracts financed by government money; so long as his sources of credit are controlled by political forces; so long as his home, or his business, is subject to mortgage held by government. . . . When the individuals who

20. *Ibid.*, 252.
21. Robert L. Lund, Howard E. Coffin, Charles W. Burkett, and Earl Reeves, *Truth about the New Deal* (New York, 1936), 80.

represent government place the individuals who cast the votes under obligation to them for their daily bread, then the voter ceases to be free to control his government and is definitely on the road to being a subject.[22]

The extreme opponents of the administration censured almost every action of the President:

If we are to preserve democracy we must go back to economic freedom. By his persistent advocacy of "socialistic" experiments, his extravagant waste of money, his reckless expansion of public credit, his policy of inflation and tinkering with the currency, his bureaucracy, his catering to class hatreds, his repudiation of promises and the loss of faith in government which his policies have caused—by all this and more, Mr. Roosevelt has endangered our entire heritage of political and economic freedom. Such is THE MENACE OF ROOSEVELT AND HIS POLICIES.[23]

In Kershner's opinion, Roosevelt's program was a serious threat to the American heritage of freedom, property, character, and culture:

If President Roosevelt cannot be stopped by votes, court decisions or a change of policies, we are headed straight for the breakdown of our credit, our economic and political systems, to revolution, regimentation and ruin. To the siren song of borrowed billions and with the colors of inflation nailed to its masthead the Administration is steering this country to the destruction of our priceless heritage of American freedom, to some form of collectivism or dictatorship and the suffering, injustice and lower standard of living which they involve.[24]

The attack on New Deal policies and the defense of the "priceless" heritage were accompanied by biting satirization of some of the leaders in the administration: "no matter how skeptical one may be of the virtues of members of Congress, there cannot be the slightest doubt of our having a Cabinet of Sunday school teachers assisted by the pick of the white-haired boys of the country." [25] "The streaming vapidities of Mr. Ickes' speech put me in mind of Tennyson's brook—they seem to go on forever." [26]

Kershner was critical of the ability of the New Dealers: "Inflation comes on apace, and our great heritage of economic and civil liberty is threatened with destruction, all in the name of wishful thinking, fancy imported ideas, impracticable and unworkable theories invented by parlor pinks and brain trust professors, most of whom never have

22. S. Wells Utley, *The American System: Shall We Destroy It?* (Detroit, 1936), 216–217.
23. Howard Eldred Kershner, *The Menace of Roosevelt and His Policies* (New York, 1936), 132.
24. *Ibid.*, from the Introduction, X.
25. Francis Neilson, *Sociocratic Escapades* (New York, 1934), 28.
26. *Ibid.*, 52.

managed a business, faced the necessity of meeting a payroll or earned a dollar." [27]

Undoubtedly another factor in the extreme antagonism of the right-wing business interests to the spirit and program of the New Deal was that the business community faced a loss of social status if the regulatory and reform measures were successful. The attack on business practices and upon business itself toppled the "Lords of Creation" [28] from their positions of leadership and was a challenge to the ethics of the business world, which had been the ethics of all American society in the twenties. The moral standing of the businessman was in question. He was under fire from many quarters—with the Senate investigation of investment banking from 1932–35, the hostility toward "economic royalists," the attempt to distinguish between "good" business and "bad" business: "Never before in the history of the country had the anatomy, morphology, intelligence, morals, and functioning of the banking and stock-trading business been so fully laid bare to national gaze and understanding." [29]

This investigation of investment banking was interpreted by many as an indictment of all brokerage and investment firms:

The Senate Investigation Committees performed a service in revealing and exposing the truth about speculation and investment finance. But simultaneously the public acquired a deep prejudice against all investment bankers. The government as yet has done little to discourage such blanket indictments of a class or group. Failure to distinguish between those who deserve punishment and those who do not has created embarrassments and problems which have retarded and delayed economic readjustment.[30]

The growing publicity given to business violations of public trust established the businessman as a public enemy. At least, such was the judgment of Edgar M. Queeny, president of Monsanto Chemical Corporation: "The public has been played upon for ten years, on the front page and over the radio, by many studied instances wherein fraud has been practiced by businessmen; wherein trust has been abused by businessmen and labor has been denied its right by businessmen. Thus, the businessman has been portrayed as a grasping, heinously selfish, public enemy." [31]

Probably these reflections on the morality of the business community contributed as much as anything else to the bitterness which the opposition felt toward the New Deal program. To many, this

27. Kershner, 42.
28. Charles and Mary Beard, 189.
29. *Ibid.*, 159–160.
30. David Lawrence, *Beyond the New Deal* (New York, 1934), 119.
31. Edgar M. Queeny, *The Spirit of Enterprise* (New York, 1943), 71.

censure of business morality was a challenge to the very foundations of American civilization:

our thinking of late years has undergone a fundamental change. Successful business, and that is the only kind which denotes progress, has been discredited, and successful business men are held up to scorn as Public Enemy No. 1, while the public bows in adulation before the unsuccessful, the inefficient, the lazy, and the sub-normal; those endowed with ambition, thrift, energy, and resourcefulness are treated with contempt, and those possessing these formerly desirable qualities are plundered in order that the loot may be given to those who do not possess them. The financial losses of the depression have been heavy, but they are insignificant as compared with the intellectual and moral degeneration which has swept over the American people, and which definitely threatens the destruction of their civilization.[32]

No attempt will be made here to determine whether the criticism of the business community was justified. Later, it will be necessary to consider whether the attack on business ethics may have affected business willingness to undertake large-scale investment expenditures. For the present it is sufficient to recognize that business leadership was extremely sensitive to the charge that it had violated the public trust. Moreover, a transformation had undoubtedly occurred in the public attitude toward the business community. The ethics of the business world were condemned; the businessman's standing in the community was jeopardized. The discovery that a man was connected with business enterprise was sufficient reason for mistrusting his motives. More fundamentally, the antagonism toward the business community generated uncertainty as to the type of economy which would persist when the New Deal reforms had been effected.

SUMMARY

The bitter division of opinion between New Deal spokesmen and business representatives has been presented. No judgment will be made here as to the relative degree of merit on either side, but certainly these antagonisms influenced the course of economic events in the period. Political and social beliefs may well have been important factors in determining the nature and scale of private investment commitments, the direction of consumption expenditures, and the extent of government intervention. The emotional attitudes of the times must always be kept in mind as among the factors which affected government action, consumption, and investment decisions.

32. Utley, 282.

CHAPTER 5

Government Fiscal Policy

THE CHANGES in net government contribution to income, which are used here as an indication of the net effects of government spending, have been given heavy emphasis as a cause of both the recession and the revival of 1937–38.[1] Marriner Eccles, for example, asserted that the "too rapid withdrawal of the government's stimulus . . . accompanied by other important factors, . . . [led to the] rapid deflation in the fall of 1937, which continued until the present spending program of the government was begun last summer."[2] The acceptance of this viewpoint among high-ranking officials gives added significance to an investigation of government fiscal policy.

Assessment of the role of government fiscal policy requires examination of both the impact of budgetary deficit or surplus and the effects of specific taxes and expenditures.[3] In this chapter analysis will be directed primarily to the over-all effects of the net contribution of government to income rather than to the effects of particular taxes and expenditures on investment decisions. The impact of particular taxes, such as undistributed profits taxes, capital gains taxes, etc., is considered in Chapter 14.

THE ROLE OF NET GOVERNMENT CONTRIBUTION TO INCOME AND FISCAL POLICY IN THE RECESSION

From the outset, a presumption can be established that the decline in net government contribution was at least of positive significance in the 1937–38 recession. Net government contribution fell $3.3 billion, from $4.1 billion in [calendar year] 1936 to $.8 billion in 1937.[4] Both the monthly net government contribution and monthly personal

1. Net income-increasing expenditures of government, as used here, are equal to the sum of all income-increasing expenditures minus the sum of all income-decreasing receipts. The data and concept are from Villard, *op. cit.*
2. Eccles, *op. cit.*, 190.
3. The reason for dividing the problem into two parts can be seen clearly in the following way. Two economies might both have balanced budgets yet quite dissimilar tax policies. Consequently, different responses might be expected from investment in the two instances.
4. Villard, 323.

70

incomes are graphed in Figure 8, for the period 1936–38. The sharp rise incident to the payment of the soldiers' bonus in June 1936 stands out boldly in both series. Net government contribution declined sharply at the beginning of 1937 and actually became negative, or income-decreasing, in August 1937. The question, therefore, is not whether government fiscal policy was a factor in the recession but what position it occupies in the list of contributory factors.

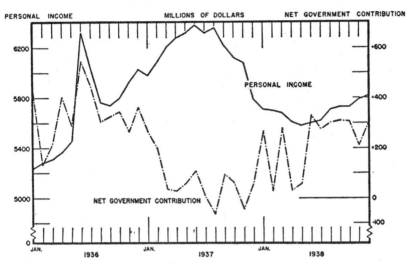

Fig. 8. Net government contribution to income, and personal incomes, by months, 1936–38. Net income-increasing expenditures of all government units from Villard, 323, Table 21. Personal incomes, seasonally adjusted, from *Survey of Current Business, National Income Supplement, 1951, 213.*

THE DECLINE IN INCOME MUCH LATER THAN THE DECLINE IN NET GOVERNMENT CONTRIBUTION TO INCOME

The most telling argument against treating the decline in net government expenditures as the primary cause of the recession is the lag which took place between this decline and the eventual decline in income. It was more than six months following the decline in net income-increasing expenditures of government before personal income began to fall. Figure 8 shows that net government contribution to income declined sharply beginning with January 1937, whereas income continued to rise through June 1937. It was not until September 1937 that the first real decline in income occurred. It would appear, therefore, that the decline in net government contribution was felt, at most, only indirectly in the national economy. Angell observed this lag in the decline of income behind the decline in net government contribution and concluded that the latter was not "a principal immediate cause" of the former: "Despite this depressing influence, however, the absolute figures for national income on a monthly basis held up all through 1937, so that the total income for 1937 was higher than that for 1936. It was not until the first 2 months of 1938 that income definitely dropped to lower levels. This lag of the drop in income behind that in deficit spending (by a full year) is so large that the second change cannot be regarded as the principal *immediate* cause of the first." [5] From Figure 8 it can be seen that income had dropped significantly by November 1937. In fact it was then 6% under the year's peak. Nevertheless it was January 1938 before personal income fell below the average in 1936. Thus the point which Angell made about the lag between the decline in government spending and the decline in national income remains valid.

THE DECLINE IN NET GOVERNMENT CONTRIBUTION AND THE MULTIPLIER

Once the lag between the movement in net government contribution to income and that in national income is established, it becomes necessary to consider whether the working out of the multiplier could account for a lag of such length. The first question is the length of time which it takes for government expenditures to be reflected in income statistics. Professor Villard concluded in his study on income-increasing expenditures of government and the multiplier that on the average these expenditures should be received as income again in a month: "A conservative estimate would be to assume that net income-increasing expenditure by the government will take a month on the average to reappear as income, as against the four-month period required by general expenditure; the correct period may be even less." [6]

The reasons why the government income period may be assumed to be considerably shorter than the general income period are fairly obvious. Since a large proportion of government expenditures in the 1930's became income as received [7] (examples are the payments for personal services, relief, and interest), it is reasonable to conclude that the government income period is substantially shorter than the general business income period. A further factor is that Villard excluded from net income-increasing expenditures those which presumably accrue to idle balances.

5. Angell, *op. cit.,* 230.
6. Villard, 254.
7. Expenditures on materials in a public works construction program are a major exception.

Suppose, therefore, that the multiplier is two, the average income period is three to four months, and the government income period is one month. Then almost 90% of the multiplier effects on income will have been experienced within a seven- to nine-month period.[8] On the basis of these assumptions, if there were a direct relationship between the decline in net government contribution and national income, then a decline in national income should follow shortly after the decline in net government contribution. But the first substantial decline in national income did not occur until September 1937, whereas net government contribution declined over $100 million from December 1936 ($365.7 million) to January 1937 ($264.0 million). The multiplier effects of this decline were undoubtedly experienced in the first or second month of the year, but they do not appear in income statistics. Clearly, if the decline in net government contribution were the principal cause of the recession, some decline in national income should have been evident by the spring of 1937. By this time net government contribution had declined over $300 million per month.[9] Yet income continued to rise, and reached its peak in June 1937.

THE SOLDIERS' BONUS OF JUNE 1936

A complicating factor in the behavior of the personal income series in the period was the payment of the soldiers' bonus in June 1936. This payment of $1,700 million, of which $1,400 million was cashed by December 1936, gave a boost to income in the summer months of 1936. What its multiplier effects were is difficult to estimate. Since all payments were immediately income when made, most of the effects on income must have been experienced within six to eight months, assuming a multiplier of two. This single burst of expenditure gave the peculiar pattern to the income stream which is shown in Figure 8.

What were the effects of this expansion in expenditures upon income in the first half of 1937? There appears to be no reasonable theoretical basis for demonstrating that the multiplier effects of the bonus payments could have raised income to the extent that it increased in the first half of 1937. In fact some anticipatory spending

8. As a hypothetical example, suppose net income-increasing expenditures of government were increased by $100.00 in the first month. The multiplier effect at the end of four months would be $50.00, followed by $25.00 and $12.50 in successive periods, a total of $87.50 as a result of the multiplier effect. This illustration is adapted from Fritz A. Machlup, "Period Analysis and Multiplier Theory," *Quarterly Journal of Economics, 54* (1939–40), 15. In the same article Machlup discusses the appropriate time period for the multiplier. Villard, 254–257, and Angell, 138, also estimate the time period of the multiplier. With the Villard assumptions 75% of the secondary effects would have been experienced in 8 months (assuming one-half of primary expenditure to be re-spent).

9. It averaged only $65 million per month in the second quarter of 1937.

may have occurred which conceivably could have reduced the size of the multiplier to be applied against the bonus payments. Moreover, because the payments were made without reference to income status, and were essentially a windfall, it might be argued convincingly that the multiplier was less than two, and that most of its effects on income were immediate. In any event the multiplier was probably not *over* two, since part of the money was hoarded, used to liquidate consumer credit, deposited in savings accounts, or drawn off for business purposes. The effects on income were noticeable almost immediately in income statistics because over 70% of the certificates were cashed within the first two and a half months, and the largest expenditures out of these receipts were in June and July.[10]

While it must be presumed that the effects of the bonus expenditures were worked off by the early part of 1937, it is possible that these expenditures, along with the other factors which were raising the level of income, helped to create more favorable expectations about future profits and sales. These developments, in turn, led to an expansion of private investment expenditures in the first half of 1937. Only in this very indirect sense can it be argued that the bonus expenditures in the summer and fall of 1936 contributed to the expansion of the level of income from January to June 1937.

MORE ARGUMENTS AGAINST NET GOVERNMENT
CONTRIBUTION AS A PRIMARY FACTOR IN THE
RECESSION

Other authors have argued that the decline in net government contribution has been overrated as a causal factor in the recession. For example, Hardy believed that an explanation of the recession in terms of the decline in net government contribution is superficial. In his opinion, the fundamental question was why the national income could not be maintained without net government contribution: "If national income is prevented from declining only by the existence of a government deficit and does decline when government financing stops, the phenomenon to be explained is why the national income does not maintain itself without this artificial aid."[11] The problem, continued Hardy, was why the recipients of income failed to spend or re-invest funds received. In other words, the important factors were those responsible for the constriction in investment spending. Although the evidence examined so far in this chapter supports the belief that the

10. "The largest bonus expenditure occurred in June and July, but some expenditures appear to have been deferred until October, November, and even December." Rolf Nugent, *Consumer Credit and Economic Stability* (New York, 1939), 213.
11. Hardy, "An Appraisal," 173.

decline in net government contribution was not the most important cause of the recession, Hardy's analysis appears to beg the question. If national income and employment did decline because net government contribution ceased, then Hardy should have concluded that the decline in net government contribution was an important causal factor in the turning point. It may be important to emphasize the problem of private investment outlays and their failure to increase as government spending declined. But this is not relevant in an evaluation of the actual causal significance of the decline in net government contribution itself.

Slichter suggested another ground for thinking that the decline in net government contribution was less important in the recession than previously believed. He observed that "despite the drop in the government's contribution to incomes, the value of output of consumers' goods did not outrun consumer purchasing power." [12] However, it should be noted that Slichter's argument is not conclusive if, in fact, output may be adjusted quickly to demand.[13] On the basis of inadequate data he also concluded that profits continued to rise in spite of the decline in net government contribution. Although profits for the first two quarters of 1937 were above those in the same quarters in 1936 as he reported,[14] the peak profit rates were obtained in the fourth quarter of 1936, and profits were less in each of the succeeding quarters of 1937.[15] Nevertheless, in his opinion the decline in net government contribution was not without unfortunate repercussion, inasmuch as it happened to coincide with consumer resistance to higher prices and a drop in business spending. Again, there is little evidence that there was an actual drop in business spending. The stronger position would be that the offsetting increase which did occur in business spending as government spending declined was not sufficient to do much more than hold income constant, and in considerable part represented unintended investment in inventories.[16]

Professor Schumpeter was another writer who believed that only moderate importance should be attached to the decline in net government contribution as an explanation of the recession. Most of the increase in national income from 1933 to 1937 he attributed to the effects of net government spending. But he argued that there had been

12. Slichter, "The Downturn of 1937," 102.

13. In this connection cf. Lloyd A. Metzler, "Three Lags in the Circular Flow of Income," *Income, Employment and Public Policy* (New York, 1948), 25–28. He examines empirical data on the lag in adjustments of output behind sales and concludes that this lag is likely to be sizable.

14. However, third quarter profits in 1937 were less than in the third quarter of 1936.

15. Barger, *op. cit.*

16. The position of inventories in the recession is discussed later in Chapter 12.

no excessive expansion or speculation in response to these spending policies, and since there was no monetary strain the importance of the decline in net government contribution should not be exaggerated.[17]

One further fact tends to lessen the causal importance of the decline in net government contribution. In the crucial period January to June 1937 the decline in net government contribution was not as drastic as the monthly averages on a yearly basis would indicate.[18] Thus in the January to June period the average contribution was still $110 million per month, and averaged $165 million per month in the first three months of the year. Fine adjusted the Krost-Currie figures [19] on net Federal Government contribution by assuming that a considerable portion of the tax revenues in 1937 were not income-decreasing and therefore should not be subtracted from government expenditures.[20] He estimates a net Federal Government contribution in 1937 of $2 billion (Villard's estimate is $834 million) compared with $4.3 billion in 1936.[21]

Gayer also noted that net government contribution was positive even though declining. He attributed responsibility for the recession not to the decline of net government contribution but to the failure of private net income-increasing expenditures to expand:

The drastic decline in the monthly contribution this year from the levels prevailing during the preceding three years probably did not in itself bring about the business recession, since there continued to be a net contribution, small though it was. But it appears clear that private income-increasing expenditures did not expand in 1937 at a rate sufficient to offset the decline in the Federal contribution. Thus the rate of recovery slackened and resulted in a positive reaction.[22]

The evidence would seem to support those who tend to minimize the direct responsibility of the decline in net government contribution for the recession. The flow of consumer goods did not outdistance

17. Schumpeter, *op. cit.,* 1032.
18. It should be recalled that this contribution includes that of all governments, federal, state, and local.
19. Also the basis for the Villard estimates.
20. Of course, all tax revenues are income-decreasing; that is, they tend to reduce disposable income. But in the special sense in which Villard and others used the term, tax revenues which come from otherwise idle balances and do not reduce consumer expenditures are said to be nonincome-decreasing. Wide disagreement is possible over the classification of the various tax revenues.
21. Fine, 112–114. In any event the decline in net government contribution took some time and was not as drastic as first consideration would indicate. This should have softened its impact on the national economy.
22. Arthur Gayer, "Fiscal Policies," *Papers and Proceedings, American Economic Review,* 28 (1938), 102.

consumer purchasing power; the decline in national income was too remote in time from the decline in net government contribution to have been caused by the latter; [23] and finally the decline in net government contribution appears to have been somewhat less drastic than initial consideration of the data might indicate. It is therefore difficult to escape the conclusion that net government contribution has been overrated as an explanation of the recession. Other factors must have been responsible for the appearance of the turning point in economic activity. Whether the recession would have occurred had net government contribution remained at a substantial level has not been answered. Some speculation on this question will be presented in the section below, which considers the relationship between net government contribution and the formation of public policy.

THE ROLE OF NET GOVERNMENT CONTRIBUTION TO INCOME AND FISCAL POLICY IN THE REVIVAL

Here again the timing of the resumption of government spending is most important. As in the recession, where the early decline in net government contribution cannot be regarded as the principal reason for the later decline in income, also in the revival the marked increase in net government contribution and the increase in national income occur so close together in time that doubt is thrown upon the one as the cause of the other. Again, Angell expresses this viewpoint: "After the 1937–1938 slump, deficit spending was rapidly revived, and before the end of 1938 was nearly back to the average levels of 1934–1936. . . . Industrial production, car loadings, factory employment and income likewise picked up after the middle of 1938, and indeed recovered so nearly synchronously with the increase in deficit spending that it is again difficult to regard one change as the direct cause of the other." [24] However, it is not as easy to minimize the renewal in net government contribution as the cause of revival. This is particularly true if Villard is correct in assuming that the effect of government expenditures should be seen in income data within the month. It was not until June that the Department of Commerce personal income series began to rise, along with the Federal Reserve Board index of industrial production. It seems possible, therefore, that the increase in net government contribution to income which began in June 1938 might well have been partly responsible for this rise. The coincidence of the two requires explanation. As Professor Wernette says, in noting the coincidence between net government contribution

23. Implicitly, this means that nongovernment spending expanded sufficiently to offset the decline in net government contribution.
24. Angell, 232.

and the revival of business, "It is perhaps only a coincidence, but it is a fact that the magnitude of the income-increasing federal expenditure began to rise rapidly in the spring of 1938, and that business improvement set in shortly thereafter." [25]

The *Economist* was uncertain as to the responsibility which the spending program had in promoting the recovery. Its overseas correspondent believed that the case was as good for credit manipulation, or for the natural forces of cyclical recovery, as for the spending program :

> In the recovery to date, no clear influence can be attributed to the spending programme, though that is not to say that it has had no influence. Many commentators, however, doubt whether the spending programme has exerted any perceptible influence yet, and expect its impact to be felt later in 1938 or even not until early 1939. The association of the upturn with the gold desterilisation of April is even more difficult to detect statistically, although one can make a plausible connection between it and the June spurt in the stock market, and thence, by psychology, with business activity. In short, one can make an almost equally convincing case by arguing that the revival was caused (a) by the natural forces of cyclical recovery, (b) by the spending programme or (c) by credit manipulation. We cannot yet give any of our questions a definite answer.[26]

Closer examination of the economics series reveals, however, that the troughs of many of the important indices of business activity occurred before the June increase in government expenditures, and that there were clear signs of reviving business activity before that date. Orders for nondurable manufactured goods, corporate bond prices, net demand deposits of member banks, the total industrial production index, the Standard Statistics Company index of industrial common stock prices, freight car loadings, retail sales, department store sales, production of minerals, and private construction contracts, all had begun to rise before the actual expansion in government spending.[27]

While there were these signs of impending revival, even they may have been partly in anticipation of the favorable stimulus to be given to the economy by the resumption of large-scale government spending. In this connection it should be recalled that the President's message asking for a new "spend-lend" program of over \$4.5 billion was sent to Congress April 14, 1938. However, at least two extremely important series, private and total construction contracts, could not have been affected by his proposals because they had begun to rise as early as March 1938. Nevertheless it would seem that more weight should

25. Wernette, 179–180.

26. *Economist, 132* (1938), 494.

27. The location of the troughs of each series is taken from Burns and Mitchell, *op. cit.,* "Cyclical Turns in 1937–1938 Recession," Table 19, 88–89. The complete table is reproduced as Table 5 in Chapter 3.

be given to net government contribution as a cause of the revival than as a cause of the recession.

NET GOVERNMENT CONTRIBUTION TO INCOME AND PUBLIC POLICY IN THE RECESSION

The final evaluation of the position of net government contribution in the recession and the recovery must be from the standpoint of its relationship to public opinion and the formation of public policy. Here the public made two insistent demands upon government in the period preceding the recession, which indirectly affected the position of net government contribution. One such demand was for a soldiers' bonus, which greatly increased the Treasury deficit and consequently the net government contribution to income; the other was from the business community for a balanced budget.

PAYMENT OF SOLDIERS' BONUS UNTIMELY

In retrospect, the soldiers' bonus was distributed when it was least needed to sustain employment and output in the economy. The bonus undoubtedly contributed to the bottlenecks and the speculative buying of the fourth quarter of 1936. Fine stressed the maladjustments in price and output which resulted from this unusual increase in purchasing power, particularly since it was directed toward the purchase of durable consumer goods: "The very bad timing of the bonus payment in the middle of 1936 served to accelerate the already rapid pace of business recovery to a rate which could be maintained only by a great volume of new private capital investment or by repeated federal expenditures of sums comparable to the bonus payment." [28] Bad though it may have been, it is difficult to see how public policy could have been otherwise in the light of the political implications of the bonus payments.

PSYCHOLOGICAL EFFECTS OF BALANCED BUDGET

This added drain on Treasury resources kept the budget out of balance. But as the prospect improved for a balanced budget in fiscal year 1938 (the year beginning July 1937) praise came from the business community. The *Economist* stressed the desirability of offsetting the budget deficits of other years through surpluses in years of prosperity. In its opinion, fiscal year 1938 was a good one in which to begin.[29]

The National City Bank of New York in its *Monthly Letter* favored an end to government deficit spending so that private expenditures might make up the drop:

28. Fine, 115.
29. *Economist, 128* (1937), 383.

In this country the time is favorable for the turn from Government to private expenditures. The effort is to taper off the Government deficit, and if the intentions are realized Government borrowing except for re-funding purposes will no longer be a major factor in the business situation. The prospect that private expenditures will make up for the drop, and more, is highly promising, in view of the outlook for investment in build-ing and other capital equipment. However, it is imperative that no ob-stacles be put in the way of trade or investment. Excessive costs of build-ing and capital goods would hamper improvement in that field, and too rapid rises in consumer goods would cause maladjustments threatening trade.[30]

As the final two sentences in this quoted passage make clear, the Na-tional City Bank was not unaware of what would happen to business if additional business investment were not made. The same *Letter* was even more explicit on this point: "This means that when Treasury ex-penditures are tapered off the general business situation must be sound, relations must be in balance, and inducements to private investment must exist; otherwise business will contract." [31]

It is also evident that financial opinion regarded the decline in net government contribution as a stimulus to business. Of course it did not have such a favorable effect, but this may have been partly because so few people knew that the budget was approaching a balance. Kimmel expressed the belief that the business population was largely unaware that the budget was balanced.[32]

Regardless of whether it was generally realized that the budget was in the process of being balanced, the financial journals believed that the time was appropriate again for business to become the "mainspring" of the economy. The National City Bank viewed the cessation of the gov-ernment deficit as a favorable development, since it would tend to exert a tempering influence upon business and speculation and would act to reveal any weaknesses in the production structure before they became serious. It predicted that businessmen would take up the slack: "if from now on the Government borrows less, there is reason to believe that business and private operators will borrow more." [33]

Business interests believed further that government spending had added greatly to the fears of "inflation," since it was largely financed by credit creation.[34] It may be assumed, therefore, that the prospect of a balanced budget must have been reassuring to business interests.

30. National City Bank of New York, *Monthly Letter* (1937), 31.
31. *Ibid.*, 31.
32. Lewis H. Kimmel, "Social Security Finances," *Conference Board Bulletin, 11* (1937), 118. Cf. also, in this connection, Wernette, 179.
33. National City Bank of New York, *op. cit.*, 19.
34. Midland Bank Review, "The Slump in America: When Will It End?" (June–July 1938), 2.

It seems quite clear that the business community regarded with favor the movement in the direction of a balanced budget. Continuous pressure to that end was exerted on public policy-makers, and it is not surprising that they were less aware of the deflationary prospects of the balanced budget than of the favorable effects which were supposed to arise from the practice of "sound" finance. The business community wanted the budget balanced, and got what it had urged. But with the balanced budget the net contribution of government to income ceased. If it is argued that this contribution should have been maintained at a high level because the recession occurred when it began to decline, there remains the question of how such action could have been politically feasible when there was such an incessant demand for a balanced budget. Even after the depressive effects of the decline in government contribution became evident, businessmen maintained that it had in fact been inflationary and dangerous in its influence. The trouble with this decline was that it occurred before business was "unleashed" to take up the slack.[35] Because of this fear of inflation, which many policy-makers shared with most businessmen, and in view of the opposition which businessmen expressed toward a chronic government deficit, it seems unlikely that net government contribution could have been continued at a high level.

EXPANSION IN PRIVATE SPENDING INADEQUATE

What, then, can be said concerning the relationship of net government contribution to the recession and to public policy? In retrospect it can be seen that private investment expenditures failed to take over the role which net government contribution had been playing, that of raising income to higher levels. It is not correct, however, to assert, as have some writers, that private spending failed to expand when net government contribution declined. In the six months following the decline in net government spending, income either increased slightly each month or remained at the high level attained when net government contribution began its decline. This means that private spending did increase to offset the decline in public spending, but the sharp rise in income which had accompanied increases in the latter was not maintained.

Government policy-makers might have emphasized that the threat of inflation was only temporary because of bottlenecks which would soon be eliminated. Yet they still would have encountered strong public opposition to chronic budget deficits and the continuation of net government contribution at a high level.

Suppose for the moment, however, that these political objections

35. T. E. Hough, "The 1937 Bond Market," *Bankers Magazine, 136* (1938), 62.

could have been overcome, and that the level of net government contribution could have been maintained in the first six months of 1937 at $340 million per month, the average monthly rate in 1936. In the first four months of 1937, net government contribution at this rate of $340 million per month would have added $800 million more than was actually added to the income stream. Since this was the period when pressure on prices was the greatest, the final collapse in prices in the middle of April might well have been more spectacular, or possibly delayed until later in the spring. On the other hand, this level of contribution in the spring might have done much to prevent the recession from gaining headway, unless business spending declined because of the continued government deficit. It is likely, though, that by the summer of 1937 the political pressures for a balanced budget would have become intense.

Little is to be gained by further conjecture as to the course of events if government contribution had remained high, since that was politically impossible anyway. Business demanded a balanced budget and the immediate government concern was with inflation, both factors which promoted a decline in net government contribution.

NET GOVERNMENT CONTRIBUTION TO INCOME AND PUBLIC POLICY IN THE REVIVAL

A number of analysts have been critical of government fiscal policy in the revival. Most criticisms center around the delay in resuming large-scale government spending following the precipitate decline in national income. Professor Hansen criticized the government for its failure to resume spending much earlier and at an expanded rate. Fine also considered the lag in the government spending program to be its chief weakness: "A major criticism that can be levied against the program is the rather considerable delay between its inauguration and the development of the recession during 1937." [36]

This lag resulted because the government still clung to the belief that a balanced budget was the best way to promote revival:

The basic need today is to foster the full application of the driving force of private capital. We want to see capital go into the productive channels of private industry. We want to see private business expand. We believe that much of the remaining unemployment will disappear as private capital funds are increasingly employed in productive enterprises. We believe that one of the most important ways of achieving these ends at this time is to continue progress toward a balance of the federal budget.[37]

36. Fine, 121.
37. Henry Morgenthau, "Federal Spending and the Federal Budget," *Proceedings of the Academy of Political Science, 17* (1938), 536–537.

Hansen and Fine seem justified in their criticism. The lag appears to have reflected the unwillingness even of the administration to incur a deficit or a further expansion in the public debt. The administration shared the business belief in the need for a balanced budget, and consequently was reluctant to take steps which would unbalance it.

IMPLICATIONS OF ERRORS IN POLICY

It scarcely seems necessary to emphasize the need for greater awareness of the deflationary aspects of new taxes. The new social security taxes of 1937, a levy of one billion dollars, bore important responsibility for the near-balancing of the budget. Yet government and business seemed little aware of their deflationary character.[38]

A second deficiency in fiscal policy was the failure to give adequate consideration to the problems faced in the change-over from a government- to a business-driven economy. Only a few realized that the first six months of 1937 were the transitional period between the two. A notable exception among government policy-makers was Eccles, who early in 1937 recognized the changing character of the economy:

Sometime in 1936 and early 1937, with the increase in tax revenues and the decline in government borrowings, I believe that increased private expenditures in the production of durable goods became the factor of major importance; recovery became self-generating and proceeded under its own momentum.

This transition is significant not only from the point of view of the success of the government spending program as a recovery measure, but also as marking the beginning of a new period with new problems.[39]

Although aware of the changing relationship of the government to the economy, Eccles was mistaken in believing that the transition had already been effected. Too little attention appears to have been directed toward the physical and psychological problems of stimulating business expenditures. It would also seem that Eccles failed to convey to other policy-makers his belief that the production of durable goods was "the factor of major importance." Either this or he was unable to win them over to his viewpoint. In any event President Roosevelt, in his attack on rising prices, placed the government on record as opposing further assistance for the durable goods industries at the very moment (April 1937) when the transitional problems were the greatest. Clearly fiscal policy to be successful must give careful attention to the delicate problems which may arise as net income-increasing ex-

38. Cf. Social Security Board, *Unemployment Compensation, What and Why?* Publication No. 14 (March 1937), 10–11.

39. Marriner S. Eccles, "Controlling Booms and Depressions," *Fortune* (April 1937), 88c.

penditures of government decline and business enterprise takes over.

The bonus payments provide a case study of the effects on the economy of an unusual expansion in government expenditures. These expenditures caused a bulge in the income stream and added fuel to the pressure on prices. They contributed to the temporary scarcities in many lines which made more difficult the transition from a government- to a business-driven economy.[40]

The time lag in the revival of net government contribution is also evidence of the inflexibility of the spending program. Action must be taken quickly if net government contribution is to achieve the greatest success in combatting recessive tendencies. The eight-month lag between the drop in industrial production and the President's proposal for a new spending program appears to have been unfortunate. In the future there may be less opposition to unbalancing the budget as a means of preventing recession, yet in the spring of 1949, as recession appeared imminent, government officials and members of Congress demanded either new taxes to keep the budget balanced or a reduction in government expenditures. Thus the resistance to unbalancing the budget was still very great and almost no one spoke out for a flexible spending program to combat the "readjustment." The lesson of 1937–38 seems to be that, once it becomes evident that production is sagging, action should be taken immediately, the sooner the better. If such action will eventually be taken anyway, as in 1937–38, then postponement of action only risks deepening the trough or prolonging the period of recession.

The experience in 1937–38 reveals other weaknesses of the deficit spending mechanism. Not only is timing and direction of spending crucial, but successful "compensatory spending" apparently requires a reasonably accurate forecast of the future course of events.[41] Even

40. This leads to the general comment that there seems to be a need for analysis of the impact which government spending has upon production and distribution processes. The methods of government contracting and purchasing and their relationship to private buying and production present a field of analysis which is largely undeveloped. (A recent contribution in this field is the study of John P. Miller, *Pricing of Military Procurements* [New Haven, 1949].) The effects of government spending on prices, output, and employment require investigation. It is also important to examine the interrelationships of government and private spending. The effects of government spending on the national economy may well depend upon the point in the production process where the spending is injected, and upon the extent to which the spending is competitive or supplementary to private spending.

41. It seems doubtful that government policy-makers in 1936–37 operated upon the theory of compensatory spending, where this is defined as the acceptance of deficit financing for achieving a high level of national income when an adequate volume of private investment is absent. Fine believes that it was not until the spring of 1938 that government leaders actually came around to the compensatory theory of government spending, operating earlier under the theory of "pump priming." *Op. cit.*, 117–119.

after individuals receive income from government there is a time lag
before this money becomes income again. Consequently the necessary
volume of expenditures may be considerably greater at one time than
another, in order to produce equal effects on income.

For example, when the business situation is deteriorating the stimulating effects of government spending may materialize in time only to
lessen the severity of the recession. It is to be hoped that government
policy-makers in the future may improve their forecasting, with the
aid of the additional statistical data which have now become available,
and by profiting from the experience of the past.[42] The impression derived from the action taken in the 1936–38 period, however, is that
policy-makers did not even make consistent use of the facts which they
had. The interrelationships of the net government contribution, the
price level, physical output, and business spending were not clearly
understood, if indeed they were perceived at all.

Finally a consideration for the future is whether it may be concluded from the experience in 1936–38 that the termination of net government contribution before full employment is reached will auto-
matically lead to recession. Such a conclusion would be contrary to
the theory of "pump priming" which relies upon using government
spending to create more favorable expectations about the future on the
part of businessmen. Private expenditures are then expected to carry
the system on up to full employment. In 1936–38 the government
stimulus to income was reduced long before the system had attained
full employment. But since some expansion in private spending took
place thereafter, there appears to be no necessary reason why private
spending might not respond vigorously to a reduction of government
spending under different conditions than in 1936–38. It would seem
reasonable, therefore, to assume that the effects which a change in
government spending will have on the economy are dependent upon,
among other things, the phase of the business cycle in which it occurs,
and to an even greater extent upon the companion policies of government. Fine rejected the conclusion that the 1936–37 sequence of events
proves that the government dare not reduce its contribution to income
before full employment is reached: "It would be entirely unwarranted
to deduce from the 1937 episode an argument against reducing the
federal contribution at any point short of full employment or the inference that compensatory fiscal policy is the sole solution to the problem of idle resources. Rather, the conclusion may well be drawn that
the above experience has demonstrated the deficiencies inherent in
compensatory spending as a monistic cure." [43]

42. Cf. Angell, 240–242.
43. Fine, 115.

SUMMARY

The experience with net government contribution in the recession and revival indicates the need to appraise the total effects of any new tax levies and to give broad consideration to the difficult problems faced in the transition from an economy propelled by government spending to one dependent upon private spending. These problems include the timing of net government contribution, the effects of government spending upon prices and production, the importance of anticipatory spending if the program is to be successful, and the need to relate net government contribution to other government policies.

CHAPTER 6

Federal Reserve and Treasury Policy

THE POSITION and contribution of monetary policy in the recession and revival must now be examined. In spite of the fact that interest rates were at an unprecedentedly low level and easy credit conditions persisted throughout the period, the deflationary actions of the Federal Reserve and Treasury authorities are believed by some to have been a prominent cause of the recession. These monetary conditions will be considered in two chapters. The various actions taken and the theory behind Federal Reserve and Treasury operations are summarized in the present chapter. Chapter 7 will evaluate the causal relationship of monetary policy to the recession and the revival.

BACKGROUND OF FEDERAL RESERVE ACTION

The stated objective of the Board of Governors of the Federal Reserve System was the promotion of economic stability: "It should be the declared objective of the Government of the United States to maintain economic stability, and it should be the recognized duty of the Board of Governors of the Federal Reserve System to use all its powers to contribute to a concerted effort by all agencies of the Government toward the attainment of this objective." [1] A more immediate objective was to maintain easy credit conditions in the interest of a full recovery. At the same time the Board was on its guard against unwise credit expansion. Most of its actions in 1936–37 were guided by the latter purpose.

As early as September 1935 the Federal Advisory Council, through the Board of Governors of the Federal Reserve System, urged "that there should at all times prevail sufficient flexibility to prevent undue expansion and contraction in the credit structure of the country." [2] The Federal Open Market Committee in its meetings on October 22 to 24, 1935, agreed unanimously that "there is nothing in the business or credit situation which at this time necessitates the adoption of any policy designed to retard credit expansion." [3] Nevertheless, it was concerned over the huge expansion in bank deposits and reserves:

1. *Federal Reserve Bulletin*, "Objectives of Monetary Policy," *23* (1937), 828.
2. *Ibid., 22* (1936), 5.
3. Board of Governors of the Federal Reserve System, *Twenty-second Annual Report* (1935), 231.

the Committee cannot fail to recognize that the rapid growth of bank deposits and bank reserves in the past year and a half is building up a credit base which may be very difficult to control if undue credit expansion should become evident. . . . the Committee is of the opinion that steps should be taken by the Reserve System as promptly as may be possible to absorb at least some of these excess reserves, not with a view to checking some further expansion of credit, but rather to put the System in a better position to act effectively in the event that credit expansion should go too far.[4]

As indicated in this statement, the critical economic factors which most impressed the Open Market Committee were the increases in both demand deposits and bank reserves. Demand deposits for all banks, which had fallen from $55,289 million on December 31, 1929 to $37,998 million on June 30, 1933, had recovered to $48,964 million by December 31, 1935. This was approximately the level in 1925–26. For all member banks, demand deposits had almost regained the levels of mid-1929.[5] Deposits of this volume, if turned over at the "normal" ratio of the twenties, were adequate to support a substantial increase in national income.[6]

Excess reserves, which ranged from minus $100 million to plus $100 million in the period 1917 to 1931, averaged about $500 million in 1933. The rapid inflow of gold and the increase in domestically mined gold expanded excess reserves from $859 million on December 30, 1933 to over $3,300 million in December 1935.[7] These changes are shown in Figure 9, which plots excess reserves by quarters on a logarithmic scale. The Board estimated that "on the basis of $3,500,-000,000 of excess reserves the increase in deposits at the old ratio could have been as much as $42,000,000,000, an increase which would have considerably more than doubled the existing volume of deposits."[8]

It should be observed here that the Board appears to have been preoccupied with monetary factors in formulating its policies. Even as concern was expressed over the level of demand deposits and excess reserves, unemployment was estimated at between nine and eleven million.[9] Moreover, in the monetary field the Board's fears proved un-

4. *Ibid.*, 231–232.

5. On December 31, 1935, demand deposits were $32,159 million compared with $32,283 million on June 30, 1929.

6. Gross national product was estimated at $90.4 billion in 1925 and $95.6 billion in 1926 compared with $70.8 billion in 1935. Cf. Painter, *op. cit.*, 872–873.

7. Domestically mined gold added $375.6 million to the monetary stock from March 1, 1933, to December 31, 1936. In addition, the increase in the gold price from $20.67 per ounce to $35.00 per ounce accounted for $1.6 billion of the $4 billion gold stock increase from January 1934 through December 1936.

8. *Federal Reserve Bulletin, 22* (1936), 616.

9. "Employment Gains Continue," *American Federationist, 45* (1938), 1344;

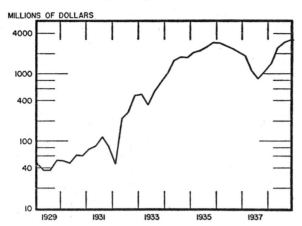

MILLIONS OF DOLLARS

Fig. 9. Estimated excess reserves of member banks, by quarters, 1929–38 (logarithmic scale). Board of Governors of the Federal Reserve System, *Banking and Monetary Statistics*, 370–372.

warranted. Demand deposits throughout the 1930's turned over at a much slower rate than in the twenties. Nevertheless, the fear of potential expansion with the huge volume of deposits and excess reserves finally led the Board to initiate a series of control actions, commencing in the spring of 1936 and terminating only when economic conditions deteriorated in the late summer of 1937.

ACTIONS OF FEDERAL RESERVE BOARD

CONTROL ACTIONS

The first of these measures, in February 1936, was an increase in margin requirements on securities from 40 to 55%. The Board believed that credit expansion in that area had played an important role in the excesses of 1929: [10]

the amount of borrowing was at about the level from which the great increase that accompanied the stock market boom of the 1920's commenced, and it was believed that the restraining influence of any increase in margin

---

National Industrial Conference Board, *Conference Board Economic Record, 2* (1940), 86.

10. The Board's concern over an excessive expansion of credit for stock market purposes could have arisen from the belief that the rise in the use of credit in the stock market in 1929 deprived legitimate business of funds, or it may have resulted from a fear that too many dollars would be made available to business, or just from the belief that a booming stock market was not a healthy development. The first position, if held, seems invalid for there is serious reason to doubt that the stock market "absorbed" credit to any significant degree. For the most definitive statement of this point of view, cf. Fritz A. Machlup, *The Stock Market—Credit and Capital Formation* (New York, 1940).

requirements, in order to be effective in forestalling any excessive growth in the use of credit for the purpose of purchasing or carrying securities by means of increased borrowing of brokers' customers and to some extent of brokers themselves, should be applied before an unhealthy development of credit in the stock market gets under way.[11]

The second measure raised the reserve requirements for member banks by 50% on August 15, 1936. By this action the Board was placed once again in a position where it could control credit conditions through open-market operations.[12] The increase was accompanied by the announcement that the easy money policy was still unchanged: "These excess reserves have resulted almost entirely from the inflow of gold from abroad and not from the System's policy of encouraging full recovery through the creation and maintenance of easy money conditions. This easy money policy remains unchanged and will be continued." [13]

After the dip caused by the increase in reserve requirements excess reserves rose again in the fall months, primarily because of the continuation of gold imports. As a result, a third control measure was taken when the Treasury announced on December 21, 1936, the inauguration of a gold sterilization program.[14] Prior to the sterilization program, the Treasury paid the commercial banks for gold imports by drawing upon its account with the Federal Reserve banks and increasing the reserves of member banks. The Treasury simultaneously replenished its balances with the Federal Reserve System by depositing certificates issued on the basis of the purchased gold. With the establishment of the gold sterilization program the Treasury bought the incoming gold as before by drawing down its account and increasing the reserves of member banks. Its depleted balances with the Federal Reserve System were replenished by selling new securities which eliminated the newly created reserves of the member banks, unless of course they were bought by Federal Reserve banks.

A final control action was the announcement of a further increase in reserve requirements by 33⅓%, effective in equal increases on March 1 and May 1, 1937. This exhausted the Board's power to increase reserve requirements. The action was viewed as a discharge of its responsibilities since it was expected "not only to counteract an in-

11. Board of Governors, *Twenty-third Annual Report* (1936), 60, Report of Action at Meeting of January 24, 1936.

12. "The reduction of excess reserves to an estimated level of approximately $1,900,000,000 brings them within the scope of control through the System's open-market portfolio which consists of $2,430,000,000 of United States Government securities." *Federal Reserve Bulletin, 22* (1936), 614.

13. *Ibid.,* 613.

14. *Ibid., 23* (1937), 1.

jurious credit expansion or contraction after it had developed, but also to anticipate and prevent such an expansion or contraction." [15]

During 1937 the increase in reserve requirements reduced excess reserves from $2,078 million in February to $1,398 million in March, and from $1,594 million in April to $918 million in May. Excess reserves reached a low of a little over $700 million in August. Figure 10 shows the effects of all these changes in reserve ratios on the excess reserve positions of the member banks. The letters A, B, and C on the chart date the reserve increases.

ACTIONS PROMOTING EXPANSION

The remaining actions of the Board of Governors and the Treasury were taken with a view to facilitating expansion. Most of them were enacted after the precipitate decline had begun and were designed to promote recovery by maintaining easy money conditions.

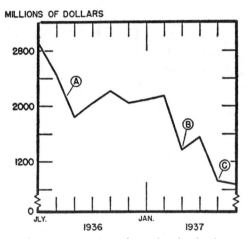

Fig. 10. Estimated excess reserves of member banks, by months, July 1936 through June 1937. Board of Governors of the Federal Reserve System, *Banking and Monetary Statistics,* 396. Letters A, B, and C date reserve increases.

The first such measure occurred, however, before the decline had begun, and consisted of open-market purchases of government securities in the amount of $94 million from March 31 to April 28, 1937. The government bond market at this time was under heavy selling pressure from member banks as they made the necessary adjustments in reserves to meet the increased requirements. The Federal Reserve made the open-market purchases "with a view (1) to exerting an influence toward orderly conditions in the money market and (2) to

15. *Ibid.,* 95.

facilitating the orderly adjustment of member banks to the May 1 increase in reserve requirements." [16]

The next action, of August 21, 1937, lowered the rediscount ratio to 1% at the Federal Reserve Bank of New York and to 1.5% at all other Federal Reserve banks. The regulations governing the eligibility of bank paper for rediscounting were also revised as of September 1937.

These actions were taken in order to meet peak seasonal demands for credit and currency. In addition, it was announced on September 14, 1937, that the Federal Open Market Committee stood ready to expand its holdings of short-term Treasury obligations by $300 million. At the same time the Treasury was requested to release approximately $300 million from the sterilized gold account, which by the end of August had mounted to $1,336 million. This action raised excess reserves from their low of $700 million in August to 1,038 million in September. These various measures had the purpose of continuing "the System's policy of furthering economic recovery through monetary ease . . ." [17]

Other expansionary actions in the fall of 1937 included the reduction of the margin requirement on securities from 55 to 40%, effective November 1, and the open-market purchase of $38 million in government securities, from November 3 to 24.[18]

It was not until after the first of the year, in the midst of declining industrial production and income, that the major actions were taken to facilitate monetary expansion. The Secretary of the Treasury announced on February 14, 1938, that net additions to the gold stock in the amount of $100 million per quarter would be permitted to become a part of bank reserves, effective from the first of the year.[19] This actually was the end of the gold sterilization program, although it was not officially discontinued until April 14, at the request of the President. At that time the Treasury transferred $1,183 million from its inactive gold account and $209 million of gold held in its working balances to its gold certificate account with the Federal Reserve banks. These funds then became a part of member banks' reserves as they were drawn upon by the Treasury to redeem Treasury notes.

On April 14, again at the request of the President, the Board of Governors of the Federal Reserve System announced a reduction in member bank reserve requirements of 12.5%. This increased member bank excess reserves by about $750 million.[20]

16. Board of Governors of the Federal Reserve System, *Twenty-fourth Annual Report* (1937), 215.

17. *Ibid.*, 205.

18. *Federal Reserve Bulletin, 23* (1937), 1068 and 1177.

19. *Ibid., 24* (1938), 181.

20. *Ibid.*, 343.

The final action was also requested by the President in his message to Congress on April 14. It consisted of a revision in bank examination procedure and in investment securities regulations of the Controller of the Currency. It was expected to result, "first, in broadening the opportunity for small and medium-sized business concerns to obtain credit from the banks on a sound basis, and, second, in relieving pressures that tend to reduce outstanding credit or prevent extension of new credit to sound borrowers." [21]

This action completed the measures to facilitate credit expansion. The sterilization fund was abandoned. Required reserve ratios, margins on securities, and rediscount rates of Federal Reserve banks were lowered. Rules governing the eligibility of paper for rediscounting were broadened and those governing the security upon which commercial banks could lend were relaxed. These measures, together with the "spend-lend" program and liberalized lending terms for construction, made up the government's program for combating the recession and initiating the revival. The extent to which these factors may have had causal responsibility for the revival will be discussed in later sections.

THEORY OF FEDERAL RESERVE OPERATIONS

The various actions of the Federal Reserve and Treasury authorities have been outlined with a brief statement of the reasons for their adoption. This section will examine in detail their general theory of operation. It is important to understand the purposes which guided the monetary authorities in their policy decisions during the period, to be aware of the various pressures to which they were subjected, and to evaluate their success in anticipating the response of the banking community.

As was noted at the beginning of the chapter, the long-run objective of the Federal Reserve policy was the promotion of economic stability. Its three principal immediate objectives were to control reserve positions of member banks by open-market operations so that the rediscount rate could be made effective, to anticipate and prevent credit expansion which in its opinion was unwise, and to maintain easy money conditions to support a full economic recovery.

It is not surprising that these policies sometimes worked at cross-purposes, combining as they did measures normally considered restrictive with an easy credit policy. Nor were the total effects of each clearly anticipated. A discussion of these three policies in turn should provide an understanding of the theory of Federal Reserve and Treasury policy and bring out any inconsistencies.

21. *Ibid.*, 563.

OPEN-MARKET OPERATIONS TO CONTROL
RESERVES OF MEMBER BANKS

A historically important means of controlling member bank reserves and credit expansion has been open-market operations. However, the increase in member bank excess reserves to over $3 billion by December 1935, compared with $2.4 billion of government securities held in the portfolio of the Federal Reserve Banks, limited the effectiveness of the System's traditional weapon of control. Full control could not be exercised when governments held were less than member bank excess reserves:

For current adjustments of the reserve position of member banks to changes in the credit situation, the Reserve System should continue to rely on the traditional methods of credit control through discount policy, and particularly through open-market operations. By the present action excess reserves will be reduced to within the amount that could be absorbed through open-market operations, should such action become desirable. Conversely, should conditions develop requiring expansion of reserves, they could be increased through open-market operations.[22]

The Reserve authorities were confronted with two alternative courses of action in any move to reduce excess reserves. Either they could engage in open-market sales to the limits of their portfolio or they could apply a uniform increase in required reserves. Open-market sales were not without supporters in the Federal Reserve system. Thus, the Federal Advisory Council strongly urged the use of open-market sales to reduce excess reserves of member banks. The Council believed government bonds were dangerous as a reserve for currency or deposits, and favored their elimination from reserve portfolios. In addition, the Council stressed the ease and flexibility of administration in open-market operations: "Under that method, Government security holdings may be permitted to run off or may be sold, rapidly or gradually, as in the judgment of the open-market committee may seem to be feasible or advisable. If at any time the effects seem to be too severe it is possible to suspend or even temporarily to reverse the policy." [23]

At the same time the Council was opposed to increasing reserve requirements: "Under the second method, namely, increase of reserve requirements, rigidity is substituted for flexibility, since it must be entirely apparent to anyone that frequent changes in reserve requirements would create a chaotic condition in planning for the future by

22. *Ibid., 22* (1936), 615.
23. *Ibid.,* 6. The two quotations in the next paragraph are also from the same source and page.

member bank management." They added, however, that if government holdings were eliminated or reduced, and it was still necessary to curb speculation, then an increase in reserve requirements should be made as "the clear and plain duty of the Board fearlessly and promptly to take such action."

Another group associated with the Federal Reserve System, the Federal Open Market Committee, opposed the sale of governments to absorb excess reserves, for two reasons: "First that it may be a shock to the bond market, inducing sales of securities by banks all over the country; second, that however it may be explained publicly, it may be misconstrued by the public as a major reversal of credit policy, since this method has never been employed except as a means of restraint, which is not desired at this time." Although opposed to open-market sales, the committee was also aware of the risk incident to raising reserve requirements: "This method of control is new and untried and may possibly prove at this time to be an undue and restraining influence on the desirable further extension of bank credit." [24]

At the joint meeting of the Federal Open Market Committee and the Board of Governors of the Federal Reserve System, on December 17–18, 1935, it was felt that there was an extreme urgency for some sort of action on excess reserves. Therefore those who favored open-market action agreed to the use of changes in member bank reserve requirements. Thus, by December 1935, the decision was made as to the method of control.[25]

RESPONSIBILITY TO ANTICIPATE AND PREVENT UNWISE CREDIT EXPANSION

The Board wanted to anticipate and prevent unwise credit expansion. As noted in an earlier section, it believed that the Federal Reserve Act "placed responsibility on the Board to use its power to change Reserve requirements not only to counteract an injurious credit expansion or contraction after it has developed, but also to anticipate and prevent such an expansion or contraction." [26] Accordingly, the Board was alert to the dangers from possible excessive credit creation in the future as well as to specific excesses in the present.

But there is no evidence that the Board at any time considered that an unwise expansion of credit had already taken place. Its restrictive

24. Board of Governors of the Federal Reserve System, *Twenty-second Annual Report* (1935), 232.

25. See, however, the report of meeting on November 20, 1936, of the Federal Open Market Committee when the method of control was discussed once again. Board of Governors of the Federal Reserve System, *Twenty-third Annual Report* (1936), 81–82.

26. *Federal Reserve Bulletin, 23* (1937), 95.

actions were all taken with a view to preventing some future, rather than current, extension of credit.[27]

Reserve ratios were increased, as a part of this anticipatory program, to eliminate excess reserves before any injurious credit expansion could take place. Huge excess reserves meant not only that open-market operations could not be completely successful in controlling the volume of member bank reserves but the Board also feared that these excess reserves at any time might be made the basis for unwise and dangerous credit expansion: "The portion of existing excess reserves which will be absorbed by the Board's action, if permitted to become the basis of a tenfold or even larger expansion of bank credit, would create an injurious credit expansion." [28]

The Board of Governors was undoubtedly conditioned in its attitude toward excess reserves by an expectation that in any period of prosperity existing or additional deposits would be turned over at roughly the average income velocity of the twenties, three times per year as compared with under two in the early years of the depression.[29] Actually this did not happen,[30] which explains in part the Board's difficulty in anticipating the future course of economic events and determining appropriate policy.

The Board not only viewed excess reserves as a potential threat to a sound economy but believed that restrictive actions after expansion had taken place might well result in a deflationary cycle by causing severe credit liquidation. Therefore, in its opinion, "It is far better to sterilize a part of these superfluous reserves while they are still unused than to permit a credit structure to be erected upon them and then to withdraw the foundation of the structure." [31]

27. However, in late 1936 the Board was disturbed by price advances and increases in the rate of business activity in certain areas: "The rate of advance in business activity was, in fact, so fast that there were evidences of unsound developments." Board of Governors of the Federal Reserve System, *Twenty-fourth Annual Report* (1937), 2.

28. *Federal Reserve Bulletin, 22* (1936), 614. However, the Board never explained precisely what it meant by an unwise or dangerous expansion of credit. This fear of credit expansion in 1936–37 seems to have resulted from a failure to integrate the real and monetary factors. Much of this alarm at the potentialities for credit expansion appears valid only in a context where resources are fully employed so that increases in money can lead only to inflationary expansion.

29. "The present volume of deposits, if utilized at a rate of turnover comparable to pre-depression levels, is sufficient to sustain a vastly greater rate of business activity than exists today. In order to sustain and expand recovery, the country's commerce, industry, and agriculture, therefore, require a more complete and productive utilization of existing deposits rather than further additions to the amount now available." *Ibid., 23* (1937), 96.

30. Angell estimated the marginal velocity of circulation of money from 1933 to 1939 at 1.75, *op. cit.,* 152.

31. *Federal Reserve Bulletin, 22* (1936), 614.

The same justification was given for the second and third increases in reserve ratios of March and May 1937: "the Board believes that the action taken at this time will operate to prevent an injurious credit expansion and at the same time give assurance for continued progress toward full recovery." [32]

EASY CREDIT CONDITIONS TO PROMOTE RECOVERY

The Board wanted to be in a position to conduct successful open-market operations, and was opposed to any unwise credit expansion. At the same time it insisted that easy money conditions would be maintained to support a full economic recovery. Thus, at the time of the first increase in reserve ratios (August 1936), it publicly denied that its easy money policy was changed: "It does not constitute a reversal of the easy money policy which has been pursued by the System since the beginning of the depression." [33] The Board was confident that the new reserve requirements would not affect the easy money conditions then prevailing.

The Board still supported an easy money policy at the time that the March–May 1937 reserve increases were announced. It saw no reason why the new increase should raise the costs of funds to borrowers:

It is the Board's expectation that, with approximately $500,000,000 of excess reserves remaining with the banks, credit conditions will continue to be easy. . . . The Board's action does not reduce the large volume of existing funds available for investment by depositors, and should not, therefore, occasion an advance in long-term interest rates or a restrictive policy on the part of institutional and other investors in meeting the needs for sound business, industrial and agricultural credit.[34]

Before reserve requirements were ordered raised, the Board made careful surveys to determine the approximate distribution of excess reserves in the banking system. The conclusion before both the August 1936 increase and the March–May 1937 increases was that the new requirements could be met by the great majority of member banks with little repercussions on credit conditions through the use of their own excess reserves or balances with correspondent banks: [35]

As was the case when the board announced the increase of requirements in July 1936, excess reserves were widely distributed among member banks, and balances with correspondent banks were twice as large as they

---

32. *Ibid., 23* (1937), 97.
33. *Ibid., 22* (1936), 614.
34. *Ibid., 23* (1937), 96–97.
35. However, balances with correspondent banks are not on the same level as reserves. They are available as reserves for claimant banks, but are not additional reserves for the banking system as a whole.

had generally been in the past. All but a small number of member banks had more than sufficient excess reserves and surplus balances with other banks to meet a 33⅓ per cent increase in reserve requirements.[36]

Thorough surveys made by the Board show that the reserves are so well distributed that practically all member banks are in a position to meet the increased requirements either by utilizing their excess balances with the Reserve banks or by drawing upon their excess balances with correspondent banks.[37]

Nevertheless, it will be contended in the next chapter that these measures, particularly the reserve increases of the spring of 1937, played a significant role in precipitating the recession of 1937–38. The reserve increases fell most harshly on the central reserve city banks and had unexpected and undesired results.

THEORY OF FEDERAL RESERVE AND TREASURY ACTION IN THE REVIVAL

In the period preceding the recession the objectives of the Federal Reserve and Treasury authorities, as has been seen, were threefold: to restore open-market operations as an instrument of control over member bank reserves, to prevent excessive credit expansion, and to continue easy money conditions. When the recession began the facilitation of monetary ease became the single objective. Thus $300 million in gold was released from the sterilization account, rediscount rates at Federal Reserve banks were lowered, and authorization was given to the executive committee of the Federal Open Market Committee to purchase up to $300 million in government bonds:

In deciding to provide additional reserves for member banks for the purpose of meeting seasonal requirements,[38] the Federal Open Market Committee and the Board of Governors acted in conformity with the System's policy of maintaining a condition of monetary ease, a policy that has been actively pursued since the early months of 1932. Recent reductions in discount rates at the Federal Reserve banks were in harmony with this policy.[39]

The same emphasis on monetary ease caused the Board to reduce margin requirements on securities:

36. Board of Governors of the Federal Reserve System, *Twenty-fourth Annual Report* (1937), 4.
37. *Federal Reserve Bulletin, 22* (1936), 614.
38. It is interesting to note that the decision to provide reserves for seasonal expansion was made on the week end following the two-week period of severe declines in the stock market, September 1937.
39. *Federal Reserve Bulletin, 23* (1937), 965.

The provisions of the Securities Exchange Act of 1934 under which margin requirements had been established expressly authorized the Board to reduce margin requirements when it deems it appropriate to do so for the accommodation of commerce and industry, having due regard to the credit situation of the country. The members of the Board present viewed the proposed action as a step in the direction of moderating credit conditions in accord with the intent of the Securities Exchange Act.[40]

Major measures to promote monetary ease, desterilization of gold and reductions in reserve requirements, were part of the general recovery program proposed by the President on April 14, 1938:

The administration proposes immediately to make additional bank resources available for the credit needs of the country. This can be done without legislation. It will be done through the de-sterilization of approximately one billion four hundred million dollars of Treasury gold, accompanied by action on the part of the Federal Reserve Board to reduce reserve requirements by about three-quarters of a billion dollars. The Federal Reserve Board informs me that they are willing to do so. These measures will make more abundant the supply of funds for commerce, industry and agriculture.[41]

BUSINESS RESPONSE TO FEDERAL RESERVE ACTION

Federal Reserve authorities were not alone in their alarm over the size of excess reserves. Business and financial representatives gave warm support to the Reserve action on the matter. The *Commercial and Financial Chronicle* approved heartily of the increased reserve requirements: "A step long advocated in these columns was taken by the Board of Governors of the Federal Reserve System, Tuesday, when announcement was made of a 50% increase of reserve requirements, to take effect August 15. This action is thoroughly commendable and constitutes a long-delayed recognition of the dangers of wild and uncontrollable credit inflation inherent in the unprecedented aggregate of idle funds." [42] The later increases in reserve requirements were also supported as desirable steps.[43]

The National City Bank of New York noted that excess reserves after any additional increase in reserve requirements would still be sufficient to support a large increase in deposits: "It is pertinent to point out, however, that excess reserves of this magnitude would still be far in excess of levels prior to 1934, and amply sufficient to provide abundant and cheap credit for industry and trade, which must still

40. Board of Governors of the Federal Reserve System, *Twenty-fourth Annual Report* (1937), 208. Record of policy actions at meeting of October 27, 1937.
41. *Federal Reserve Bulletin, 24* (1938), 343.
42. *Commercial and Financial Chronicle, 143*, Pt. 1 (1936), 315.
43. *Ibid., 144*, Pt. 1 (1937), 323.

be considered a major objective of Federal Reserve and Treasury policy." [44]

The chairman of the Board of Directors of the Chase National Bank of New York, W. W. Aldrich, stated: "I believe that the reserve requirements should again be raised by an equal amount to the full limit allowed by the law . . ." [45]

These statements indicate that the business community regarded with favor the measures which were taken by the Federal Reserve to reduce the potential expansion of deposits in the banking system. It was the general national budgetary measures, deficit financing, devaluation of gold, and cheap money policies, which received the most pointed criticism from business.

44. National City Bank of New York, *Monthly Letter* (1936), 174. It described the sterilization program as designed to limit the effects of gold purchases on the credit base. It may be inferred that the bank approved of the new measure, particularly since it had viewed the high tide of gold imports as carrying "a constant danger of inflation." *Ibid.* (1937), 4.

45. Winthrop W. Aldrich, "Business Recovery and Government Policy," *Bankers Magazine, 134* (1937), 7. Condensed from an address.

CHAPTER 7

The Causal Significance of Federal Reserve and Treasury Policy in the Recession and Revival

THE ARGUMENTS against Federal Reserve and Treasury policy as a cause of the recession will be outlined first. Then the case for these policies as a cause of the recession will be developed. Finally consideration will be given to the contribution of Federal Reserve policy to the theory of monetary management.

ARGUMENTS AGAINST FEDERAL RESERVE AND TREASURY POLICY AS A CAUSE OF THE RECESSION

A large majority of economic analysts have denied that Federal Reserve and Treasury policy had any causal part in the recession because monetary conditions remained extremely easy throughout the period, 1936–38. Hardy argued that excess reserves were ample, even after reserve ratios were increased, to disprove any monetary stringency.[1] Wilson also insisted that the easy credit conditions were evidence that the monetary policies did not actually prove restrictive.[2] Brockie contended that "monetary explanations of the 1937–38 crisis . . . are completely lacking in strategic causal significance."[3]

Schumpeter was even more positive in his belief that the increase in reserve ratios had no effect in the 1937–38 recession. He also based his conclusion on the fact that money rates did not stiffen. In his opinion an increase in reserve ratios could have an effect on the cost of capital funds, in the presence of huge excess reserves, only if there were imperfect competition in the market. This did exist, but the slight increase in the cost of capital which resulted had no effect on business calculations: "It [increase in bond yields] was, in fact, a reaction to the increase in reserve requirement—under conditions of imperfect competition curtailment of even an unsalable excess of supply

1. Hardy, *op. cit.,* 170–171.
2. Wilson, *op. cit.,* 180–181.
3. Brockie, "The Rally, Crisis, and Depression, 1935–38," 295.

can have effect on price. But while monetary management produced this effect, it certainly did not, via the rate of interest, produce any other; for no business calculation can in practice be affected by so minute an increase." [4] The increased reserve requirements produced no strain, nor were they responsible for the sagging prices of corporate securities in the third and fourth quarters of 1937. On the basis of these observations, Schumpeter wrote off Federal Reserve policy as a factor in the recession: "Monetary policy per se may, hence, become a major factor in the near future; but it had but little to do with the prosperity of 1935 to 1937, and nothing with the subsequent slump." [5]

Slichter discounted Federal Reserve policy on different grounds. He conceded that Reserve actions might have accentuated the break in bond prices and even reduced the flow of new security issues. But he believed that this had little effect on business expansion because internal sources alone provided over three-fourths of business capital.[6]

However, Slichter believed that experience with Federal Reserve policy in the period demonstrated the limitation of monetary and fiscal methods of controlling business cycles. A number of observations prompted this conclusion. First, in this instance, a statement of policies to be carried out in the future stimulated forward buying in commodities and the subsequent price rises; second, actions could not be taken quickly enough; and third, restraints on speculation were likely to be at the risk of discouraging investment. To Slichter the problem was not to adjust the physical volume of deposits but to control their velocity.[7]

These economists were not alone in discounting Federal Reserve and Treasury policy as a causal factor in the recession. Bankers generally believed that monetary policy had little responsibility. For example, an editorial in *Bankers Magazine* questioned the importance of Federal Reserve and Treasury policy because bank reserves were abundant and money rates were not high but extremely low.[8] Aldrich also dismissed monetary factors as a cause: "The causes for the recession cannot be found in monetary factors. The low levels of bank lending rates, which persisted despite the increase in reserve requirements and the continued sterilization of gold, gave definite evidence that there was no credit strain." [9]

4. Schumpeter, *op. cit.*, 1029.
5. *Ibid.*, 1031.
6. Slichter, "The Downturn of 1937," 103–104. Hardy also minimized the importance to the business community of bank financing. *Op. cit.*, 180–181.
7. Slichter, "The Downturn of 1937," 109.
8. *Bankers Magazine*, "A Perplexed Situation," *136* (1938), 369.
9. Winthrop W. Aldrich, "Business Recession in Relation to Government Policy," *Bankers Magazine, 136* (1938), 121. See also H. B. Elliston, "Blaming the Money Managers," 103–110.

THE CASE FOR MONETARY POLICY
AS A CAUSE OF THE RECESSION

In Chapter 2 it was noted that Angell, Lewis, Sachs, Ohlin, and Meade all placed some stress on government monetary policy as a cause of the recession. Hansen's thesis on the relationship of Reserve and Treasury action to the securities markets was also outlined in that chapter. In view of this emphasis, it is necessary to investigate the possibility that monetary policy may have contributed to the recession through repercussions on the bond and security markets.

Hansen was not alone in observing the apparent responsibility of Federal Reserve authorities for the softening of prices in the bond market. A. P. Woolfson and the *Economist* elaborated at some length on this causal relationship. Woolfson believed that the banking system had developed a new relationship between reserves and deposits in which excess reserves were a "normal" requirement. The effect of increased reserve requirements was to freeze the aggregate level of loans and investments so that business demands for accommodation were met by a reduction in investments rather than by an expansion in deposits: "any increase in customers' demands for loans from the commercial banks was not met by the use of existing excess reserves, but by a reduction in investments, . . . The Federal Reserve System had put itself in the position where its fear of inflationary developments tended to induce a deflationary tendency in the commercial bank deposits and a deflation in the values of high-grade bonds." [10]

In Woolfson's opinion the quantitative controls of 1937 were inadequate in the absence of qualitative controls. The crucial weakness in the situation was not so much the freezing of the level of loans and investments as the inflationary nature of the great increase in bank loans from early 1936 to the summer of 1937. This expansion of commercial bank credit contributed to the speculation in inventories. In his judgment a sharp and continued increase in the demand for bank loans, following a sustained increase in industrial production of the magnitude which occurred in 1934–36, should be viewed with suspicion.

The most carefully documented arguments for Federal Reserve policy as an important cause of the recession were presented by the *Economist*. Its conclusions did not differ greatly from those of Hansen, but the process by which Reserve actions affected the recession and the psychological impact on the national economy were given much more attention.

10. A. Philip Woolfson, "Our New Depression—What Can We Do About It?" *Bankers Magazine, 136* (1938), 104.

Briefly, the *Economist*'s position was that increased reserve requirements fell most heavily on the central reserve city banks. This had unexpected and undesired reactions in the bond market and subsequently upon the flotation of new securities. In turn, the increased difficulty of securing new capital played a large part in the recession. The reactions in the bond market were due chiefly to the movements of funds between various parts of the country as the banking system made the necessary adjustments to the reserve changes. This argument must now be examined in detail.

EFFECT OF INCREASED RESERVE
REQUIREMENTS ON MEMBER BANKS

Although reserves were adequate for the banking system, some of the central reserve city banks ran into considerable difficulty in making the adjustment.[11] These banks already had the highest required reserves and were faced with an increased demand for business accommodation. By the August 1936 action they had to provide 6.5% more reserves. In all they required $840 million for increased reserves and $427 million for increased loans. Of this amount $520 million were available in their excess reserves, but for the rest it was necessary to realize on holdings of government bonds. The effects of these sales were masked, however, by continued buying by banks outside New York and Chicago. Government bonds held by all member banks fell by only $126 million.[12] (See Table 6.)

TABLE 6: CHANGES IN SELECTED ITEMS IN NEW
YORK CITY AND CHICAGO MEMBER BANK
BALANCE SHEETS, JUNE TO DECEMBER 1936
(In millions of dollars)

Item	New York City	Chicago	Total
1. Loans	+327	+100	+427
2. Investments	−603	+48	−555
3. Required reserves	+678	+162	+840
4. Decrease in governments held by member banks			−126

Source: Loans and investments and required reserves from Board of Governors of the Federal Reserve System, *Twenty-fourth Annual Report* (1937), 118, 120. Decrease in governments from *Federal Reserve Bulletin, 23* (1937), 178.

11. This analysis of the effects of the reserve increases on the different types of banks is adapted from the *Economist*, "Federal Reserve Policy," *129* (1937), 117–118. The data are from the *Federal Reserve Bulletin, 23* (1937).

12. The only effective pressure was experienced by the New York City banks whose investments declined over $600 million. Loans and investments increased with the Chicago banks.

When reserve requirements were increased in the spring of 1937, the New York and Chicago banks again had to obtain 6.5% of new reserves. By this time, however, there were no unsterilized gold imports to add to their reserve balances and demands for loans were still expanding. Additional pressure was exerted by the country banks who met their share of the increased reserves from balances with New York and Chicago banks rather than from their own excess reserves. The reserve city banks, too, were so pinched for reserves that they had to sell bonds.

The effects of the second reserve increase on the portfolios of the member banks are summarized in Table 7. In the first six months of 1937, New York and Chicago banks had to supply $672 million in reserves, $462 million in loans, and $542 million in balances for out-of-town banks. Reserve city banks for these same purposes required $447 million, $199 million, and $516 million respectively. In all, central and reserve city banks sold $1,232 million of government bonds. In spite of the fact that country banks were still buying bonds, holdings of all member banks fell by $856 million of government bonds, and $330 million of other bonds. Even more pressure than this was exerted upon the bond market since government bonds outstanding increased substantially in this period: "during the period of these sales there was a net increase of $1,240 millions in the total amount of Government obligations outstanding. The Government bond market had to absorb over $2,000 millions of bonds in six months with the large banks, the biggest buyers in the last four years, turned sellers." [13]

During the process of these reserve adjustments the bond market was depressed: "Although the aggregate of reserves was abundant, the internal balance of payments was adverse to New York City, which was obliged to adjust its position through the security markets, in the absence of a functioning money market. This combination of a heavy demand from the Treasury [14] and liquidation by the New York banks depressed the bond market, raised the long-term interest rate, and impeded the issue of new securities." [15]

The *Economist* concluded, therefore, that Federal Reserve action had heavy responsibility in precipitating the recession: "In retrospect over the last eighteen months, it is easy to see that the restrictive policies initiated in the summer of 1936 made a very large contribution to the present recession. The decision to mop up the excess reserves seemed reasonable and moderate at the time it was taken. But it failed

---

13. *Economist, 129* (1937), 118.
14. Quotation in preceding paragraph points out that there was an increase in governments outstanding of $1,240 million during the first half of the year.
15. *Economist, 128* (1937), 469.

to take account of the relative indebtedness of different parts of the country to each other." [16]

FEDERAL RESERVE ACTION AND THE DECLINE IN BOND AND STOCK PRICES

The *Economist*'s analysis of the causal responsibility of Federal Reserve policy in the recession gains support from examination of the changes in prices and yields of securities. A heavy selling wave of government securities occurred immediately before and after the announcement of the second reserve increase. Central reserve city banks were joined by reserve city banks in selling short-term government bills and notes in anticipation of this second increase and in order to expand the more profitable loans to business.

TABLE 7: CHANGES IN SELECTED ITEMS IN MEMBER BANK BALANCE SHEETS, JANUARY TO JUNE 1937
(In millions of dollars)

Item	Central Reserve City Banks	Reserve City Banks	Country Banks	Total [a]
1. Loans	+462	+199	+262	+925
2. Investments	−867	−365	+47	−1,186
3. Government securities	−778	−221	+143	−856
4. Change in other bonds [b]	−89	−145	−96	−330
5. Required reserves	+672	+447	+285	+1,404
6. Interbank deposits	−542	−516	−75	−1,134
7. Sales of government bonds by central reserve and reserve city banks [c]				−1,232

a. Detail may not add due to rounding.
b. Change in investments minus change in government securities.
c. The sum of −867 and −365.

Source: Data from *Federal Reserve Bulletin, 23* (1937), 822–824.

The Board of Governors was quick to admit that its action on excess reserves contributed to the heavy volume of sales of government bonds and to the increase in yields:

In February and March there was a substantial volume of sales of Government obligations, both by banks and by other holders. These sales reflected in part adjustment of reserve positions by banks in connection with the increase in reserve requirements, and in part other influences, . . . As a result of the selling of securities yields on Government obliga-

16. *Ibid., 131* (1938), 191–192.

tions, both long-term and short-term, showed sharp advances in February and March.[17]

The initial pressure on prices of short-term government issues began early in December 1936 and spread quickly to other areas. Prices of municipal bonds declined early in January 1937, long-term corporate bonds in the middle of January, long-term Treasury bonds the last week of February, and common stocks in the middle of March.[18] As will be developed below, these price declines depressed business expectations, reduced the volume of new corporate capital issues, and increased both the difficulty and costs of obtaining new capital funds.

Other writers have observed that long-term government bond prices declined *before* long-term corporate bond prices, and have concluded that there was a causal connection between the two.[19] But the revised series on long-term Treasury bonds, which excluded maturities of less than 15 years, placed the high prices in late February 1937, or at a time when corporate bond prices had already been declining for more than a month. Because of this change in the time of peak for government bond prices, attention was directed toward short-term notes where the first declines in prices actually occurred. The other analysts of Federal Reserve action in the recession, guided by the unrevised Treasury series, were unaware that the initial pressure was on short-term rates. However, the reason for the pressure here seems obvious. Business demands for accommodation were rising and provided a more profitable outlet for bank funds than low-interest-yielding government securities. Therefore, Treasury bills and notes were sold in large amounts by member banks from January through March 1937. Bills outstanding were unchanged but member bank holdings declined by $132 million. Notes outstanding declined by $506 million; member bank holdings by $497 million. Member banks reduced their holdings of bills and notes by $407 million more than would have been warranted by their share of the total decline in outstandings.[20]

The time sequences for the peak prices in the various types of se-

17. *Federal Reserve Bulletin, 23* (1937), 283.

18. The parallel between movements of interest rates in 1936–37 and in 1947–48 is striking. Short-term interest rates rose in June 1947 when Federal Reserve support was withdrawn and member banks sold low-interest-yielding securities, thereby obtaining the reserves to meet the rising business demand for loans. By November 1947, sharp declines had occurred in long-term corporate and government bond prices as member banks sold these assets in anticipation of more profitable employment of their funds elsewhere.

19. Cf. especially the *Economist, 129* (1937), 117–118; and Alvin H. Hansen, *Full Recovery or Stagnation?*

20. Board of Governors of the Federal Reserve System, *Banking and Monetary Statistics*, 77, 510. On December 31, 1936, member banks held 43.9% of total notes outstanding.

curities [21] show the early peak in prices of short-term governments. Treasury bills reached their peak on December 10, 1936, municipals the first week of January 1937, long-term corporate bond prices the second or third week in January, long-term government bond prices the fourth week of February, and stock prices on March 10. Data on yields for these various classes of securities have been plotted by weeks in Figure 11 (December 1936 through September 1937). The scale for the yields on the Treasury bills is on the right-hand side of the chart.

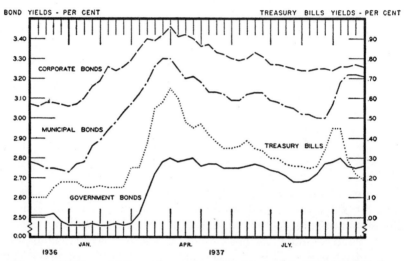

Fig. 11. Yields on high-grade corporate bonds, municipal bonds, U. S. Government bonds, and Treasury bills, by weeks, December 1936 through September 1937. Yields on high-grade corporate bonds, U. S. Government bonds from *Banking and Monetary Statistics,* 473, Table 129. Yields on Treasury bills from *ibid.,* 461, Table 123. Yields on municipal bonds from Standard and Poor's Corporation, *Long Term Security Price Index Record,* 138.

Table 8 shows that sharp declines occurred in short-term governments and corporate bond prices even as long-term governments were reaching their peak prices. On February 25, 1937, three of the five long-term government bonds listed in the table were at their peak prices and low in yields. But short-term government bond yields had increased almost .3% on the average, and corporate and municipal bond yields had risen sharply, from .1% with the City of Cincinnati 2.25% bonds to .4% with Pennsylvania Railroad 4% bonds.

21. The dates selected for the bond peaks are based on a consensus of the various indices : corporate bonds—Moody's, Dow-Jones, *New York Times,* and Standard and Poor's; municipals—Dow-Jones, Standard and Poor's, and U. S. Treasury; U. S. Government bonds—U. S. Treasury, and Standard and Poor's. The various indices agree on the peak in stock prices.

These data establish that the initial selling pressure was in the short-term low-interest governments as member banks attempted to adjust their reserve positions. Furthermore, the rise in the short-term interest rate was accompanied by marked declines in prices of all save long-term government bonds, and subsequently even these, along with common stock prices, gave way. It seems plausible to conclude that Federal Reserve action on reserve requirements touched off a series of events leading to a weakening of the securities markets which made the task of obtaining new capital funds more difficult.

TABLE 8: PRICES AND YIELDS ON SELECTED U. S. GOVERNMENT NOTES AND BONDS, AND CORPORATE, MUNICIPAL, AND STATE BONDS, SELECTED DATES, 1936–37

	1936–37 High Price	Price Feb. 25, 1937	Change from High	Yield to Maturity at High	Yield to Maturity Feb. 25, 1937
U. S. Notes					
1⅝% of 3/15/40	102.12 [a]	101.9 [a]	−1.3 [a]	0.87	1.17
1½% of 6/15/40	102.2	100.29	−1.5	0.89	1.20
1½% of 12/15/40	102.2	100.25	−1.9	0.96	1.27
1½% of 3/15/41	102.3	100.25	−1.10	0.99	1.29
1⅜% of 6/15/41	101.21	100.6	−1.15	1.00	1.31
1¼% of 12/15/41	101.3	99.30	−1.5	1.03	1.25
Average				0.96	1.25
U. S. Bonds					
2½%, 1953/49	101.22	101.17	−.5	2.32	2.36
2¾%, 1954/51	103.17	103.17	[b]	2.45	2.45
3%, 1955/51	106.28	106.26	−.2	2.43	2.44
2⅞%, 1960/55	104.29	104.29	[b]	2.52	2.52
2¾%, 1959/56	103.17	103.17	[b]	2.52	2.52
Corporate Bonds—Rails					
Atchison, 4%, 1995	117¼	111	−6¼	3.33	3.55
Chesapeake & Ohio, 4½%, 1922	128½	121	−7½	3.35	3.61
Norfolk & Western, 4%, 1996	124	118¼	−5.75	3.11	3.30
Pennsylvania, 4%, 1948	116⅝	113½	−3⅛	2.23	2.63
Virginia, 3¾%, 1966	109	104¾	−4¼	3.25	3.48
Corporate Bonds—Utilities					
Brooklyn Edison, 3¼%, 1966	105¾	102⅞	−2⅞	2.95	3.10
Consumers Power, 3½%, 1965	108	104	−4	3.07	3.28

TABLE 8: PRICES AND YIELDS ON SELECTED U. S. GOVERNMENT NOTES AND BONDS, AND CORPORATE, MUNICIPAL, AND STATE BONDS, SELECTED DATES, 1936–37 (*continued*)

	1936–37 High Price	*Price Feb. 25, 1937*	*Change from High*	*Yield to Maturity at High*	*Yield to Maturity Feb. 25, 1937*
Detroit Edison, 3½%, 1966	109½	104⅝	−4⅞	3.00	3.25
Ohio Edison, 4%, 1965	108¼	104¾	−3½	3.52	3.73
South Western Bell Telephone, 3½%, 1964	110⅛	106½	−3⅝	2.95	3.13
Municipal and State Bonds					
City of Cincinnati, 2¼%, 1956	104	102⅜	−1⅝	2.00	2.10
Fairfield County, 1¾%, 1950	96½	94⅞	−1⅝	2.05	2.20
Boston Metropolitan District, 2¼%, 1957	100	96⅞	−3⅛	2.25	2.45
St. Louis, 2½%, 1956	107⅞	105½	−2⅜	2.00	2.15
N. Y. State, 4%, 1964	131⅝	124⅞	−6¾	2.40	2.70

a. Figures after decimals are 32ds (U. S. notes and U. S. bonds).
b. New high.

Source: High price for U. S. notes and yield to maturity at high from National City Bank of New York, *Monthly Letter* (1937), 20; price and yield to maturity on U. S. notes, February 25, 1937, from *Wall Street Journal*, February 26, 1937, 14; all other data from National City Bank of New York, *Monthly Letter* (1937), 35.

However, a serious argument against a theory of causal responsibility for Federal Reserve policy in the recession is that the peak in dollar volume of new corporate capital issues for the recovery, 1933–37, of $276.1 million, occurred in June 1937, or after the break in bond and stock prices. This peak seems inconsistent with the belief that the conditions of obtaining new capital had worsened. On the other hand, if the June issues are excluded, then new capital issues fell substantially following the March stock break. The monthly rate of new corporate financing fell from an average of $137 million in the fourth quarter of 1936 and $130 million in the first quarter of 1937 to an average of $81 million in April–May 1937, and averaged only $82 million in the third quarter of 1937. With the exception of June 1937, there was a 40% decline in new issues.

Thus, even though the peak in dollar volume of new corporate capital issues occurred in June 1937 it can still be shown that the terms under which new funds were available had deteriorated, for which Federal Reserve policy through its effects on security prices bears no small responsibility. Moreover, a striking difference in the terms of new issues can be observed by comparing the composition of the new capital issues of December 1936, which was the peak month for new issues prior to June 1937 ($218 million compared with $276 million for the latter month), with that of June 1937. This comparison suggests that new corporate funds were more difficult to obtain and were available on much less favorable terms in June 1937 than in December 1936, and that special reasons account for the peak in the former month.

COMPARISON OF CAPITAL MARKETS OF DECEMBER 1936 AND JUNE 1937

In the first place, an indication perhaps of the greater difficulty in financing risky enterprises is the increased ratio of bonds to common stocks. In December 1936 new capital issues totaled $218.1 million, of which $101.1 million or 46% were bonds, the remainder being common stocks. In June 1937, they totaled $268.9 million,[22] of which $187 million or 70% were bonds and only $81.9 million or 30% were stocks. Thus in the June 1937 financing bond flotations took the place of common stock issues. The market declines had affected business expectations to the point that lenders apparently required the greater relative security of bond indebtedness.[23]

Secondly, examination of the companies participating in the new financing and of the actual magnitudes of some of the issues suggests that special reasons, rather than ease of financing, account for the peak of new issues in June 1937. Most of the issues were for companies with the highest credit ratings, whose ability to obtain new funds was relatively unaffected by the increased market pessimism. Table 9 shows the 23 largest capital issues of December 1936, which comprised 87% of the total, and the nine companies whose borrowing accounted for 92% of the June financing. The results of an effort to measure the investment quality of the various companies are summarized in Tables 10 and 11. As an indication of the risk attending marginal capital in each of the companies, the lowest Moody rating on any outstanding bond of the particular company is listed.[24] Thus,

22. Later revised to $276.1 million but the breakdown by company is available for the $268.9 million total.

23. It is possible, but extremely improbable, that the new issues were in the form of bonded indebtedness, not because of the more favorable reception accorded such issues but because the borrowers wanted their money in that form. It is not contended here that there was any trend toward a higher percentage of bond flotations in the period from December 1936 to June 1937. The higher percentage of bond flotations supplies one reason for the peak in new issues of June 1937. Cf. discussion of this point in Philip W. Bell, "Federal Reserve Policy and the Recession of 1937–38; A Note," *Review of Economics and Statistics, 33* (1951), 349–350.

24. Bonds rating Aaa, Aa, A, and Baa are considered by Moody's services to be of investment grade.

TABLE 9: NEW CORPORATE CAPITAL ISSUES,
DECEMBER 1936 AND JUNE 1937
(In millions of dollars)

December 1936		June 1937	
Company	Amount	Company	Amount

BONDS

Chicago, Milwaukee, St. Paul & Pacific Railroad Co.	3.1	Union Pacific Railroad Co.	10.4
Chicago, Rock Island & Pacific Railway Co.	2.4	Phelps Dodge Corporation	20.3
		Socony-Vacuum Oil Co.	75.0
		Safeway Stores, Inc.	15.0
Illinois Central Railroad Co.	13.9	Cincinnati Gas and Electric Co.	10.0
Kansas City Southern Railway	1.3	Buffalo Niagara Electric Corp.	12.2
Long Island Railroad Co.	2.0	Commercial Credit Co.	35.0
Consumers Power Co.	12.0		
Dow Chemical Co.	5.0		
Rochester Gas and Electric Corp.	15.0		
Armour & Co.	12.0		
Associates Investment Co.	12.0		

STOCKS

Public Service Co. of New Hampshire	1.2	DuPont (E.I.) de Nemours & Co. (preferred)	50.0
Yellow Truck and Coach Manufacturing Co.	9.0	Standard Brands, Inc.	19.0
Crown Cork & Seal Co., Inc.	6.2		
Remington Arms Co., Inc.	6.4		
Transcontinental Western Air, Inc.	2.5		
Florence Stove Co.	2.4		
Minneapolis-Honeywell Regulator Co.	2.5		
Lockheed Aircraft Corp.	1.7		
LeTourneau (R.G.), Inc.	1.0		
Black & Decker Manufacturing Co.	1.3		
Transwestern Oil Co.	10.3		
Montgomery Ward & Co., Inc.	26.1		
Sears, Roebuck Co.	35.2		
Total 23 companies	185.7	Total 9 companies	246.9
Total issues in December 1936	218.2	Total Issues in June 1937	268.9
23 companies floated 87% of total		9 companies floated 92% of total	

Source: Basic data from *Commercial and Financial Chronicle, 144,* Pt. 1
(1937), 173–175; *145,* Pt. 1 (1937), 189–190.

TABLE 10: INVESTMENT RISK OF JUNE 1937 ISSUES

	Low Rating on Long-Term Bonds	Rating on Equipment Issues
Railroads		
Union Pacific Railroad Co.	Aa [1]	Aaa
Public Utilities		
Cincinnati Gas & Electric Co.	Aaa	
Buffalo Niagara Electric Corp.	A	
Industrials		
Socony-Vacuum Oil Co., Inc.	Aaa	
Phelps Dodge Corp.	Baa	

Other High Quality Issues	*Basis for Judgment*
DuPont (E.I.) de Nemours & Co.	Substantial earnings and dividends during depression.
Safeway Stores, Inc.	Substantial earnings all through depression. Dividends also paid.
Standard Brands, Inc.	Substantial earnings and dividends during depression.
Commercial Credit Co.	Bankrupt in 1934 but reorganized. In view of contract with Chrysler Corporation to finance its cars, and short-term nature of issue, it is considered to have investment merit.

1. Only one bond issue Aa, others Aaa.

Source: Basic data from *Moody's Industrials, Public Utilities, and Railroads,* 1937.

Cincinnati Gas and Electric Corporation and Socony-Vacuum had no bond outstanding rating less than Aaa, Union Pacific none less than Aa, and Buffalo Niagara Electric Company none less than A. Dupont, Safeway, and Standard Brands Incorporated had no bonds outstanding, but their earnings records and dividend payments place them in a high investment status. Of the remaining two, the Phelps Dodge issues were rated Baa, giving them minimum investment status, and the Commercial Credit Corporation, although reorganized in 1934, possessed investment merit because of its contract for the financing of Chrysler products. This latter issue was also a short-term bond which increased its investment standing.

In contrast to the investment quality of the June 1937 issues, it can be observed in Table 11 that no company which floated new securities in December 1936 merited an Aaa rating on its lowest-grade

TABLE 11: INVESTMENT RISK OF DECEMBER 1936
ISSUES

	Low Rating on Long-Term Bonds	Rating on Equipment Issues
Railroads		
Chicago, Milwaukee, St. Paul & Pacific Railroad Co.	Ca	Baa
Chicago, Rock Island & Pacific Railway Co.	Ca	Ba
Illinois Central Railroad Co.	Ba	Aa
Kansas City Southern Railway Co.	Baa	Aa
Long Island Railroad Co.	Baa	Aa
Public Utilities		
Consumers Power Co.	Aa	
Rochester Gas & Electric Corp.	Aa	
Public Service Co. of New Hampshire	Aa	
Industrials		
Armour & Co.	Baa	
Crown Cork & Seal Co., Inc.	Baa	

Other High Quality Issues	*Basis for Judgment*
Associates Investment Co.	Finance medium-priced cars; paid dividends all through depression.
Dow Chemical Co.	Good earnings, paid dividends throughout the depression.
Minneapolis-Honeywell Regulator Co.	Relatively new company with good earnings. Dividends all through depression.

Other Risk Capital Financing	
Black & Decker Manufacturing Co.	Deficits, 1931–35, lapse of dividends.
Florence Stove Co.	Dividend lapse for over two years in depression.
LeTourneau (R.G.), Inc.	Not listed.
Montgomery Ward & Co., Inc.	Deficits in depression, in arrears on preferred stock.
Lockheed Aircraft Corp.	Speculative.
Remington Arms Company, Inc.	Very much in arrears on preferred stock.
Sears, Roebuck and Co.	Deficits 1932–33, dividend lapse.
Transwestern Oil Co.	Not listed.
Transcontinental Western Air, Inc.	Speculative.
Yellow Truck and Coach Manufacturing Co.	No dividends 1927–36.

Source: Basic data from *Moody's Industrials, Public Utilities, and Railroads,* 1936.

bond outstanding. Only three public utility issues and three railroad equipment issues were rated Aa. Among the railroad companies only the Kansas City Southern and Long Island Railroad had minimum investment rating for their marginal bonds outstanding. In the industrials, Armour and Crown Cork and Seal were rated Baa, but with the exception of Dow Chemical and Minneapolis-Honeywell, and possibly Montgomery Ward and Sears, Roebuck,[25] the remaining industrials were definitely speculative.

On the basis of these rough estimates of investment quality, no more than 39% or $86 million of the new financing in December 1936 was for companies which normally raise funds with well-rated bond issues. Even this estimate includes over $20 million of railroad equipment issues,[26] which had an investment status because of their short-term maturity. The ratings on the long-term bonds of most of these issuing railroads were below the higher investment grades. The remaining $132 million, or slightly over 60% of the total, appears to have been risk or speculative capital. The poorer tone of the capital market in June 1937 is suggested by the fact that only 8% or $22.3 million of the new capital issues were for unseasoned companies or companies with less than investment standing.[27]

Not only were 92% of the new issues in June 1937 floated by nine companies which were such "blue-chip" risks that they could borrow on comparatively favorable terms even in a worsening market, but, in addition, unusual circumstances surrounded one of these issues. The Socony-Vacuum bonds, comprising over one-quarter of the June 1937 total, were purchased privately by five large life insurance companies and thus contribute to the explanation for the peak in financing at this time. The question might well be raised of why these companies issued new securities in a depressed market. The answer seems to be that their own internal sources of funds were somewhat depleted.[28]

The final evidence on the change in the conditions under which new funds were available is the substantial increase in the cost of capital even to the seasoned borrowers. In December 1936 the Public Service Company of New Hampshire obtained $1.4 million of new capital with 20-year, 3.25% bonds priced 101.5 to yield 3.17%. By

25. However, both incurred large deficits in the middle thirties, with Montgomery Ward in arrears on its preferred stock.

26. The $12 million of bonds for Associates Investment are also included but the Montgomery Ward and Sears, Roebuck common stock issues are excluded.

27. The percentage is 21 if the Commercial Credit Corporation bonds are excluded from the investment quality group.

28. Cf. Ruth Mack, *The Flow of Business Funds and Consumer Purchasing Power* (New York, 1941), 321–324; Friedrick A. Lutz, *Corporate Cash Balances* (New York, 1945), 49; and Sachs, *op. cit.*, 13–31.

June 1937 the Cincinnati Gas and Electric Company, which has as high a credit rating as any other operating municipal utility in the country, had to give a 3.5% coupon on $10 million of 20-year bonds which were priced to yield 3.37%. This represents a .2% increase in yield and 7% increase in the cost of capital to a top quality risk. The Connecticut Light and Power Company in December 1936 borrowed $16 million in 3.25% bonds which were sold to yield 3.05%.[29] Judged by this experience, the Cincinnati Gas and Electric probably could have borrowed for around 3% at that time, so the real increase in costs of capital was nearer 10 than 7%. These data, it should be noted, measure only the increase in cost of capital to the highest grade risk. Moody's yields on Baa bonds, which are still better risks than common stocks of untried and lesser known companies, and even of most seasoned companies, rose by almost .5%, from a low of 4.49% in January 1937 to 4.93% in June 1937, or a 10% increase in the cost of capital.

It may be objected, as has been done by Schumpeter and others, that increases in costs of this magnitude can have little effect on business decisions. Apparently they had little effect on the prime quality borrowers in June 1937, measured by the amounts of their borrowing. Even with the average business, Schumpeter's position may be partially correct, but important classes of borrowers are marginal businesses or at least speculative enterprises. The increases in capital costs for this type of company can only be surmised. If, however, the current yield expectation on outstanding common stocks can be taken as a rough estimate of the cost of new capital,[30] then the rate rose by over 1%, or from 3.06% in March 1937 to 4.07% in June.[31] This suggests that the average company faced at least a 33⅓% increase in the cost of new funds. The cost nearer the margin and for individual companies in different industries must have been a good deal higher. Not only was the cost of capital increased but the deteriorating market performance gave a blow to business expectations about future profits and production.

To summarize, it has been shown that new capital was more difficult to obtain following the breaks in bond and stock prices, even though the peak in new issues occurred after these declines. Interest costs on new capital rose considerably and two factors account for the peak level of issues in June 1937. The composition of new issues changed from heavy emphasis on stocks and speculative enterprises

29. Yield data from Securities and Exchange Commission, *Security Issues of Electric and Gas Utilities, 1935–1940* (1941), 7.

30. For any new issue it is the dividend which the company believes it must expect to pay on the new capital if investment funds are to be attracted.

31. Alfred Cowles, *Common-Stock Indexes,* Cowles Commission for Research in Economics, Monograph No. 3 (Bloomington, 1939), 271.

in December 1936 to bond issues and stocks of companies having investment status in June 1937. In addition, a few companies with top credit ratings floated the new issues in that month. Although June 1937 was the month with peak new issues, the make-up of the issues and the behavior of the market suggest that new corporate capital was available on less favorable terms. The market action itself seriously depressed business expectations.

THE CONTRIBUTION OF FEDERAL RESERVE POLICY TO THE RECESSION

The relationship between Federal Reserve policy and the recession now appears clear. The increasing of reserve requirements in the spring of 1937 led to member bank adjustment of investment portfolios. A heavy selling wave, originally concentrated in short-term government bills and notes, was followed later by pressure on corporate and long-term government bond prices, and ultimately on common stock prices. An examination of the composition of new capital issues in December 1936 and in June 1937 revealed the deterioration in the terms of issues between the two dates, and the increased difficulty of obtaining "risk" capital. Under the particular circumstances of that period—declining government deficits, increasing wage rates, the unfavorable atmosphere surrounding investment decisions—Federal Reserve action appears to have had more widespread repercussions on business expectations and decisions than heretofore believed. Because of its effects on bond yields and the financial markets, and through them on business expectations, it did more than adjust the physical volume of member bank reserves. Even though monetary conditions were extremely easy, compared with any previous period, Federal Reserve policy cannot be cleared of important responsibility in the recession.

RELATIONSHIP OF FEDERAL RESERVE AND TREASURY POLICY TO THE REVIVAL

In Chapter 2 monetary policy was described by some as contributing to the revival. Both of the principal actions taken, desterilization of gold and reduction in reserve requirements, were regarded as favorable to revival. Besides the analysts cited in Chapter 2, the *Economist* mentioned the increase in excess reserves as a favorable factor supporting business optimism for recovery in the autumn of 1938.[32]

The conditions of monetary ease, to which Reserve and Treasury actions contributed, undoubtedly facilitated the recovery. However,

32. *Economist, 131* (1938), 474.

their relative importance remains uncertain. The best guess seems
to be that such actions would have done little to promote recovery
if unaccompanied by other favorable factors. The President's message
of April 14, 1938, recognized this explicitly: "By themselves, however, monetary measures are insufficient to start us on a sustained
upward movement." [33]

The response to the monetary measures which were taken prior
to the President's message on his general recovery program gives a
rough idea of their effectiveness in halting the decline then under way.
The continuation of the decline seems to indicate that the reversal [34]
in the Board's policy during the fall months of 1937 had little effect
in tempering the recession.

Federal Reserve and Treasury action appear to have affected the
recovery only as a part of the government's general program to combat the recession. These monetary measures played a role in facilitating the revival, but it is necessary to go beyond them for the important
causes. The factors behind the decisions to increase borrowing at
banks and in the investment markets, and to increase business and
consumer spending, assume the greatest importance.

LESSONS FROM EXPERIENCE IN MONETARY MANAGEMENT, 1936–38

In retrospect, the most fundamental error in monetary policy appears to have been the undue concern over inflation in the face of
large-scale unemployment of resources. It may be argued convincingly that the business and financial community in 1936–37 still
analyzed the phenomenon of rising prices in terms of the quantity
theory of money. Nor had the problem of the determinants of national income and employment become dominant in government
policy considerations. When the MV factor, in the basic equation
$MV = PT$, was observed without reference to changes in trade or
production, the huge increase in deposits carried a serious threat of
inflation.

33. *Federal Reserve Bulletin, 24* (1938), 343.
34. The *Economist* was even fearful that this reversal might lead to undesired
consequences through an excessive expansion of credit. It gave a whimsical touch
to this possibility, which, of course, did not materialize: "Up to now the Reserve
System has been concerned to increase reserve requirements, diminish surplus
reserves and throttle the inflow of foreign money, in order to prevent an inflationary
growth of credit. . . . It may be that the Federal Reserve Board has decided to
encourage further reasonable expansion by reducing reserve rates, just as Alice attempted to control her own size by nibbling first a piece of the expanding and then
of the contracting mushroom. It is to be hoped that the Reserve Board will avoid
some of the consequences which Alice found so unpleasant." *Economist, 128* (1937),
478.

It is not true, however, that all government policy makers were blind to the existence of unemployed men and resources. Marriner Eccles was among the few who recognized that no real inflation was imminent when resources were unemployed. His testimony on this point before the Senate committee investigating unemployment and relief is very revealing:

Last spring a great deal of pressure was being brought for the Reserve System to exercise a restraining influence upon advancing prices. There were many people who felt that the inflationary development that seemed to be under way last spring should be stopped by restrictive monetary policy. I disagreed with them and, briefly quoting what was said at the time, because it is better to give what was said at the time than to look back and think what you might have said, I said on March 15th . . . of 1937: "I have been and still am an advocate of an easy-money policy and expect to continue to be an advocate of such a policy so long as there are large numbers of people who are unable to find employment in private industry, which means that the full productive capacity of the Nation is not being utilized. Under such conditions, to restrict the available supply of capital and thus to make it difficult, if not impossible, to employ these people would not only be antisocial but uneconomic." [35]

Thus Eccles was apparently aware of the incompatibility of inflation with large-scale unemployment of resources. But he may still be criticized on two counts. First, he did not stress sufficiently the problem of unemployment of resources nor the temporary nature of the rises in prices which were occurring because of bottlenecks. And second, although the Board asserted again and again that its actions on reserves were neither restrictive nor meant to be so, they were widely regarded as such. Since Eccles realized that sustained inflation was not likely (in spite of the rising commodity prices) because of the unemployed resources, there appears to have been no pressing reason for taking any restrictive actions on reserves. The principal error still seems to have been the failure to adapt monetary policy properly to the problem of full utilization of resources.

In addition to this fundamental problem of the relationship of monetary policy to the employment of resources, Federal Reserve and Treasury actions from 1936 to 1938 give insight into other problems of monetary management.

(1) A minor point, but one which was regarded as important by countries losing gold, is the effects of the sterilization policy on the exchange value of the dollar. J. B. Condliffe suggested that the sterilization policy depressed the dollar's exchange value and checked the rising tendency of prices in the United States, "thereby arresting one

35. U. S. Congress, Senate, Special Committee, etc., *Hearings, 1,* 62–63.

means of righting the exchange disequilibrium between that country and the rest of the world." [36] Of course this statement is only partially true, because prices continued to rise after the gold sterilization account was set up, and much of the gold losses from the continent was of political rather than of economic origin. Nevertheless, it must be recognized that domestic monetary actions have external implications.

(2) Another lesson is that a rate structure on bonds which member banks consider "too" low may exert a deflationary influence, analogous to that of "too" high rates.[37] In the latter case the decline begins because costs of capital to borrowers prove too great. In the former case the deflationary pressure is exerted because the rates or yields to lenders are believed to be too low. This pressure may occur if interest rates in general are considered to be "too low" and are expected to rise.

If banks sell government bonds in order to make other investments, then any decline in the price of Treasury securities may be interpreted by nonbanking investors as indicating that the prices of all investment securities are going to decline. An avalanche of selling may occur as a consequence. Member banks themselves undoubtedly acted upon the premise that the rate of interest was abnormally low on government securities—the result of government manipulation in connection with the deficit financing program.

(3) In addition to the misgivings which banks had about long-term interest rates, it should be observed that adjustments in interest rates had to take effect in the bond market in the absence of a functioning money market. The *Economist* pointed out the significance of this lack: "credit management in the United States is handicapped by the absence of a money market, in that it throws upon the bond market and the long-term interest rate functions of adjustment for which they are by no means suited." [38]

(4) A fourth problem was the timing of the various actions taken by the Federal Reserve. As early as September 1935 there was considerable agitation for the tightening of reserve requirements, yet the first increase in reserve requirements was not taken until almost a year later. Had restrictive measures been adopted earlier it is possible that the advance in prices in the middle of 1936 might not have gotten under way.

Just as government leaders were slow in announcing a new recovery program, so the Board delayed in reducing reserve require-

---

36. J. B. Condliffe, *World Economic Survey, 1936/37* (Geneva, 1937), 55.
37. Cf. *Economist, 132* (1938), 275.
38. *Ibid., 128* (1937), 470.

ments and desterilizing gold until April 1938. Yet as early as October 1937 the Swedish economist Ohlin proposed reducing reserve requirements and desterilizing gold to aid in American recovery:

Whatever the reasons or justification for the fear of inflation which called for certain financial measures of a restrictive kind early in 1937 and late in 1936, e.g. the increase in the reserve requirements and the decision to sterilize gold, it seems perfectly clear by now that there is no reason for any such fear of inflation. Hence, it is difficult to see why the reserve requirements should not be lowered again and perhaps some more gold desterilized.[39]

(5) Questions have also been raised about the Board's conception of its responsibility in the exercise of monetary controls. As was noted earlier in this chapter, Slichter believed that Federal Reserve policy, 1936–38, illustrated the limitations of monetary and fiscal controls for the business cycle. Woolfson made the same criticism. He was of the opinion that the administration had committed a serious error of judgment in believing that monetary authorities could produce stability in the country's credit and commodity price structure through credit control measures.[40]

Actual developments lend support to the statements. But both analysts seem to err in believing that the Reserve authorities felt monetary controls, by themselves, could produce economic stability. An excellent summary of the Board's conception of the place that monetary measures occupy in promoting economic stability was contained in a statement on the objectives of monetary policy sent to the chairman of the Senate Committee on Agriculture and Forestry, August 2, 1937. The Board believed that monetary authorities could make a contribution to economic stability through maintaining an easy flow of funds for productive enterprise, but expressed strong opposition to using monetary policy alone. It then summarized its position: "the Board believes that economic stability rather than price stability should be the general objective of public policy. It is convinced that this objective cannot be achieved by monetary policy alone, but that the goal should be sought through coordination of monetary and other major policies of the Government which influence business activity, including particularly policies with respect to taxation, expenditures, lending, foreign trade, agriculture and labor." [41]

This statement shows clearly that the Board was under no illusions as to the effectiveness of monetary controls in promoting price or

39. Ohlin, *op. cit.*, 18.
40. Woolfson, 101–105.
41. *Federal Reserve Bulletin, 23* (1937), 828.

economic stability. It therefore adds support to the basic criticism which Slichter and Woolfson made of reliance on monetary and fiscal policy for control of business fluctuations. Nevertheless this experience with Federal Reserve controls serves neither to discredit their use nor to suggest that monetary controls be abandoned. But it does emphasize the necessity for recognizing also the psychological and real factors which affect the conditions of economic stability.

(6) In Chapter 6 it was shown that the Board was under constant pressure from businessmen, bankers, and government policy-makers. The demand from these various sources for the reduction of excess reserves was perhaps even more insistent than the demand for reduction of the government deficit and the balancing of the budget. Businessmen and bankers were so afraid of inflation that even had the Board been opposed to action on reserves it probably would eventually have had to yield to this pressure for reserve changes as a means of combatting "inflation."

Businessmen, bankers, and government leaders feared inflation because of the potential expansion which might take place upon the basis of the existing reserves of the banking system. In retrospect, this belief appears to have been based in large part upon misleading conceptions of what was a normal relationship between reserves and deposits. Most of the agitation for reserve action appears to have been prompted by belief that a velocity of deposit turnover such as had been "normal" in the past would soon be attained again. Thus Eccles asserted: "Normally banks have a negligible amount of excess reserves. When we return to this normal situation, credit control measures will be felt more quickly and are likely to be more effective." [42]

The velocity ratio in the twenties was so nearly constant that it appeared to establish a normal turnover for deposits. But this velocity was not regained in the thirties. Likewise, to maximize earnings, excess reserves were kept to a minimum in the twenties but in the changed environment of the thirties they became a normal characteristic of the banking system. These developments suggest how difficult it is to determine which economic relationships will persist relatively unchanged through several business fluctuations, and which will break rather sharply with the past. In evaluating the failure of Federal Reserve policy it must be kept in mind that the Board acted upon the basis of the experience in the twenties, which, however, proved to be an inadequate guide for the thirties. This experience prevented it from realizing that the huge volume of excess reserves in the thirties had created a situation in which they were a require-

42. Eccles, "Controlling Booms and Depressions," 88d.

ment of conservative banking policy. Some of the factors which encouraged the maintenance of excess reserves have been suggested by Samuelson:

Despite the common tendency to regard excess reserves as being an unnecessary surplus, the bank *feels* that it needs them. The legal ratio is only a lower limit, but not necessarily operative. Thus in Great Britain, where no legal ratios exist, the customary ratio felt to be needed is the only relevant one.[43]

In a footnote he added:

This does not imply that the banks feel the reserves to be necessary to cover possible withdrawals. It is more and more being realized that reserves do *not* perform the function of till money. Rather they are felt to be necessary for the maximization of income over time in a world where uncertainty dictates a diversification of portfolios. This the Reserve authorities overlooked when they raised reserve requirements in 1936–1937. They were unprepared for the resulting pressure on the market for governments, since they regarded excess reserves as surpluses. Actually, the banks tried to reëstablish old excess reserve ratios. The fact that they did not succeed in doing so—on balance the public acquired few governments from the banking system—is still compatible with the hypothesis that they attempt to do so.[44]

(7) Another important lesson to be learned from this experience in monetary management is the need to recognize the possible differential effect of an over-all increase in reserve ratios. Increases in reserve requirements have been criticized as a method for controlling reserve positions: "Merely an antidote after the poison has been absorbed, such a method operates in averages upon a banking system which is highly individualistic and may set in motion disturbances and frictions with repercussions of great significance." [45] Actually the Board was aware that its action might bring unwanted repercussions because of the differences in reserve positions of individual member banks. In fact, it was this realization which led to the controversy between the Federal Advisory Council, the Federal Open Market Committee, and the Board of Governors of the Federal Reserve System over the desirability of using blanket reserve changes or aggressive open-market sales to effect the reductions in excess reserves.

Not only was there controversy over the method of control, but

43. Paul A. Samuelson, "Fiscal Policy and Income Determination," *Quarterly Journal of Economics, 56* (1941–42), 594. Cf. also G. Griffith Johnson, *op. cit.,* 135–136.
44. Samuelson, 594.
45. G. Griffith Johnson, 136.

the Board, before taking action, was extremely careful to survey the distribution of excess reserves among the member banks, not once but several times. Therefore it cannot be charged with failing to recognize problems of readjustment which might arise from over-all reserve increases. But in spite of the Board's knowledge of the distribution of excess reserves it did not assess correctly the repercussions which occurred.

(8) The unforeseen and disastrous consequences which accompanied the blanket increase in reserve requirements emphasized the necessity for providing more selective credit controls. The delicate problem of how to maintain low interest rates and easy money conditions and at the same time prevent unwise credit expansion is still unsolved. The dilemma arises because any change severe enough to be effective in controlling credit expansion is likely to reduce the degree of monetary ease.[46] If it can be shown that the market for loanable funds is imperfect, then selective credit controls may be in order also on the supply side.

(9) The experience in 1937–38 seems to lend support to the position taken by Sproul and others [47] that a sudden relaxation of Federal Reserve control of the long-term interest rate, or the institution of drastic credit restriction, might have greater impact on business financing and expectations than is desired. The experience with such action in the recession of 1937–38 has now been examined and leads to the conclusion that Federal Reserve policy contributed to that recession. The tools of control employed in this period were very rough and imperfect, and their use appears to have been unnecessary and unwise in view of the underemployment of resources. Nevertheless, it should not be inferred from this experience that similar action by the Federal Reserve System is inadvisable at all times. There is considerable reason to believe that the economic forces of expansion in 1945–48 were in many respects unlike those from 1936 to 1937. Thus if Federal Reserve controls had been employed more vigorously from 1945 to 1948, the response might have been quite unlike that in 1936–37.[48]

46. This dilemma has been pointed out by Professor Metzler, who also proposed a solution, selective controls on the terms of lending. "Inventory Cycles in the United States," an unpublished paper, 25–26. Portions of this paper were reprinted in *Income, Employment and Public Policy.*

47. Cf. *New York Times*, January 27, 1948, p. 35. Speech of Allan Sproul before midwinter meeting of the New York State Bankers Association, Monday, January 26, 1948. The forces favoring inflation were so strong in the spring of 1951 that the experience attending the unfreezing of interest rates probably was not a fair test of possible repercussions under more normal circumstances, nor were the measures taken exceptionally drastic.

48. Hansen has objected, however, to immoderate use of monetary measures to

CONCLUSION

This completes an assessment of the contribution of Federal Reserve policy in the recession of 1937–38 to the theory of monetary management. There is no evidence that the Board was not conscientious and careful in the decisions made. For the most part, the actions taken were those which the business and financial community was urging. In spite of this general agreement that these actions were both necessary and desirable, they had undesired and unfortunate consequences. It is difficult to avoid mistakes of this nature. The best hope seems to be through utilizing the experience of the past and keeping a general awareness that variables in the economic world are closely interrelated. An encouraging development has been the added attention paid to the relationship between monetary and real factors. Such errors in monetary policy are less likely to be committed in the broader framework which deals with the determination of national employment and the flow of national income.

---

control inflation, for reasons quite similar to those reviewed in this section. Such a control he suggests "would probably be found to operate indirectly via a general shattering of confidence (through the effect on the securities market) rather than in terms of the direct effect of higher interest rates on investment and consumption decisions. Those who glibly talk about controlling the inflation by monetary policy have failed to consider that moderate measures by themselves are relatively ineffective, while drastic measures may easily turn the economy into a tail spin." *Monetary Theory and Fiscal Policy* (New York, 1949), 161.

CHAPTER 8

Price-Cost Relationships, the Recession, and Investment Expenditures

IN CHAPTER 2 it was explained that two different interpretations were given to the changes in price-cost relationships. From the viewpoint of those who emphasized investment factors, the increase in costs impinged unfavorably upon profits and businessmen's expectations, and initiated the decreased rate of investment which precipitated the recession. But from the underconsumption viewpoint, prices rose faster than costs, particularly that part of costs represented by labor income, so that consumers were priced out of the market and the recession began. The rising level of inventories played a role in either approach. The interpretation under the investment emphasis was that inventories accumulated when autonomous investment expenditures were insufficient to sustain or increase the level of income. According to the consumption theorists, consumption expenditures tailed off and inventories accumulated excessively because profits rather than wage earners' incomes went up. This description of the division of opinion over the causal role of price-cost relationships is undoubtedly too simplified, but does point up a real cleavage of opinion. Price-cost relationships will be discussed in this chapter, primarily from the standpoint of their investment significance. Chapter 10 will evaluate their position in the underconsumption explanation of the recession, and Chapter 12 will consider the role of inventories.

A GENERAL APPROACH TO PRICE-COST RELATIONSHIPS

Maladjustments in price-cost relationships are present in any business fluctuation, and have been accorded causal responsibility in most recessions and depressions. The recession of 1937–38 is no exception. In many cases, however, little attention has been given to establishing the relationship between prices and cost in specific areas. Of course in all depressions this relationship is unprofitable in many sectors of the economy. But to say only that the recession was "caused" by price-cost relationships is no more meaningful than to say that price is determined by demand and supply. This is not to imply that analyses which relate prices and costs to business fluctuations are valueless. But it is essential to determine in which areas changes in prices and costs assume importance.

As early as November 1936 the sharp general increase in both prices and cost suggested the possibility that some price-cost maladjustments might well develop in specific areas. The National City Bank of New York, which emphasized the price-cost approach to business fluctuations, forecast that the recovery might end because of the type of forward buying, the inventory and price increases then under way: "Experienced observers recognize that when this type of buying appears business is more likely than not to be nearing the top of an upward movement, and ready for a tapering off while the accumulated purchases are absorbed. This view of the matter inspires caution, as possibly suggesting a resting period in the recovery some time in 1937." [1]

The basic problem of this chapter is to determine whether the price-cost margin narrowed and affected current or expected profits unfavorably so that business investment expenditures were reduced. First, the changes which occurred in the prices of commodities and raw materials and in wages and labor costs will be described. Then their impact upon the profitability of investment expenditures will be investigated.

THE INCREASE IN PRICES OF COMMODITIES AND RAW MATERIALS IN 1937

The Bank for International Settlements gave a concise picture of the price movements in 1937. These movements coincided roughly with the quarterly periods. Prices rose sharply during the first quarter, stimulated by exaggerated expectations of increased demand from consumer and government armament orders. At the same time, industrial companies were protecting themselves against further advances in the prices of raw materials and thus bought more than was justified by normal needs. As a result inventories accumulated in certain sectors of the economy, while stocks of raw materials were depleted in other areas. In the second quarter there was an equally sharp fall in prices as speculative transactions were liquidated. In the third quarter prices were relatively stable, but were followed by a sharp decline in the fourth quarter when demand contracted even as more abundant supplies arrived on the market. [2]

The four phases of the price movements during the year can be

1. National City Bank of New York, *op. cit.* (1936), 154.
2. Bank for International Settlements, *Eighth Annual Report* (Basle, 1938), 6–7.

seen clearly in the Bureau of Labor Statistics index of raw material prices. These prices rose from 85.6 in December 1936 to 90.1 in March 1937. They then declined to 86.1 in June, or almost to the December 1936 level; declined to 84.4 in September; and fell another 9 points to 75.4 in the last quarter of the year.

The price ranges of the nonferrous metals also gave a rather spectacular picture of the fluctuations in the period. In the five months from November 1936 to March 1937, copper increased from 9.75 to 17 cents per pound, lead from 4.65 to 7.75 cents, and zinc from 5.22 to 7.85 cents. By November 1937, only a year from the date of the first figures quoted, copper had fallen to between 10.75 and 11 cents per pound, lead to 5 cents, and zinc to 5.25 cents.

There is considerable difference of opinion over whether these advances in prices were a "normal" or "abnormal" development. Sachs believed that the increase was a perfectly normal phenomenon. Prices of commodities, having been more drastically depressed, generally show faster and greater increases than does production as business rebounds from depression lows. The corrective adjustment follows: "such advances are followed by correctives with accompanying recessive or readjustive business; and so, commodity prices within a year from such a spurt are generally lower due to the new supplies which the functioning productive economy and capital markets release." [3] The stimulus to the economy from the rise in commodity prices prepares the way for a healthy prosperity: "In the final phase of better than normal business, the economy, as a result of new financing and induced additional capacity, gains in production more than in prices, and that constitutes the healthy phase of prosperity." [4]

The National City Bank of New York also regarded the price increases as a normal development. It was desirable for prices of farm products and raw materials to increase because this tended to restore the price relationships between the various parts of the economic system which existed before the 1929–32 depression. At the same time, some apprehension was felt lest a rise in prices of manufactured goods might prevent further increases in business activity. In the bank's opinion, when forward buying began to decline the recovery movement would slow down: "Such fluctuations, however, are normal in the business situation. They are not to be regarded as disturbing, as a disruption of the general equilibrium, though strikes or an excessive rise in industrial costs and prices, would be." [5]

The National City Bank also expressed the opinion that delays

3. Sachs, *op. cit.*, 24.
4. *Ibid.*, 24–25.
5. National City Bank of New York, *op. cit.* (1937), 4.

in deliveries and difficulty in obtaining materials might affect the economy favorably by stimulating new industrial capacity which would temper the boom in some lines.[6]

The break in commodity prices in April 1937 was regarded as a normal readjustment following the speculative excesses of the fall and winter of 1936–37: "In the commodity markets the congestion which forced prices up was intensified by speculation and by temporary difficulties in increasing output, and it has been relieved in the natural way, through resale of speculators' holdings and a rising trend in production." [7] With respect to the drop in metal prices, the bank concluded that only speculators had been hurt, because very little metal for trade purposes had been purchased at these high prices. Profits appeared to be obtainable even by high cost producers in most lines, and lower prices were a favorable development for consuming industries.

Schumpeter was among those who disagreed with these interpretations of the price rises as a "normal" development. He insisted that the violent rise which occurred in the fourth quarter of 1936 was abnormal, heralding "inflation" rather than prosperity.[8]

Angell believed that the rise was a normal development, signaling the beginning of an " 'automatic' self-generated end of the expansion phase. . . ." [9] It was developments such as these which led businessmen to revise their current anticipations downward, and made the end of the expansion inevitable.

The important considerations here would appear to be not so much whether the price rises were normal or abnormal as the effects which they may have had upon investment expenditures. Before this problem can be investigated, the principal changes in wage and labor costs must be traced.

Rise in Wage and Labor Costs

The outstanding development in wage and labor costs was their considerable increase over the 1929 levels. Hourly wage rates rose almost 21% by 1937, while real weekly wages increased by 9%. This increase, in the face of the large volume of unemployment, requires explanation.

Part of the explanation lies in the legislation of the 1930's. The NRA and the NLRB strengthened the bargaining position of labor and promoted united effort to achieve increased take-home pay. Even

6. *Ibid.* (1936), 156.
7. *Ibid.* (1937), 61.
8. Schumpeter, *op. cit.*, 1018.
9. Angell, *op. cit.*, 231.

more fundamental than legislative changes, however, is the firm belief which many Americans hold that America must remain the land of highest wages because these wages have been responsible for the heights to which American production, income, and employment have climbed. The complex of ideas involved is perhaps best described as "Henry Fordism," which is a belief in the cure-all value of high money wages.

This belief has been widely held, and not only in the ranks of labor. Large-scale business, encouraged by the President, attempted to hold wages steady in 1930 in the face of the declining demand for goods and services as well as for labor. And nonlabor groups have given support to higher wages during more prosperous times. Ohlin seems to have sensed the importance of this psychological attachment to the high wage standard: "The American labor movement sincerely believes that higher wages create better markets and therefore are a road leading to greater general prosperity and higher production. The American public seems very largely to share this view. . . . For they believe higher wage rates to be in the best interest of the whole nation." [10]

The increases in wage rates under the National Industrial Recovery Act were undoubtedly facilitated by a strong conviction of the desirability of higher wage rates.[11] The great advance in wage and labor costs cannot be understood without recognition of this fact.

The next question is whether wages rose more rapidly than prices and profits. At present it seems impossible to obtain a clear answer. The data are not available from which to draw any very reliable conclusion. It is possible that a comparison of the changes in average hourly wage rates and in general wholesale prices or prices of finished goods might give a rough measure of the increase in wages relative to prices and profits. This comparison suffers, of course, from the obvious weaknesses that the hourly wage rate is not necessarily a measure of labor productivity, nor are price indexes a very reliable guide to profit performance, in view of the changes which occur both in productivity and industrial capacity. Nevertheless over a short period of time an increase in average hourly wage rates, relative to prices, might be presumed to indicate a reduction in either the current or the prospective price-cost margin. Hence it is conceivable that such measurements might establish a decline in profitability of investment.

10. Ohlin, *op. cit.*, 16.

11. But as Hansen has said: "The Administration, and with it public opinion, has never faced the utter fallacy of trying to boost income, output and employment by raising costs. . . . We have apparently yet to learn that high *wage rates* do not of themselves guarantee a high labor income and full employment." *Full Recovery or Stagnation?* 287.

A comparison of average hourly wage rates in manufacturing and the general wholesale price index, for the period December 1936 through March 1937, shows that average hourly wage rates increased by 3.8% (from 63.8 to 66.2 cents per hour) and wholesale prices by 4.3% (from 84.2 to 87.8 cents per hour). Prices of finished goods increased by only 3.1% in the same period. But in the six months from December 1936 through June 1937 hourly wage rates advanced 11% (from 63.8 to 70.8 cents per hour), whereas wholesale prices advanced only 3.6% (from 84.2 to 87.2). In the very important period, March through June 1937, wholesale prices actually declined by 0.7% as wage rates rose by 5.7%. Insofar as these wage increases were not offset by increased productivity, or declining costs as the result of increased volume, it might be reasoned that the prospects for profits were worsening during this period.

These data contain a suggestion, therefore, that wage rates did rise more rapidly than other prices and profits. In Chapter 13 it will be shown that the profitability of investment was very likely reduced in the second quarter of 1937, whatever the cause. In the present chapter consideration must now be given to the possibility that price-cost changes affected the profitability of investment in selected areas.

Price-Cost Changes and the Profitability of Investment

To test the direct effects of changing price-cost relationships on the profitability of investment, it would be most desirable to have data on per unit cost, per unit prices, total sales, etc., by months. But these statistics are not available. Therefore, the best that can be done is to draw inferences from changes in prices and costs for certain industries such as railroads, building, electric power and light, and steel.

RISE IN WAGES AND COST OF MATERIALS IN RAILROADS

One study showed that average prices paid by one of the larger railroads for 68 classes of materials increased by 17% from September 1936 to September 1937. No claim is made that these figures represent the prices paid by all the railroads for the materials and supplies, and the volume and other data are lacking with which to compute the weighted effects of price changes on railway equipment. Nevertheless, the comparison does relate to important materials actually used by railroads. The study concluded that "this year's purchases of materials and fuels, and also equipment . . . will cost

the railroads at least $150,000,000 more than the same purchases
would have cost in 1936." [12]

Since the increase in income from September 1936 to June 1937
was only about 7%, it seems likely that the 17.2% increase in cost
of railroad materials, accompanied by increased labor costs, goes a
long way toward explaining the failure of railroad investment in
1937.

It is interesting to note that non-American commentators were
prominent among those who emphasized the unfavorable cost developments in both the housing and railroad industries. Thus the
Economist regarded the rising labor cost in building and railroads as
decidedly unfavorable to investment. [13]

Ohlin pointed out that the increase in wages, taxes, and prices of
materials reduced net earnings to the point where the financial status
of the railroads was impaired, the weaker roads were unable to buy
needed equipment and the stronger roads pursued a "wait and see"
policy: "it seems clear that the decline in railroad profits and purchases is one of the major factors which explains the recession of the
last few months." [14]

Among American economists, Slichter placed the most emphasis
on the unfavorable cost developments in the railroad industry:

A clear and important instance of a reduction of commitments because of
fears that higher costs would destroy profits is furnished by the railroads.
. . . In the second quarter [of 1937], it became evident that profits would
be little larger than the negligible returns of the second quarter of 1936,
and that a wage increase might destroy them altogether. Consequently,
after April the railroads virtually withdrew from the equipment market
and after July drastically reduced expenditures on maintenance. [15]

The impact of these wage and material cost increases on net railway income was felt by the middle of 1937. [16] Thus, by July, as can
be observed in Table 12, net income of class 1 roads had begun to
decline very slightly over the same months of the preceding year, even
though total revenues were still $16 million ahead of July 1936. In
the third quarter of 1937 income was one-third less than in 1936.
Important also to investment decision was the fact that net income,
which had been substantial in the third and fourth quarters of 1936,
was only moderate in the first and second quarters of 1937.

12. "Railway Material Costs Up 17 Per Cent in 12 Months," *Railway Age, 103*
(1937), 792.
13. "The Economic Outlook in America," *Economist, 129* (1937), 248–249.
14. Ohlin, 12.
15. Slichter, "The Downturn of 1937," 105.
16. The inflexibility of rates prevented the use of price rises as a partial compensation for the cost increases.

It would seem that the decline in net income affected investment decisions quickly, for new orders for freight cars fell from the peak rate of 13,046 in April to 3,903 in May and to 528 in June. They never exceeded 1,625 cars in the remaining months of 1937. New orders for each of the months from January 1936 through December 1937 are also shown in Table 12.

TABLE 12: TOTAL OPERATING REVENUES AND NET
RAILWAY INCOME FOR CLASS I RAILWAYS,
AND NEW ORDERS FOR FREIGHT CARS BY ALL
BUYERS, 1936–37

Month	Operating Revenue (millions of dollars)		Net Income (millions of dollars)		New Orders for Freight Cars	
	1936	*1937*	*1936*	*1937*	*1936*	*1937*
January	299.1	331.7	−7.8	−4.5	1,050	10,881
February	300.4	321.9	−11.6	−5.0	7,236	10,532
March	308.3	377.7	−8.2	24.9	627	6,200
April	313.4	351.5	−2.2	3.8	3,650	13,046
May	320.9	352.4	−2.3	1.3	9,667	3,903
June	330.6	351.7	9.0	18.4	4,320	528
July	349.7	365.1	19.4	19.2	4,469	1,030
August	350.5	359.6	21.0	7.2	3,225	1,490
September	357.1	363.1	26.5	16.1	3,100	1,195
October	391.3	372.9	46.6	17.0	1,310	21
November	358.4	318.2	30.2	−5.5	1,710	1,625
December	372.1	300.3	49.2	−5.7	19,922	1,350

Original Source: Interstate Commerce Commission for operating revenues and net income; and *Railway Age* for new orders for freight cars.

Secondary Source: Data from *Survey of Current Business, Supplement, 1940,* for operating revenues and net income; and *1938,* for new orders for freight cars.

Although railway net income did not begin to decline markedly until August 1937, new orders for freight cars fell off after April. This suggests the possibility, at least, that the prospects of declining profits began to affect railroad investment decisions in the late spring of 1937.

RISE IN WAGES AND COST OF MATERIALS IN
BUILDING INDUSTRY

The building field is another area in which there is some evidence that increases in costs served as a deterrent to investment. The cost of common labor in construction rose over 21% from its 1929 peak. This cost change, along with the sizable increases in other labor and material costs, probably resulted in the tabling of a considerable volume of proposed housing. Ohlin emphasized this point in his discussion of the profitability of investment in new housing:

If, for instance, in the course of the first half year of 1937, building costs went up 15 or 20% above the 1929 level, while the general income level in the United States measured in dollars was probably something like 10% below the pre-depression level, then a great deal of building that would have been profitable under the conditions ruling last year is now unprofitable. It is not surprising, therefore, that last spring and summer a great many building plans were put back into the drawers as a result of the increase in costs in the preceding twelve months.[17]

The Midland Bank asserted that the costs of building a house were twice as high in the United States as in England. In its opinion, these high costs were chiefly responsible for the failure of the building industry to revive following the depression.[18]

If the demand for housing was relatively elastic with respect to price, as the evidence seems to indicate, then the price increases which occurred from the middle of 1936 to the middle of 1937 probably seriously dampened this demand. Material costs rose by 10% from September 1936 to March 1937, and skilled and common wage rates in construction rose by 7 and 6% respectively. At the same time (March 1937) one of the first series to decline was the index of private construction contracts, and the housing construction component showed the greatest relative decline. Thus there is some indication of a high degree of sensitivity of housing construction to changes in cost. Slichter attributed the decline in residential construction to the rising costs. Residential construction was sustained for a time because of the relatively inelastic urgent demand. But soon the backlog was used up and the demand then became sensitive to price changes. Speculative building for resale was particularly responsive to the rise in costs.[19] In Slichter's opinion, conditions in the spring of 1937 called for efforts to reduce rather than raise costs: "Evidently the smart thing for the building industry to have done in the spring of 1937, after it had become evident that the backlog of inelastic demand for housing was being worked off and that the industry would have to be sustained by an elastic demand, would have been to cut building costs instead of raising them."[20]

Increases in costs of themselves might have been expected to reduce demand for home ownership, but, in addition, a comparison of

17. Ohlin, 10.
18. *Midland Bank Review, op. cit.,* 4.
19. Slichter, "Corporate Price Policies," 27–29.
20. *Ibid.,* 29.

rents and construction cost indexes shows that there was no incentive for rental construction. The rise in rents was greatly exceeded by the rise in construction costs. The data presented in Table 13 show that the National Industrial Conference Board rent index increased by 10.8% from July 1936 to June 1937. However, the construction cost indexes for brick residences rose by 18.9% in Atlanta, 16% in New York, and 12.4% in San Francisco. The increases were even greater with frame construction, being 22.7% in Atlanta, 18.0% in New York, and 13.2% in San Francisco. St. Louis was the only city studied where the profitability increased. There the increase in cost of brick construction was 7.4% and of frame construction 7.7%. It seems quite unlikely that substantial increases could have occurred in the demand for rental construction where rises in construction cost relative to rental values reduced so sharply the profitability of new rental construction:

the unfortunate effects of the uneconomic rise in costs in late 1936 and early 1937 are vividly demonstrated. Just at a time when vacancies were greatly reduced and when it appeared that the oversupply of housing facilities provided in the twenties had been largely absorbed, costs of construction increased substantially to offset this fundamental correction in the demand factor. Although the supply of productive factors in the construction industry might have been dissipated somewhat during the depression, no evidence can be found which indicates that a shortage of building labor or materials existed in early 1937. In view of this fact, monopoly pricing of both labor and materials must be held responsible for the deterring effects ensuing from the increase in costs of new housing in 1937.[21]

The failure of housing construction assumes more importance when it is realized that in a good year in the 1920's these expenditures alone amounted to as much as 30% of total gross capital formation and 7% of national income.[22]

The decline in housing expenditures suggests, therefore, that some of the housing demand was responsive to price changes. There also appears, however, to have been a certain section of the housing market which was relatively insensitive to income or price considerations, because a serious recession did not occur in housing expenditures. Thus the housing series, among the first to decline, was also among the first to revive. This revival commenced in February 1938, two months before the new "spend-lend" program was announced and

21. Hayes, "A Study of the Recession of 1937," 206. This conclusion is based largely on the data and analysis presented by Lowell J. Chawner in *Residential Building*, Housing Monograph Series, No. 1, 1939.
22. Estimates based on residential construction of $5 billion, gross capital formation of $18 billion, and national income of $75 billion.

TABLE 13: INDEXES OF RENT AND RESIDENTIAL CONSTRUCTION COSTS, 1936–37

(1929 = 100)

	Rent Index	Atlanta	BRICK New York	San Francisco	St. Louis	Atlanta	FRAME New York	San Francisco	St. Louis
1936									
Jan.	80.3	85.9	69.5	101.8	82.6	83.8	67.4	96.8	76.2
Feb.	80.5	87.7	70.4	103.8	83.8	85.9	68.5	98.4	77.0
March	81.2	89.5	70.4	109.1	84.9	87.0	68.5	98.8	78.2
April	82.5	89.5	71.2	104.1	84.9	87.0	68.9	98.8	78.2
May	83.8	88.9	71.2	102.9	85.5	86.4	68.9	97.7	79.0
June	84.3	87.5	71.9	103.4	85.5	84.7	69.3	98.0	79.0
July	84.9	86.6	71.9	103.4	85.0	84.2	69.3	98.0	78.3
Aug.	86.2	86.6	72.6	108.9	84.0	84.2	70.0	101.0	77.2
Sept.	87.3	87.0	72.6	109.2	84.0	84.8	70.0	101.6	77.2
Oct.	87.8	88.9	72.6	109.6	83.7	85.3	70.0	102.1	77.7
Nov.	88.5	89.1	72.7	109.9	85.2	87.8	70.0	102.3	78.4
Dec.	88.9	90.0	73.2	109.9	85.2	88.7	70.5	102.3	78.4
Avg.	84.7	88.1	71.7	105.9	84.6	86.1	69.3	99.7	78.0
1937									
Jan.	89.3	93.6	74.4	113.4	88.1	94.1	71.9	106.1	81.6
Feb.	90.0	95.8	75.8	108.6	88.9	96.1	73.6	106.1	82.6
March	91.5	98.5	76.5	110.5	89.2	98.0	74.6	108.2	82.9
April	92.6	103.3	76.5	112.2	89.8	103.8	74.6	110.2	83.3
May	93.6	103.3	76.8	112.2	89.7	103.8	74.7	110.2	83.2
June	94.1	103.2	83.4	116.2	91.3	103.3	81.8	110.9	84.3
July	94.7	99.9	84.9	116.2	90.6	99.4	82.6	110.9	83.5
Aug.	95.4	100.1	85.1	123.1	90.1	99.6	82.8	120.7	82.9
Sept.	96.3	100.4	86.5	122.5	92.3	99.9	84.2	119.9	85.5
Oct.	97.0	99.3	84.1	118.3	91.6	98.4	81.3	112.0	84.6
Nov.	96.8	99.3	83.5	118.3	90.9	98.4	80.7	112.0	83.9
Dec.	96.4	96.8	83.0	114.5	90.3	95.9	80.5	108.1	82.9
Avg.	94.0	99.4	80.9	115.5	90.3	99.2	78.6	111.3	83.4

Source: Basic data from Lewis, *op. cit.*, 40, Table 9. He used the rent index of the National Industrial Conference Board with the base shifted from 1923 to 1929, and the construction cost indexes of E. H. Boeckh and Associates, Inc., with the base shifted to 1929. The latter index was derived from contractors' records of wages and material costs.

four months before the upturn in income and industrial production. It occurred when income was declining and seems to have resulted from a shift in the demand curve, rather than from any change in demand due to change in price. One qualification should be added. The Federal Housing Act was amended in February 1938 so that terms for houses valued under $6,000 were liberalized. Also the new guarantee was raised from 80 to 90%. At the same time the effective interest rate was reduced from 6 to 5%. Thus these changes in price could account for part of the change in demand.

In summary, it would appear that prices in the building industry were distinctly unfavorable to an expansion of effective demand. There seems little reason to doubt, therefore, that a certain amount of investment expenditure in housing was curtailed by the price-cost relationship in the spring of 1937.

RISE IN WAGES AND COST OF MATERIALS IN THE
ELECTRIC POWER AND LIGHT INDUSTRY

The electric power and light industry is another for which some price-cost data are available. Output in 1937 exceeded that in 1936 by 9.2%. Production was 15% greater in both the first and second quarters of 1937 than in the same quarters of 1936. Third quarter production was 11% greater than in 1936. The recession reduced fourth quarter production to 1.1% above that in the fourth quarter of 1936. The important development, however, from the price-cost standpoint, was that total revenues increased 6.7% over 1936, or $136 million, but income, before interest and dividend requirements, increased only 0.7%, or $5 million. The explanation is, of course, that costs increased and limited the rise in net income.[23] For example, fuel costs increased by $20 million, wages and salaries by $25 million, provisions for retirement and depreciation by $15 million, and maintenance by $15 million.[24] Therefore, even though there was a large increase in production, net income was virtually unchanged. This probably means that the profitability of investment began to decline sometime in the first half of 1937. At the very least, it must have been evident that profits were due to decline in the near future.

THE STEEL PRICE RISES OF DECEMBER 1936 AND
MARCH 1937

The sharp increases in steel prices in December 1936, and especially

23. Here again, as with the railroads, the inflexibility of rates prevented the use of price increases to compensate for the rise in costs.
24. These data are all taken from the Edison Electric Institute, *Statistical Bulletin No. 5* (1937), 5.

those in the first week of March 1937, probably led some of the large buyers of steel to reduce their investment expenditures. It has already been indicated, in the section on the railroad industry, that beginning in the second quarter of 1937 railroad investment became increasingly sensitive to cost calculations. The coincidence of the large increases in steel prices and the declining profits in the railroad industry account at least partially for the revision of expectations which led to a virtual cessation of railroad investment.

However, Lewis in his study of the steel industry denied that changes in steel prices seriously affected the total volume of steel demanded or produced: "In summary, while price changes and anticipated price changes affect the timing of steel purchases, the large fluctuations in the total volume of steel production during the 1936–1939 period cannot be attributed to changes in the levels of steel prices. On the contrary, the evidence compels the conclusion that the influence of the level of steel prices on the total consumption of steel was relatively unimportant." [25]

Even though the actual volume of steel produced may not have been sharply affected by the price policies for steel, the psychological importance of price increases in this basic metal must not be overlooked. Moreover, as was suggested above, the actual price rises probably helped to restrict investment expenditures in certain areas.

PRICE-COST RELATIONSHIPS IN OTHER AREAS

An attempt was made to determine the effect of cost increases in certain consumer goods industries such as textiles and rubber tires and tubes. In the case of the former it was found that textile production reached its peak in the first half of 1937. Industry representatives believed this was due to "over buying" on the part of textile users.[26] The abnormal demand and the operation at capacity in 1937 for the first time since 1927 belie any marked effect of price-cost developments on textile production or investment decisions.

In the rubber tire and tube industry, price-cost relationships also appeared to have had little effect on production or investment decisions. The four large rubber companies recorded tremendous increases in profits in the first and second quarters of 1937 over the same quarters in 1936. Here again, as in the textile industry, the existence of considerable excess capacity made possible huge increases in production at a profit even in the face of substantial increases in wage and

---

25. Lewis, 4.
26. U. S. Congress, Senate, Special Committee, *Hearings, 1*, 296. The statement referred to was that of Claudius T. Murchison, president of Cotton-Textile Institute, Inc.

material costs. Therefore, on the basis of the sketchy data available, it would seem that investment planning was not restricted by any narrowing of the price-cost margin in either the textile or rubber tire and tube industries.

RELATIONSHIP OF PRICE AND COST CHANGES TO THE RECESSION

The analysis in this chapter has suggested that rises in prices from a cost standpoint contributed to the recession through their disturbing effects upon the prospects for profits.[27] In any event, the general rise in costs was a deterrent to continued recovery:

There can be no doubt that the rise in costs of production was one of the main causes of the precipitous decline in industrial activity of the United States during the second half of 1937. With a more gradual advance in wage rates the chances were that a greater number of unemployed would have been absorbed by industry, increasing the purchasing power in the hands of the public without the same risk of an early setback. Not even the most extensive distribution of purchasing power by the government nor the persistent pursuit of a cheap-money policy succeeded in bringing about a lasting recovery when costs rose so much as to be out of line with current prices of finished articles.[28]

However, there may be a tendency to overemphasize the importance of general cost increases. It is worth noting that the United States had a much smaller increase in wholesale prices during the period than did most other major countries. Table 14 shows the percentage increases in wholesale prices for the various important nations, from May 1936 to May 1937. The increase for the United States was 11.2% compared with 20.4% in the United Kingdom, 18.5% in Canada, and 17.8% in Sweden.[29] Yet these countries enjoyed a much more substantial recovery than did the United States. Furthermore, these cost increases were accorded little causal responsibility in the recessions which subsequently occurred in these nations.

SUMMARY

A general rise in prices and costs was not necessarily a factor leading to the recession. Therefore, the effects of price changes in particu-

27. Underconsumptionists would interpret these events otherwise. From their viewpoint the increase in prices, relative to the increase in labor income, gave rise to the recession through its disturbing effects on consumption expenditures. These interpretations of the price-cost problem will be discussed in detail in Chapter 10, on consumption factors.

28. Bank for International Settlements, *Ninth Annual Report* (Basle, 1939), 10.

29. Condliffe, 83. The only major country with a smaller rise in prices was Germany.

TABLE 14: THE MOVEMENT IN WHOLESALE PRICES
IN MAJOR NATIONS, MAY 1936 TO MAY 1937

(1929 = 100)

Country	May 1936	May 1937	Per Cent Increase May 1936 to May 1937
France	59.6	87.7	+47.1
Latvia	70.9	93.4	31.7
Chile	191.2	241.9	26.5
Netherlands	61.2	76.9	25.7
Japan	87.5	109.6	25.3
Switzerland	65.2	79.7	22.2
Belgium	66.9	81.4	21.7
United Kingdom	80.5	96.9	20.4
Norway	88.6	105.4	19.0
Canada	75.1	89.0	18.5
China	101.2	119.7	18.3
Sweden	84.3	99.3	17.8
Denmark	95.5	111.4	16.6
Italy	79.2	91.7	15.8
Finland	91.8	106.1	15.6
Greece	111.3	128.3	15.3
India	63.8	73.0	14.4
Poland	55.8	62.2	11.5
U.S.A.	82.5	91.7	11.2
Bulgaria	56.7	62.6	10.4
Hungary	71.1	78.5	10.4
Australia	84.4	91.9 [a]	8.9
Peru	103.4	112.5	8.8
Yugoslavia	66.6	72.2	8.4
New Zealand	93.5	100.9	7.9
Czechoslovakia	76.5	82.4	7.7
Austria	83.2	88.8	6.7
Argentina	101.5	104.0 [b]	2.5
Germany	75.7	77.2	2.0
Union of South Africa	86.0	85.0	−1.2

a. April
b. October 1936

Source: Adapted from Condliffe, 83.

140

lar areas have been traced and analyzed. It has been shown that the increase in prices of raw materials and wages reduced current and prospective profits in areas such as the railroad, building, and electric power and light industries. Insofar as developments in these specific areas may be generalized,[30a] and to the extent that investment expenditures were reduced by the prospect of declining profits, the rise in costs reinforced the recessive tendencies. The more important of these cost changes will be investigated further in the next chapter, on the relationship between monopoly, price flexibility, and the turning point in the recession.

30. It is not possible to do so, however, with the textile and the rubber tire and tube industry.

CHAPTER 9

Monopoly Factors and the Recession

THIS CHAPTER considers imperfections in the market, price flexibility, and the turning point in the recession. At the outset, it should be understood that the discussion deals mainly with cyclical rather than secular problems of monopoly. Therefore, less consideration will be given to problems which are essentially long-run, such as the optimum allocation of resources or the wisest distribution of income, than to the effects of monopoly on short-run spending-saving decisions. The long-term relationships of monopoly pricing and control to investment expenditures merit less attention in so short a period as 1933–38. Analysis of a turning point is not greatly assisted by an answer to the question of whether there has been a trend toward more or less competition in the economy.[1] Moreover, the behavior of investment expenditures in the "sleepy sort [of monopoly] which does not strain after every gnat of profit, but prefers a quiet life" [2] is not the main problem under investigation in this chapter. Instead, the problem is to investigate the possibility that monopoly pricing contributed to the recession by affecting the direction and flow of income.

THE GOVERNMENT ATTACK ON MONOPOLY

Government officials and policy-makers denounced the rises in many of the important prices as monopoly-inspired. The major administration leaders, one by one, publicly criticized "monopolized" prices and monopolists. Eccles suggested that antitrust action be broadened to assist in an attack on monopoly prices.[3] As already noted, Henderson, in April and May 1937, attacked monopoly increases in prices and the President criticized increased prices, particularly in the durable goods industries.[4]

In December 1937, after the recession had begun, Assistant Attorney General Robert Jackson entered the fight by blaming monopo-

1. However, recent studies would indicate no substantial change in concentration. Cf., for example, G. Warren Nutter, *The Extent of Enterprise Monopoly in the United States, 1899–1939* (Chicago, 1951).
2. J. R. Hicks, *Value and Capital* (London, 1939), 265.
3. Eccles, "Controlling Booms and Depressions," *180*.
4. Cf. Chapter 2.

lists and big business for the country's many economic ills.[5] Harold Ickes followed with an attack on "America's 60 Families." [6] On January 1, 1938, Henderson charged that the breakdown of the recovery resulted from a shortage of purchasing power. People could not purchase the full output of farms and factories. Prices were rising faster than wages, and monopolies were responsible for the price rise: "Were monopolies responsible for this price rise which crippled workable relationships in the American economy by reducing the general public's capacity to consume? My answer is emphatically yes. I believe the unbalance in prices was touched off by the monopolistic prices." [7] It has already been pointed out that Harry Hopkins believed the recession was caused primarily by unwarranted price increases accompanied by the failure of consumer purchasing power to keep step with production.[8] His recommendation was for flexible corporate prices.

A final statement of the Administration's attitude toward monopoly came from the President when he asked for a national study of the concentration of economic power, and the effect of that concentration upon the decline of competition.[9] This last action was regarded by some critics as a face-saving gesture. Nevertheless, it was objective evidence that the Administration intended to support its indictment of monopoly pricing with a full-scale investigation. Following the 1929–33 depression there had been proposals for such an investigation, but it is unlikely that hearings would ever have been held but for the spectacular collapse of production and income in the fall of 1937: "in all probability there would have been no TNEC had it not been for the setback which recovery suffered early in 1937. The TNEC was, therefore, in part a product of the historic past and in part the immediate result of the recession of 1937." [10]

FACTORS PROMOTING MONOPOLY AND PRICE RIGIDITY

Attention must now be given to the structural and market elements which served to strengthen the forces of monopoly and price administration.

LEGISLATION

Without a doubt, legislative action in the thirties played an important role in increasing monopoly and price rigidity. The NRA

5. *New York Times,* December 30, 1937, 6.
6. *Ibid.,* December 31, 1937, 6.
7. *Ibid.,* January 2, 1938, 2.
8. Cf. Chapter 2.
9. *New York Times,* April 30, 1938, 2.
10. Lynch, *op. cit.,* 16.

received sharp criticism for its part in this. Perhaps even more important, the opposition of many producers to "unfair" practices [11] (among which price competition is generally regarded as the most "unfair") found expression in the restrictive codes of the NRA, so that these attitudes continued to affect future price policies even after the act was invalidated. Most of the spirit of the codes was eventually legalized in state unfair practices acts and in federal legislation—the Miller-Tydings and Robinson-Patman Acts. This occurred even though governmental policy was opposed to legislation for industry groups.[12]

ORGANIZATION OF THE LABOR MARKET

The labor market was an area where structural changes led to increased price rigidity. Rigidities in the pricing process were promoted by the efforts of the AFL and the CIO, spurred on by the enactment of the NRA and later the Wagner Labor Act, to organize the labor market. The development of industry-wide bargaining made it possible for labor to obtain substantial wage increases in competitive industries. In monopolized areas, the enhanced bargaining strength made it certain that wage concessions could be exacted. The rapid expansion in the degree and strength of labor organization encouraged wage flexibility as prices and production rose, and served to increase wage rigidity and inflexibility as prices and production fell.

CORPORATE PRICE POLICIES

In addition to structural changes which increased price rigidity, two other institutional factors, corporate price policies and transportation costs, bore considerable responsibility for the existing price inflexibility.

At least three types of corporate price policies promoted price inflexibility—outright collusion, nonprice competition, and the character of the distributive margin.[13] Collusion is of course one basis for monopoly pricing, and nonprice competition includes all of the factors

11. John P. Miller, *Unfair Competition* (Cambridge, Mass., 1941), 332–358.

12. "In large part the postulate that the interests of the industry group and the public interest are compatible has been repudiated by official policy, although the philosophy and technique of the NRA has been applied to isolated parts of the system, notably in the control of the bituminous coal industry and in the legislation permissive of resale price maintenance." *Ibid.*, 400. The oil industry has also been organized in much the same fashion.

13. An excellent discussion of these aspects of corporate price policies is contained in Saul Nelson and Walter G. Keim, *Price Behavior and Business Policy*, Temporary National Economic Committee, Monograph No. 1, 1940.

influencing the differentiation of products and the special agreements affecting sales which avoid price competition.

The distributive margin is of particular interest because of its relative inflexibility, which accounts largely for the greater inflexibility of retail prices than wholesale prices. The very great mark-up from manufacturer to consumer is a large part of the total cost to the consumer,[14] and current selling practices make this markup extremely inflexible. The legislation of the thirties and forties may well have increased the degree of inflexibility in the distributive margin: "resale price maintenance legislation—the so-called 'Fair Trade Acts,' together with the Federal Miller-Tydings Enabling Act—have increased the rigidity of the prices of many trade-marked commodities. It is possible that the state 'Unfair Practices Acts' and the Robinson-Patman Act have reduced the flexibility of distributive margins in certain markets." [15]

INFLEXIBLE TRANSPORTATION COSTS

Many of the same observations apply to transportation costs, which are also a large item in final cost to the consumer and also tend toward inflexibility. Their relative importance may be seen when it is noted that the total value of manufactured products in 1929 was $65.6 billion of which $8.8 billion was transportation costs. Because transportation costs are relatively inflexible, they become proportionately much more important when commodity prices are low or falling. Their importance lessens when commodity prices are high or rising.[16]

These institutional factors contribute to the rigidity of the pricing system. Nevertheless it should be emphasized that neither such factors nor price rigidities themselves provide an explanation for turning points in economic activity. They may well have important effects on human welfare through their impact on the distribution of resources and income. But they must be judged to have been of little immediate importance in causing the recession of 1937–38, or any other turning point, unless it can be shown that there were measurable changes in the degree of monopoly which then initiated changes in income, production, and employment. Further consideration will be given to this point in the section below on changes in the degree of monopoly and the turning point. But first the theoretical and statistical measurements of monopoly power must be described.

14. The markup ranges up to 100% in the electrical appliance industry.
15. Nelson and Keim, 52. The restrictive effects of these regulations have been partly moderated by the development of private brands.
16. *Ibid.*, 271. One consequence of the highly inflexible railroad rates was to accelerate the trend toward the use of other forms of transportation.

Measurements of Monopoly

Theoretical Measurements of Monopoly Power

Two important measures of monopoly are those proposed by Lerner and Bain.[17] Lerner's measure [18] assumes that a divergence between price, or average receipts, and marginal costs indicates the existence of monopoly. Conversely, an identity of price and marginal cost demonstrates the absence of monopoly. Thus in his analysis the degree of monopoly power is measured by the ratio of the difference between price and marginal cost to price. Where P equals price and C equals marginal cost, the index of the degree of monopoly power is P minus C over P. This index can have a value varying between zero and one, between a perfectly competitive price situation and increasing degrees of monopoly pricing.

Bain's test for monopoly is an abnormal profit rate. He proposes to compare the profit rate with the going rate of interest,[19] defining the profit rate as follows: "It is in any short period the ratio of the net earnings of that period (quasi-rents less depreciation computed as indicated) to the replacement cost of service value of those assets of the firm which it could economically hold at a minimum and produce its present output. The profit rate (through comparison with the rate of interest) is therefore an indicator of the deviation of the earnings behavior of the firm from a selected norm." [20] Any deviation between this profit rate and the rate of interest over time is a "probable indication of monopoly or monopsony." [21]

It should be noted that there is a fundamental difference between the Lerner and Bain measures. The Lerner measure is relevant for the problem of optimum resource use, whereas the Bain measure directs attention to the effects of monopoly activity on income distribution. The argument in this chapter is that a change must occur in income

17. Cf. also K. W. Rothschild, "The Degree of Monopoly," in *Economica, New Series 9* (1942), 24–39.

18. Abba P. Lerner, "The Concept of Monopoly and the Measurement of Monopoly Power," *Review of Economic Studies, 1* (1934), 157–175.

19. Joseph S. Bain, "The Profit Rate as a Measure of Monopoly Power," *Quarterly Journal of Economics, 55* (1940–41), 271–293.

20. *Ibid.*, 287–288.

21. The complete statement from Bain is: "A persistent deviation over a period of years, however, is an indication of a failure of the competitive mechanism to force an approximation to equilibrium, and therefore a probable indication of monopoly or monopsony power, or less probably of pure competition with persistent impediment to entry." *Ibid.*, 288. It should be noted, however, that a deviation between the profit rate and the interest rate may reflect difference in risk rather than imperfect competition.

distribution and subsequent spending out of that income if monopoly factors are to be charged with some causal responsibility in the recession. From this standpoint the Bain measure appears to be more revealing. However, the task of assembling the relevant data prohibits the use of the measurement in this study.

From the theoretical standpoint there are defects in both of these measures. In Bain's measure it is not possible to separate the monopoly and the monopsony contributions to total monopoly power. His measure also cannot indicate differing degrees of monopoly among various firms and industries, whereas the Lerner measure can. However, a limitation of considerable importance on the Lerner measure is that the relevant decisions may be made on the basis of current marginal cost and user cost [22] rather than on current marginal cost alone.

Another question which should be raised when applying the Lerner measure is what effect differences in advertising expenditures may have on the degrees of monopoly power shown for two firms. An answer to this question requires a distinction between costs which are productive from a social viewpoint and those which are not. This becomes a more general problem than one of advertising expenditures alone, since even expenditures to improve a product may or may not be productive from a social standpoint.[23]

Besides having theoretical weaknesses, these measures and others that have been proposed defy precise measurement. Marginal costs for the individual firm, and even more for the industry, appear beyond adequate measurement. Analysts have resorted to extreme simplification and have abstracted from pure marginal cost theory in order to use the Lerner measurement of monopoly. This has been necessary to fit the available price and cost data into a statistical measurement of monopoly power.[24] Lerner has suggested that it would be desirable to obtain the standard deviation of monopoly power for society as a whole.[25] How far that goal is from realization becomes apparent from consideration of the almost insurmountable difficulties which are faced in a statistical determination of the index of monopoly power for even an individual firm.

22. Alfred C. Neal, *Industrial Concentration and Price Inflexibility* (Washington, 1942), 69. However, Lerner has indicated to me privately that his definition of costs would include user cost also.

23. This problem in using the Lerner measure was pointed out to me by John P. Miller of Yale University. I am indebted to Professor Lerner for the suggestion made above that the problem is broader than advertising expenditures, requiring consideration of the social productiveness of any costs incurred.

24. One such attempt has been made by John T. Dunlop, "Price Flexibility and the 'Degree of Monopoly,'" *Quarterly Journal of Economics*, 53 (1938–39), 522–34.

25. Lerner, 175.

Bain also is aware of the very serious problems of measurement in determining the normal competitive cost basis for calculation of abnormal profits. Nevertheless he expresses the belief that, with painstaking study, company books can be reasonably well adjusted.[26] The problem of measurement, if not insuperable, is certainly of sizable proportions.

STATISTICAL MEASUREMENTS OF CHANGE IN
DEGREE OF MONOPOLY POWER

In spite of its limitations, theoretical and statistical, the concept of monopoly power which rests upon differences between price and marginal cost still appears to be the most promising area for empirical investigation.

The Neal method of analysis and results. A major contribution in this field of measurement has been made by Alfred C. Neal.[27] Indices on price, per unit direct cost, and overhead and profits margin enabled him to study changes in prices relative to changes in direct costs during the periods 1929–31 and 1929–33. For the 1929–31 comparison he used 106 industries which accounted for 59% of the total value of manufactured products in 1929. For the 1929–33 comparison he used 85 industries which accounted for 57% of the total value of products in 1929. The test for price flexibility was whether the absolute change in prices was *less* than the absolute change in direct cost. If the absolute change in prices was greater than that in direct costs, prices were considered flexible. Neal's objective was to test the generalization that industrial concentration was the major factor influencing price flexibility and variations in production.

Even though the statistics were for the 1929–33 period, his findings will be summarized. They give a good indication of the types of quantitative results which may be obtained by comparing changes in the relationships between price and average direct costs. Furthermore, the results are interesting in themselves because of the confirmation or contradiction they provide for many of the generalizations which have been made on the effect of price rigidity and concentration of economic power in the 1929–33 depression.[28]

First, for the 1929–1933 period, there was a slight tendency, as has been claimed by proponents of the concentration thesis, for production to fall most where price fell least. . . . Neither price change nor production

26. Bain, 293.
27. Neal, *op. cit.*
28. His study was directed largely to the conclusions advanced by Gardiner Means in "Industrial Prices and Their Relative Inflexibility," Senate Document No. 13, 74th Congress, 1st Session (1935); National Resources Committee, *The Structure of the American Economy,* Pt. I; and other writings.

change, however, is to be explained by concentration. Rather, differential price changes are explicable by differential unit direct cost changes, and differential production changes are to be explained in terms of demand shifts which are a consequence of the nature of the demands concerned.[29]

Secondly, differential price behavior among industries for both comparisons (1929–1931 and 1929–1933) is to be explained for the most part by differential unit direct cost behavior rather than by concentration.

Thirdly, concentration does not even explain the *difference* between actual price declines and those which could be expected on the basis of changes in direct cost. This conclusion is reasonable in view of the differences in cost structures among industries.[30]

In the fourth place, however, concentration did have a small but significant influence upon the decline in the difference between unit price and unit direct cost—the overhead-plus-profits margin. This margin tended to decline least where concentration was high; most where it was low. The relationship is not clear-cut, but it is consistent with theoretical presumptions.[31]

In his chapters 5 and 6, Neal has emphasized the qualifications and limitations of his analysis. But with all these shortcomings it would still be desirable to have comparable data and computations from 1933 to 1937–38. Unfortunately the magnitude of the job is such that it cannot be undertaken here. Most of the material for Neal's analysis was taken from Frederick C. Mills' studies,[32] which end before the important years 1936–38. A similar study for the entire period 1933–37 [33] would seem to be the only practical way to get some indications of possible changes in the degree of monopoly, as they affect resource use.

Comparative price movements as an indication of monopoly. Because the statistics for application of the Neal method have not been assembled, the only practical method for indicating monopoly seems to be to use comparative prices. The method is simple. Where prices of individual commodities not only failed to decline in the sharp collapse of production and income during 1937–38 but actually rose to new heights, it may be reasoned that these prices were "administered" and indicate the presence of monopoly. Likewise it may be assumed that those prices which rose least from 1933 to 1937 were probably

29. An example is the greater stability of demand for farm products than for commodities like consumer goods.

30. In industries with high ratios of overhead costs to price, the decline in price could greatly exceed the decline in direct costs.

31. Neal, 165–166.

32. Frederick C. Mills, *Economic Tendencies in the United States* (New York, 1932) ; and *Prices in Recession and Recovery* (New York, 1936).

33. Because of the sharp intrayear reversal in the direction of production and income in 1937, changes in price-cost relationships might be obscured by the use of available annual data.

the product of monopoly forces. The components of the Bureau of Labor Statistics' index of wholesale prices have already been analyzed both for the peak price in the years 1936–38 and for the amplitude of fluctuation from 1933 to that peak period.[34] The 650 individual commodities were divided on the basis of flexibility of prices into 10 groups of approximately equal size. The most inflexible prices, those which reached their peaks in December 1938, were designated as Group I; the most flexible, those which reached their peaks in January through December 1936, as Group X. No group was designated as II because the frequency of price peaks in December 1938 was so great that 158 observations met the timing criterion for Group I. The time specifications and frequencies for each of the groups are shown in Table 15.

TABLE 15: DISTRIBUTION OF COMPONENTS OF BUREAU OF LABOR STATISTICS INDEX OF WHOLESALE PRICES ACCORDING TO PEAK MONTH, 1936–38

Group	Group Limits	Number of Items
I	December 1938	158
II	———	—
III	July to November 1938	40
IV	April to June 1938	57
V	December 1937 to March 1938	61
VI	September 1937 to November 1938	67
VII	June 1937 to August 1937	73
VIII	April 1937 to May 1937	62
IX	January 1937 to March 1937	71
X	January 1936 to December 1936	61
	Total	650

Source: Basic data from Nelson and Keim, *Price Behavior and Business Policy,* Temporary National Economic Committee, Monograph No. 1, 209, Table 26.

The amplitude data will not be analyzed in detail. It would appear, however, that those which increased least during 1933–37 tended to be the prices which were inflexible in both the 1937–38 recession and the 1929–32 depression.[35]

Table 16 presents a sample of the types of prices which are included in each group, with the most attention directed toward the relatively inflexible prices. This distribution of prices shows a tendency for the

34. Nelson and Keim.
35. *Ibid.,* 47. The study confined itself mainly to the 1929–37 period, in which there was "apparently a marked relationship between the extent of decline between 1929–33 and the percentage of recovery from 1933 to 1937." *Ibid.,* 170.

TABLE 16: DISTRIBUTION OF SELECTED PRICES ACCORDING TO 1936-38 HIGH

Relatively Inflexible					Relatively Flexible				
Group I		III	IV	V	VI	VII	VIII	IX	X
grape juice	lamp black	farm implements	most	bitum. coal	shoes	cows	corn	flaxseed	ginger ale
plain soda	chrome green	steel rails	iron	peanuts		steers	oats	beans	anthracite
collars	whiting	trucks	and	alfalfa seed		hogs	rye	cottonseed oil	
sisal	wall board	asphalt	steel			most fruits	cotton products	most ores	
fuel oil, Okla.	plate glass	gas				meats		cotton products	
Calif. petrol	sewer pipe					cotton products			
hand tools	plaster								
aluminum	slate								
nickel cathode	tar								
heating boilers	electric iron								
sinks	electric range								
bath tubs	gas range								
paving brick	oil range								
lime brick	vacuum cleaners								
hollow building tile	washing machine								
roofing tile	electric refrigerator								
Douglas fir lathe	truck tires								
chestnut	bus tires								
cypress	newsprint								
redwood	plate glass mirrors								
enamel	most tobaccos								
outside white paints	iron oxide								

151

Source: Basic data from Nelson and Keim, 190–207, Table 26.

low prices of farm and food products, textiles, and most ores to coincide with or to precede the general decline in production and income. The same table reveals that the prices of gas, fuel oil and petroleum, aluminum, nickel, a large number of chemicals, and of durable goods such as electrical appliances, plumbing and heating equipment, as well as of most construction raw materials, iron and steel products, and agricultural machinery equipment reached new highs for the 1936–38 period in the months following April 1938, or directly in the face of the severe decline in production and income.

A qualifying statement must be made concerning the reliability of the movements in some of these price indexes. An excellent analysis of the basic weaknesses of some of the components in the Bureau of Labor Statistics index of wholesale prices [36] demonstrates that the inflexibility of those of yellow pine lumber, crushed stone, aluminum, lime, asphalt, and a half dozen other commodities is largely fictitious. This is because these represent only the published or trade journal prices, and not the return actually realized by the manufacturer or supplier. Therefore care must be taken in the interpretation of an individual price series. In addition, noncyclical factors of a secular, seasonal, or even casual nature may have affected the timing of some of these series. Nevertheless it may be presumed that the prices which rose as demand fell were administered prices.[37]

The analysis in this section has suggested the industrial areas where prices were apparently determined according to administrative decision, and where as a consequence there may have been sufficient changes in the degree of monopoly power to have contributed to the turning point in the recession.[38] Of course the analysis does not measure the changes which may have occurred in monopoly power from 1933 to 1938, nor even establish the presumption of such changes, but it does direct attention to the most likely areas where monopoly power may have been enhanced.

Is General Price Flexibility Desirable?

An elaborate analysis of the problem of general price flexibility will not be undertaken here.[39] However, it may be suggested that many

36. National Resources Committee, 173–185.

37. It is, of course, possible for a firm to have the ability to administer prices and yet not use that ability.

38. This does not appear to be inconsistent with the observation made on the preceding page that many prices which were relatively inflexible in both the 1929–33 depression and the 1937–38 recession were also relatively inflexible during 1933–37. The degree of monopoly power could have increased for some of these industries even with inflexible prices if there were reductions in their variable costs. However, it would seem that it was not extraordinary price rises in these areas which evidence or establish any change in the degree of monopoly power.

39. In this section I have drawn heavily upon discussion with Max Millikan of Massachusetts Institute of Technology and Eugene V. Rostow of Yale University.

policy recommendations have been based on the application of tools of partial equilibrium analysis to general equilibrium conditions. Given a change in one price, partial equilibrium analysis assumes all other prices and incomes constant. This analysis obviously cannot be used to determine the consequences of general price flexibility in a situation where "all other prices and income" cannot be considered constant.[40]

In the framework of the analysis employed in this study, an answer to the question raised above depends upon the effects which general price flexibility may have upon the inducements to invest, inducements to consume, or upon the relatively autonomous changes in the financial position of government. An appraisal of the desirability of general price flexibility to promote an expansion in income and employment depends upon the assumptions made about the changes which occur in the aforementioned areas. For example, the classical position [41] was that employment and output would rise when resources were underemployed, if prices were completely flexible. This would occur either because a fall in prices would increase the effective money supply, interest rates would fall, and investment increase, or because the decline in prices would increase the real value of consumers' cash balances so that intended consumption would increase and intended saving decline. However, there appears to be no guarantee that either of these developments will occur. It is just as likely (and recent experience would suggest more likely) that a decline in prices will lead to an expectation of their declining further, so that investment and/or consumption expenditure and employment and output decline in a deflationary spiral.[42] Furthermore, under current accounting practices, a fall in prices leads business firms to overstate their losses. This reduces correspondingly the incentives for investment.

One other factor must be considered in examining the effectiveness of general price flexibility in stabilizing the economy. Investment

40. See Keynes, *op. cit.*, 258–260. As considerations of this sort are pointed out in elementary economics courses, it would seem unnecessary to stress them here were it not for the fact that so many policy recommendations are understandable only in the light of such an error in methodology.

41. The classical economist sometimes relied on changes in relative prices to stabilize the volume of employment. This position must meet the arguments advanced above concerning the distinction between partial and general equilibrium and the very practical objection that the wage earner may not be able to reduce his real wage rate. Cf. Keynes, 13.

42. Where general elasticities of expectation are greater than 1, any change in prices is not expected to be permanent but to be followed by even greater changes in the same direction. Thus no incentive is provided under such assumptions for the buying commitments necessary to stem the deflation or stabilize the system. Cf. Hicks, chaps. 20 and 21; and Oscar Lange, *Price Flexibility and Employment*, Cowles Commission for Research in Economics, Monograph No. 8 (Bloomington, 1944), chap. 5.

spending in contrast with consumption spending is generally made according to a plan which compares current revenues and costs with future revenues and costs. Therefore, if future prices are expected to decline, a decrease in current prices will act more powerfully to restrict current investment than consumption expenditures.

The remarks so far have been directed toward the problem of general price flexibility on the downside. The price instability which may attend general price flexibility on the upside is illustrated on a small scale in the sharp price boom which commenced in September 1936 and ended in April 1937. Here price flexibility was definitely destabilizing because the elasticity of expectations with respect to future price changes was greater than 1. Not only did the increases in prices of commodities fail to reduce the excess demands for these commodities, but the belief that prices would continue to rise increased the excess demand. This situation appears to be the special case minimized by Lange in his discussion of stability conditions and price flexibility.[43]

The short duration of the boom, from September 1936 to April 1937, indicates that some price rigidities developed to puncture it, that is, there was a relative increase in the demand for those goods whose prices were reasonably stable and at the same time a shift away from those whose prices had risen sharply. But the rapidity of the rise in the early stages is evidence of the extreme instability which may accompany general price flexibility. Of course the problem here was given a somewhat unusual twist because resources were unemployed. It has been suggested that complete price flexibility is desirable in such a situation because it contributes to the speed with which unused resources are bid into production and stimulates the new capacity necessary to break out of any bottlenecks of supply. The weakness in these arguments is that high elasticity of price expectations encourages short-term investment in inventories. This in turn results in a higher level of output which is only temporary, because it is based on a given rate of increase in prices. These various objections weigh heavily against price flexibility on the upside, not only when resources are fully employed but when they are unemployed as well.

This discussion has been largely speculative. One thing which has

---

43. Lange, 20–28. In Lange's terms, the monetary supply was elastic but even so its effects were not positive. The expectation that prices would continue to rise was so great that the real demand for balances did not increase. Where more profit could be obtained by a slow response of supply there was no incentive to exchange goods against money. Later, as prices fell, it is probable that the quantity of money for exchange against goods did not increase rapidly enough to offset the prospects of subsequent declines in prices of goods.

been established is that a general fall (or rise) in prices will have different effects upon employment and output according to the impact which these price changes have upon investment, consumption, or government decisions. No simple generalization seems possible. The accepted opinion today is that general price flexibility is unwise in a business fluctuation because of this problem of elastic price expectations.[44] The dangers which arise from elastic price expectations are so great that serious doubts must be expressed as to the advisability of supporting general price flexibility as a device for stabilizing income and employment. Moreover, the state of our knowledge about the effects of price changes on the propensity to consume or to invest is so uncertain that it appears unwise to base public policy on forecasts in these areas. It should be apparent that the use of price changes to alter the real supply of money, and thus to change the interest rate, is a very cumbersome and impractical mechanism. Direct government intervention (fiscal policy) should achieve this objective at less cost.

CHANGES IN DEGREE OF MONOPOLY AND THE TURNING POINT IN THE RECESSION

Changes in the degree of monopoly affect changes in particular rather than general prices. However, the framework of analysis used in the discussion of general price flexibility also provides the basis for investigating the changes in the degree of monopoly. There must be a change in the latter which changes the flow of income before consumption, savings, or investment are affected. Once more it is important to emphasize that the mere existence of monopoly does not explain turning points in economic activity.

Two questions must be raised concerning any change in the degree of monopoly and its relationship to the 1937–38 recession. First, how would any such change affect economic activity? Second, were there changes in the degree of monopoly in specific areas which may have altered the direction of economic activity? Consideration will first be given to the possible effects of such changes upon consumption and investment expenditures.

44. Hicks, chaps. 21 and 22; also Lange, chap. 13. Both Hicks and Lange conclude that some rigid prices may be desirable for economic stability. Thus Lange concludes: "if long-range price expectations are prevailingly elastic, less monetary management, and also less government expenditure, are required when some important price (or prices) in the economy is (or are) rigid, than when all prices are perfectly flexible. For rigidity of some important price (or prices) will produce directly the intratemporal substitution effects and expansion effects needed to stabilize the economy, without going through a general fall of prices, a consequent increase in the real demand for cash balances, and, finally, a greater increase in the real quantity of money to create a positive monetary effect," 87–88.

CONSUMPTION AND INVESTMENT EFFECTS

An increase in prices relative to costs could have helped to precipitate the recession if the increased flow of profit-income reduced the marginal propensity to consume to the point where *ex ante* savings became excessive. But profits remained extremely low throughout the period, and there is no conclusive evidence to support the claim that consumption declined relative to income immediately preceding the recession.[45] These reasons make it seem unlikely that any increase in the degree of monopoly could have affected the recession by initiating changes in the consumption area.

The other way by which any change in the degree of monopoly might have affected the recession was through its repercussions upon the profit expectations of businessmen and subsequently upon their investment expenditures. An increase in prices may have restricted investment commitments by raising costs in certain crucial areas. In the preceding chapter it was suggested that since costs did rise in particular areas prospects for future profits were dimmed. Accordingly, investment expenditures were reduced, because as costs rose current operations became less profitable and future operations appeared so. To the extent that these cost increases resulted from monopoly action and were greater than those which would have occurred under competitive pricing, changes in the degree of monopoly power may have contributed to the turning point in the recession by decreasing the profitability of investment expenditures. The evidence suggests that changes in the degree of monopoly were more effective in reducing investment expenditures than in restricting the flow of consumption expenditures.

WERE THERE SIGNIFICANT CHANGES IN THE DEGREE OF MONOPOLY?

The NRA undoubtedly led to marked changes in the degree of monopoly in many areas. But by 1936–37 these effects must have been worked out. It is improbable that further changes in the degree of monopoly arose from this source.

The labor field stands out as the most important in which a significant change may have occurred in power monopoly, although, of course, not in the degree of monopoly as defined above. The phenomenon of substantial increases in wage rates accompanied by large-scale unemployment can be explained only by an increase in monopoly which also re-enforced monopolistic pricing and price rises in other areas. Demands by labor for increased wages could be more easily

45. See the discussion in Chapter 10.

agreed to and met in those areas where it was possible to administer prices. The ready assent to wage demands encouraged by the monopoly power not only raised prices in the affected industries but by increasing their costs also supported upward movements of wage scales in other industries. This undoubtedly restricted some of the investment decisions which were sensitive to changes in cost.

In areas other than the labor market it seems less likely that significant changes occurred in the degree of monopoly in the technical sense. For example, although pricing was subject to monopoly controls in both steel and housing, there is no conclusive evidence that the degree of monopoly changed in either area.

SUMMARY

At present, direct measurement of changes in the degree of monopoly and the effects of monopoly pricing seems impossible. Under such circumstances it may well be that the most fruitful investigation is "a qualitative analysis of the characteristics of industrial markets (including numbers, degree of differentiation of the product, etc.,) in order to find where monopoly power may be expected to exist and where (assuming profit maximization) it is exploited." [46]

The desirability of general price flexibility was shown to depend upon the assumptions made about the changes in consumption, savings, or investment which occur when prices are perfectly flexible. Knowledge is lacking about the changes which are most likely to occur in any of these areas. However, it has been suggested that the high elasticities of price expectations which accompany general price flexibility are undesirable, with or without full employment of resources. Therefore, it would seem more effective and wiser to employ government monetary or fiscal policies rather than completely flexible prices to promote increases in output and employment.

The significance of monopoly pricing and price rigidity in the recession and revival lies in their direct influence on costs and their indirect effects on investment decisions. The only definite change in monopoly power which could be established was in the determination of wages. There it seems very likely that its increase may have contributed to a reduction in investment expenditures through its impact on costs in particular areas.

46. Bain, 272.

CHAPTER 10

The Relationship of Consumption
Expenditures to the Recession*

THE FAILURE of consumption spending has been accorded important causal responsibility in the recession of 1937–38. The strongest statement of what may be called the "simple" underconsumption interpretation of the price-cost relationships in the period came from various governmental representatives. For example, as was noted in Chapter 2, Leon Henderson forecast a major business recession because prices were rising so rapidly that purchasing power was failing to keep pace. Too much of the money flow was into profits and savings where it failed to find profitable investment outlets because of the reduced consumer purchasing power.[1]

In addition many attribute the imperfect recovery of certain of the investment components in the national product of the peculiar nature of that recovery. From this viewpoint, producers' durable equipment expenditures expanded during the 1935–37 period because investment decision was closely geared to consumption expenditures.[2] But the relatively long-term commitments, such as characterized the twenties and which normally result in expansion of plant capacity, were notable for their absence. The recession itself resulted largely because consumption expenditures "flattened" out. The failure of consumption expenditures reacted unfavorably upon the derived producers' durable equipment expenditures (the acceleration principle) and produced the phenomenal involuntary investment in inventories.[3]

This chapter proposes to examine two related propositions which arise from the considerations just raised. One is that a failure in consumption expenditures was an important cause of the 1937 downturn. Thus, if consumption expenditures had continued to rise, income, pro-

* Portions of this chapter were presented before the annual meeting of the Econometric Society in New York, December 27–30, 1949.
1. Quoted in Lynch, *op. cit.*, 18–19.
2. In the first three quarters of 1937 these expenditures surpassed even their peak levels of the twenties. Cf. Barger, Table 11, 114–119.
3. Secular stagnation is also advanced by some to explain the absence of long-term investment commitments.

duction, and output would also have continued to expand. The other is that most investment expenditures in the process of the recovery from 1933 to 1937 were *induced* by consumption expenditures. Here, if investment expenditures had not been so closely dependent upon consumption, the recovery movement would have continued uninterrupted by recession. Attention will first be given to the recession as a consequence of a failure in consumption expenditures. Then the inquiry will be directed toward the broader question of whether the recovery was "consumption inspired," so that investment failed to take hold as in previous recoveries and thus left the economy more vulnerable to recessive tendencies.

LIMITATIONS OF DATA

Before appraising the consumption developments a word of caution must be introduced concerning inferences drawn from the available economic series. In the first place, statistical data in themselves prove nothing about causation. The most that can be said is that the data are consistent or inconsistent with a particular hypothesis.[4] In the second place, many of the series display serious inconsistencies within themselves and may render any generalizations drawn from them quite untrustworthy.[5] The weaknesses of many of the series will be evident in the following pages. Yet the series require exhaustive analysis to illuminate these weaknesses and to challenge some of the established generalizations drawn from these data or from even more inferior data.

In the third place, the available economic series permit only the most cautious and guarded conclusions about percentage changes in the several variables. The lack of comparability of the basic statistics limits their reliability. For example, the series on both adjusted income and consumption expenditures have broader coverage [6] than does the series on the production of consumers' goods, but neither is adequately deflated by any of the various price indexes. And the narrow coverage of the series on production of consumers' goods seriously impairs its usefulness. Moreover, as will be shown below, selection of a series based upon one set of data rather than another can affect any conclusions drawn. In addition it must be recognized that the monthly and quarterly data on consumption expenditures, and, for that matter, on personal income, are subject to sizable error, the exact magnitude of which is unknown. Therefore, any particular in-

---

4. An elementary proposition in statistics.
5. This seems to be particularly true of the data used in aggregative analysis.
6. Barger concludes that the accuracy of the adjusted income series exceeds that for the outlay series. For a definition of adjusted income see Fig. 1, p. 4.

come or expenditure figure may be considerably in error. But in spite of the weaknesses in the data they are the best yet compiled, and are superior to those which were available for analysis in the period immediately following the recession. These more extensive and better data require examination to see how consistent they appear to be with the underconsumption version of the recession.

THE RECESSION AS A CONSEQUENCE OF A FAILURE IN CONSUMPTION EXPENDITURES

The available data appear inconsistent with the belief that the recession was due to a failure of consumption expenditures. This appears so even though two major indices of consumer behavior, department store sales and consumer installment credit, indicate some slackening of consumer demand in the period immediately preceding the recession. The index of department store sales remained virtually constant from October 1936 through September 1937, and in the next section it is shown that the rate of expansion of consumer installment credit declined from the beginning of 1937.[7] But a broader measure of consumption, Barger's quarterly data on total consumption expenditures,[8] shows the greatest absolute and relative increase in consumption expenditures for the third quarter of 1937, even as income and production were beginning to decline. Also, according to monthly data of the Department of Commerce, consumption expenditures hit their peak in September 1937, the very month of the precipitate decline in income and production. In addition, as is indicated below, consumers' income was apparently not outdistanced by the production of consumers' goods during 1936–37, nor does it appear that consumption expenditures declined relative to consumer income (marginal propensity to consume). The consumption function (average propensity to consume) also appears to have been unchanged.

THE BEHAVIOR OF CONSUMER INSTALLMENT CREDIT

Haberler has concluded that consumer installment credit "while not negligible, was not a very important factor"[9] in the economic fluctuations from 1929 to 1940. This seems particularly true for the period 1936–37, if changes in consumer installment credit are compared with the fluctuation in other variables such as net government contribution, net change in business inventories, or producers' durable equipment expenditures.

7. Only a slight decline for the first eight months, however. See discussion below.
8. Barger, Table 11, 118.
9. Gottfried Haberler, *Consumer Installment Credit and Economic Fluctuations* (New York, 1942), 12.

Table 17 gives two different sets of comparisons for the change in consumer installment credit [10] in the years 1935, 1936, and 1937. Comparison 1 is for the average monthly change in the eight-month period, January through August of each year. In Comparison 2, the computations are for the nine months from December through August, the additional month being December which experienced a sizable increase each year because of the holiday spending. The average monthly increase in consumer installment credit was $17 million or 15% less in 1937 than in 1936, and was actually $12 million greater than in 1935. In some individual months of 1937 there were even

TABLE 17: ESTIMATED AVERAGE MONTHLY INCREASE IN CONSUMER DEBT, SELECTED PERIODS 1935–37

(In millions of dollars)

Comparison 1

January 1935 through August 1935	+85
January 1936 through August 1936	+114
January 1937 through August 1937	+97

Comparison 2

December 1934 through August 1935	+59
December 1935 through August 1936	+87
December 1936 through August 1937	+64

Source: Basic data from Holthausen, *op. cit.*

greater increases than in the corresponding months of 1936. When the comparison is made between December and August, the average monthly rate of increase in 1937 was $23 million less than in 1936, but $5 million greater than in 1935. In Table 18 the data on consumer installment credit have been converted to an index based on 1929 = 100. On this basis there was more than a 15% change in consumer credit from January to August 1936 compared with slightly over 10.5% from January 1937 to August 1937.

The relatively small declines in the rate of increase of consumer credit in the first eight months of 1937 seem to confirm Haberler's judgment of the unimportance of consumer installment credit. Nevertheless its expansion probably led to a somewhat more rapid advance in the production of durable consumer goods than would otherwise have been expected.[11] Also, because there was a decline in the rate of consumer credit increase in 1937, even though slight, Haberler's

10. In the main, consumer installment credit merely reflects purchases of consumer durables, but the credit data are available on a monthly basis, 1936–38.
11. Haberler, 13.

further conclusion seems justified: "the fact that the turning points in the curve of net credit change precede the turns in general business may perhaps indicate that installment credit helped to precipitate the downturns of the business cycle in 1929 and 1937 and to start the upturn in 1933; . . ." [12]

TABLE 18: INDEX OF TOTAL SHORT-TERM CONSUMER CREDIT, DECEMBER 1934 THROUGH DECEMBER 1937

(1929 = 100.0)

	1934	*1935*	*1936*	*1937*
January		61.0	76.3	94.1
February		60.6	76.0	93.4
March		62.3	78.1	95.7
April		64.8	80.9	97.9
May		66.2	84.2	100.6
June		68.1	86.0	102.7
July		68.8	87.1	103.1
August		70.0	88.3	104.3
September		71.4	90.3	105.7
October		72.9	92.2	106.3
November		74.5	93.1	105.9
December	62.8	77.8	96.6	106.6

Source: Basic data from Holthausen.

RELATIONSHIP OF PRODUCTION OF CONSUMER GOODS TO ADJUSTED INCOME

In Tables 19, 20, and 21, comparisons are made between the production of consumers' goods, adjusted income, consumption expenditures, and salary and wage income. (However no comparisons should be drawn between the salary and wage income and adjusted income data because of the dissimilar sources.) Table 19 compares changes in production of consumers' goods from the first to the fourth quarter of 1936 with the changes in deflated adjusted income and consumption expenditures for the same period. [13]

From the first to the fourth quarter of 1936 production of consumers' goods increased by 14.5% [14] and deflated adjusted income

12. *Ibid.*, 143.
13. The comparisons were also made with an index of salaries and wages selected to represent labor income. The results were unaffected by this substitution except for a shift in timing. An ideal measure of consumer income for use in testing the theory that prices and production of consumers' goods outran labor income would include salaries not exceeding a certain level (say $5,000), wages, and income of small proprietors.
14. Production of consumers' goods includes an upward adjustment of 1.5%,

by 9.7%. It would seem reasonable to assume that the somewhat greater increase in production of consumer goods was to permit a "normal" addition to inventories. Yet the lack of comparability between income and production series is so great that even such a de-

TABLE 19: CHANGES IN PRODUCTION OF CONSUMERS' GOODS, CONSUMPTION EXPENDITURES, ADJUSTED INCOME, AND SALARY AND WAGE INCOME, FIRST TO FOURTH QUARTER 1936

	1st Quarter	*4th Quarter*	*Per Cent Change*
Production of consumers' goods (100 estimated long-term trend) [a]	84	95	14.5
Consumption expenditures before price correction (in millions) [b]	14,901	16,430	10.3
Percentage change in consumption corrected for price change [c]			7.2
Adjusted income before price correction (in billions) [d]	15,264	17,246	12.9
Percentage change in adjusted income corrected for price change [c]			9.7
Salary and wage income before correction for price change (1935–39 = 100) [e]	93.8	103.1	9.9
Percentage change in salary and wage income corrected for price change [c]			6.8
Cost of living (1923 = 100) [f]	83.5	85.9	2.9

a. Federal Reserve Bank of New York. Production of consumers' goods includes an upward adjustment of 1.5%, since the Federal Reserve Bank of New York discounts a secular trend of slightly under 2% per year.

b. Barger.

c. Corrected for price change with National Industrial Conference Board cost-of-living index.

d. Barger.

e. Average of three months in each quarter. Based on Department of Commerce income data.

f. National Industrial Conference Board.

duction may be unwarranted. Nevertheless the difference between the increase in production and the increase in income does not appear to be large enough to give vigorous support to the argument that consumer income failed to keep up with the production of consumers' goods.[15]

since the Federal Reserve Bank of New York index discounts a secular trend of slightly under 2% per year.

15. Of course it does indicate that there was a relative increase in savings which had to be offset by investment.

Consumer income and consumers' goods production were even more closely related from the fourth quarter of 1936 through the second quarter of 1937. As shown in Table 20, production of consumers' goods and real consumer income declined by the same proportions, 2.2% for production, and 2.9% for adjusted income. But in the crucial period from the second to the third quarter of 1937 the differences between production and income change are so sizable that the results may have some significance even with imperfections in the

TABLE 20: PRODUCTION OF CONSUMERS' GOODS, CONSUMPTION EXPENDITURES, ADJUSTED INCOME, AND SALARY AND WAGE INCOME,[a] FOURTH QUARTER 1936 TO SECOND QUARTER 1937

	4th Quarter	2d Quarter	Per Cent Change
Production of consumers' goods (100 estimated long-term trend)	95	92	−2.2 [b]
Consumption expenditures before price correction (in millions)	16,430	16,124	−1.9
Percentage change in consumption corrected for price change			−5.0
Adjusted income before price correction (in billions)	17,246	17,327	0.5
Percentage change in adjusted income corrected for price change			−2.9
Salary and wage income before correction for price change (1935–39 = 100)	103.1	110.7	7.4
Percentage change in salary and wage income corrected for price change			4.0
Cost of living (1923 = 100)	85.9	88.7	3.3

a. For sources of data see Table 19.
b. Series adjusted as in Table 19.

data. Here, as may be seen in Table 21, the production of consumers' goods declined slightly (.6%) even as real income increased by 6.4%. Any inference drawn from the data for this important period would be directly opposed to the proposition that incomes were outdistanced by the production of consumers' goods.[16] In Figure 12, personal incomes and consumer expenditures computed from Department of Commerce data, and production of consumers' goods (data from Federal Reserve Bank of New York) are graphed by quarters for the

16. However, the stimulus to accumulate inventories may have disappeared with the decline in consumption expenditure from the fourth quarter of 1936 to the second quarter of 1937. In light of this it is possible that the production at an *unchanged* level was higher than desired.

period 1936–38. Upon the basis of these three tables and Figure 12, it seeems reasonable to conclude that the case for the failure of income to keep up with production of consumers' goods has yet to be established.

TABLE 21: PRODUCTION OF CONSUMERS' GOODS, CONSUMPTION EXPENDITURES, ADJUSTED INCOME, AND SALARY AND WAGE INCOME,[a] SECOND TO THIRD QUARTER 1937

	2d Quarter	3d Quarter	Per Cent Change
Production of consumers' goods (100 estimated long-term trend)	92	91	−0.6 [b]
Consumption expenditures before price correction (in millions)	16,124	17,264	7.1
Percentage change in consumption corrected for price change			6.5
Adjusted income before price correction (in billions)	17,327	18,528	6.9
Percentage change in adjusted income corrected for price change			6.4
Salary and wage income before correction for price change (1935–39 = 100)	110.7	110.1	−0.5
Percentage change in salary and wage income corrected for price change			−0.9
Cost of living (1923 = 100)	88.7	89.1	0.4

a. For sources of data see Table 19.
b. Series adjusted as in Table 19.

Slichter also has examined some of the data on income and consumers' goods production. He compared labor income (nonagricultural income adjusted for the bonus payment) with the Federal Reserve Bank of New York index of production of consumers' goods, inflated by the change in cost of living (index not identified). He concluded more positively that "the value of output of consumers' goods did not outrun consumer purchasing power. In so far as one tended to outrun the other, incomes tended to outstrip production." [17] In a footnote to this statement, he continued: "Only in the fourth quarter of 1936 did the production of consumers' goods outrun labor incomes by a noticeable amount. In the second quarter of both 1936 and 1937, labor incomes definitely outran the retail value of the output of consumers' goods."

17. Slichter, "The Downturn of 1937," 102.

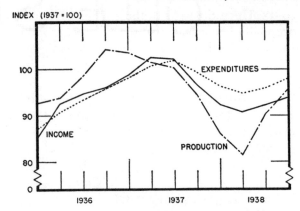

Fig. 12. Production of consumers' goods, consumers' incomes, and consumers' expenditures, by quarters, 1936–38. Production of consumers' goods from Federal Reserve Bank of New York, Research Department, "Production and Trade Indexes" (1944). Quarterly averages were computed from monthly data and the index was shifted from a base of 100 = long-term trend to 1937 = 100. Consumers' incomes from *Survey of Current Business, National Income Supplement, 1951*, 213. Consumers' expenditures computed from tables in William C. Shelton and Louis J. Paradiso, "Monthly Estimates of Total Consumer Expenditures, 1935–42," *Survey of Current Business* (October 1942), 8–14. Consumers' incomes and expenditures are seasonally adjusted.

THE POSITION OF THE CONSUMPTION FUNCTION— RELATIONSHIP OF CONSUMPTION EXPENDITURES TO ADJUSTED INCOME

The case for a shift in the consumption function is even less convincingly supported by the data. Upon referring to Table 19 again, it will be noted that income increased by 12.9% from the first to the fourth quarter of 1936, and consumption expenditures by 10.3%. The limits of accuracy of the data would seem to prohibit any significance being attached to a difference in percentage change of this magnitude. Likewise, the difference between the increase in income of .5% from the fourth quarter of 1936 to the second quarter of 1937 and the decrease in consumption expenditures of 1.9% is within the limits of accuracy of the data. (See Table 20 again.) Finally, in the vital period between the second and third quarters of 1937 income increased by 6.9% accompanied by a 7.1% increase in consumption expenditures (shown in Table 21, but not in Figure 12).[18]

18. The personal income and consumption expenditure statistics which are graphed in Figure 12 come from the Department of Commerce and differ from Barger's, which are used in Tables 19, 20, and 21 and are discussed in the text. However, the rise in consumption expenditure as personal incomes declined slightly from the

The importance of the decision as to which particular series should be analyzed is well illustrated if quarterly salary and wage income, instead of quarterly adjusted income,[19] are compared with quarterly consumption expenditures. From these data there is evidence that consumer expenditures fell off relative to consumer income from the fourth quarter of 1936 to the second quarter of 1937. Thus, although production of consumers' goods declined 2.2%, real consumer income increased by 4.0%, yet deflated consumption expenditures declined by 5.0%. (See Table 20.)

Slichter explains this phenomenon by suggesting that there was considerable resistance to increased prices of consumers' goods, even though such increases on the average were very small (the cost-of-living index increased by only 3.3%). There may have been prices on individual commodities which showed substantially greater increases, so that some changes in individual propensities to consume may very well have resulted. But it may be questioned whether the moderate over-all increases in prices could account for a general lag in consumption expenditures. The data in this period, therefore, seem to be consistent with an underconsumptionist, oversaving explanation for the recession. But if salary and wage income change are also compared with the change in consumer expenditures from the second to the third quarter of 1937, the data are consistent with just the opposite conclusion. The production of consumers' goods was only slightly reduced (.6%), as was real income (.9%), and deflated consumption expenditures rose sharply (6.5%). These data seem to indicate that the recession was immediately preceded by an increase in the propensity to consume and a decline in savings.

One possible interpretation of the underconsumptionist position is that the turning point in economic activity occurs because the curve describing the consumption function shifts downward. This initiates a sequence of events which reduces income and the level of voluntary saving. The problem of verifying this theory in the period 1937–38, or for that matter in any period, is that neither the exact shape nor position of the consumption function is known.[20] However, regardless of the assumption made about the form of the historical consumption function, it seems unreasonable to assume that there has been any downward shift or change in slope where consumption expenditures

---

second to the third quarter of 1937, which is shown in Figure 12, also supports the belief that consumption expenditures did not decline relative to personal incomes.

19. However, quarterly disposable income, if available, would appear to be the proper variable to relate to quarterly consumption expenditures.

20. This suggests a stability in the consumption function which may not be at all consistent with reality. See discussion in the symposium on the consumption function, *Review of Economics and Statistics, 28* (1946), 197–224.

increase almost as much as income. This should be particularly true for a short period such as is under consideration in this chapter.

CHANGES IN THE MARGINAL PROPENSITY TO CONSUME

A further test of the relationship between consumer expenditures and incomes during the period 1935–38 was made by calculating marginal propensities to consume for various time units. Table 22 shows the results obtained from the Barger quarterly data.[21] The effects of the bonus payment on the relationship between consumption and income are clearly seen in that the marginal propensity to consume was at its lowest in the second quarter of 1936, which included the June bonus payment. The significant marginal propensities to consume for analysis of the recession are those of the fourth quarter

TABLE 22: MARGINAL PROPENSITIES TO CONSUME, BY QUARTERS, 1935–38

Year	Quarter	Consumption	Change in Consumption	Income	Change in Income	Marginal Propensity to Consume [a]
			(In millions of dollars)			
1935	1	13,667		13,639		
	2	13,831	164	13,909	270	.61
	3	14,008	177	14,126	217	.82
	4	14,414	406	15,190	1,064	.38
1936	1	14,901	487	15,264	74	6.6
	2	15,378	477	17,762	2,498	.19
	3	15,834	456	16,572	−1,190	b
	4	16,430	596	17,246	674	.88
1937	1	15,952	−478	16,705	−541	.88
	2	16,124	172	17,327	622	.28
	3	17,264	1,140	18,528	1,201	.95
	4	17,067	−197	17,472	−1,056	.19
1938	1	14,998	−2,069	15,832	−1,640	1.3
	2	14,749	−249	15,780	−52	4.8
	3	15,517	1,038	16,359	579	1.8
	4	16,728	1,211	17,420	1,061	1.1

a. Ratio accurate to only two figures.
b. Ratio negative.

Source: Basic data from Barger. Data are seasonally adjusted.

21. The quarterly data show greater changes in both income and consumption than the monthly figures, and thus tend to be more accurate. The annual figures, although more accurate, are not examined because they are correspondingly less meaningful in a study of the turning point in a fluctuation.

of 1936 and the first three quarters of 1937. Quarter to quarter comparisons reveal no change in the rate of consumption relative to income in the first quarter of 1937, a decline in the second quarter, and then an increase to almost unity in the important third quarter. From these data it seems unlikely that a decline in consumption spending initiated the recession.

Additional data from the Department of Commerce permit several other comparisons between consumption and income. Estimates have been obtained of consumption expenditures by months and quarters, seasonally adjusted. Marginal propensities to consume by monthly, quarterly, and six-month periods have then been computed using Department of Commerce personal income data and these consumption expenditures. The results are summarized in Tables 23, 24, and 25. The monthly marginal propensities to consume (Table 23) un-

TABLE 23: MARGINAL PROPENSITIES TO CONSUME, BY MONTHS, 1935-38

Year	Month	Consumption	Change in Consumption	Personal Income	Change in Income	Marginal Propensity to Consume [a]
		(In millions of dollars)		(In billions of dollars)		
1935	Jan.	3,966.7		4.62		
	Feb.	4,090.1	123.4	4.78	.12	1.
	March	4,090.1	No change	4.83	.05	0.
	April	4,080.6	−9.5	4.96	.13	b
	May	4,047.4	−33.2	4.97	.01	b
	June	4,170.8	123.4	4.97	No change	
	July	4,128.1	−42.7	4.99	.02	b
	August	4,189.7	61.6	5.07	.08	.8
	Sept.	4,218.2	28.5	5.11	.04	.7
	Oct.	4,223.0	4.8	5.12	.01	.5
	Nov.	4,294.1	71.1	5.16	.04	2.
	Dec.	4,298.9	4.8	5.22	.06	.1
1936	Jan.	4,346.3	47.4	5.24	.02	2.
	Feb.	4,360.6	14.3	5.28	.04	.4
	March	4,436.5	75.9	5.31	.03	3.
	April	4,488.7	52.2	5.37	.06	.9
	May	4,569.3	80.6	5.45	.08	1.
	June	4,635.8	66.5	6.34	.89	.1
	July	4,683.2	47.4	6.04	−.30	b
	Aug.	4,702.2	19.0	5.76	−.28	b
	Sept.	4,697.4	−4.8	5.74	−.02	.2
	Oct.	4,782.9	85.5	5.80	.06	1.

TABLE 23: MARGINAL PROPENSITIES TO CONSUME,
BY MONTHS, 1935–38 *(continued)*

Year	Month	Consumption	Change in Consumption	Personal Income	Change in Income	Marginal Propensity to Consume [a]
		(In millions of dollars)		(In billions of dollars)		
	Nov.	4,825.6	42.7	5.93	.13	.3
	Dec.	4,854.0	28.4	6.04	.11	.3
1937	Jan.	4,839.8	−14.2	5.98	−.06	.2
	Feb.	4,911.0	71.2	6.09	.11	.6
	March	5,005.9	94.9	6.21	.12	.8
	April	5.039.1	33.2	6.28	.07	.5
	May	5.091.3	52.2	6.32	.04	1.
	June	5,058.1	−33.2	6.38	.06	b
	July	5,105.5	47.4	6.32	−.06	b
	Aug.	5,119.7	14.2	6.36	.04	.4
	Sept.	5,129.2	9.5	6.22	−.14	b
	Oct.	5,119.7	−9.5	6.12	−.10	.1
	Nov.	4,963.2	−156.5	5.98	−.14	1.
	Dec.	4,877.8	−85.4	5.79	−.19	.4
1938	Jan.	4.896.7	18.9	5.71	−.08	b
	Feb.	4,820.8	−75.9	5.70	−.01	8.
	March	4,787.6	−33.2	5.68	−.02	2.
	April	4,797.1	9.5	5.61	−.07	b
	May	4,735.4	−61.7	5.58	−.03	2.
	June	4,749.6	14.2	5.60	.02	.7
	July	4,816.1	66.5	5.62	.02	3.
	Aug.	4,797.1	−19.0	5.71	.09	b
	Sept.	4,830.3	33.2	5.73	.02	2.
	Oct.	4,863.5	33.2	5.73	No change	
	Nov.	4,930.0	66.5	5.79	.06	1.
	Dec.	4,972.6	42.6	5.82	.03	1.

a. Ratio accurate to only 1 figure.
b. Ratio negative.

Source: Income data from U. S. Department of Commerce, *Survey of Current Business, National Income Supplement, 1951*, 212–213, Table 48. Consumption data computed from Shelton and Paradiso. All data are seasonally adjusted.

doubtedly are the least reliable of the calculations because they are computed on the basis of small changes in both consumption and income. Nevertheless they provide no evidence that consumption was lagging relative to income. Whereas the marginal propensity to consume in the months from November 1936 through January 1937

never exceeded .3, from February through May of 1937 it was above
.6 (with the single exception of .5 in April) and reached a peak of
1 in May. It should be recalled that Henderson's observations about
the relative failure of purchasing power were dated in this period. In
the month of June consumption declined as income rose, and in August the marginal propensity to consume was only .4. In the other
summer months of July and September, however, income declined

TABLE 24: MARGINAL PROPENSITIES TO CONSUME—
A SECOND COMPARISON—BY QUARTERS, 1935-38

Year	Quarter	Consumption	Change in Consumption	Income	Change in Income	Marginal Propensity to Consume [a]
		(In millions of dollars)		(In billions of dollars)		
1935	1	12,142		14.23		
	2	12,299	157	14.91	680	.23
	3	12,541	242	15.17	260	.93
	4	12,811	270	15.50	330	.82
1936	1	13,135	328	15.82	320	1.0
	2	13,694	555	17.16	1,340	.41
	3	14,078	384	17.54	380	1.0
	4	14,463	385	17.78	240	1.6
1937	1	14,762	299	18.28	500	.60
	2	15,188	426	18.98	700	.61
	3	15,359	171	18.91	−70	b
	4	14,961	-398	17.88	−1,030	.39
1938	1	14,505	−456	17.10	−780	.58
	2	14,278	−227	16.79	−310	.73
	3	14,448	170	17.06	270	.63
	4	14,762	314	17.35	290	1.1

a. Ratio accurate to only two figures.
b. Ratio negative.

Source: Income data from U. S. Department of Commerce, *Survey of Current Business, National Income Supplement, 1951*, 212–213, Table 48. Consumption data computed from Shelton and Paradiso. All data are seasonally adjusted.

but consumption rose. Thus these data, too, revealed no such outstanding change in the relationship between consumption and income
as has been suggested by proponents of the underconsumption hypothesis.

The quarterly marginal propensities to consume (see Table 24), computed from the Department of Commerce data, appear to lend the most support to the underconsumption argument. Thus the marginal propensity to consume exceeded 1 in all but the second quarter of 1936 (which reflects the bonus payment)', but fell to .6 in both the first and second quarters of 1937. In the crucial third quarter, however, consumption increased by 171 million but income fell by 70 million, so even these calculations fail to establish any relative decline in consumption in the period immediately preceding the recession.

TABLE 25: MARGINAL PROPENSITIES TO CONSUME, BY SIX-MONTH PERIODS, 1935–38

Year	6-Month Period	Consumption	Change in Consumption	Income	Change in Income	Marginal Propensity to Consume [a]
			(In millions of dollars)			
1935	1	24,441		29,140		
	2	25,352	911	30,670	1,530	.60
1936	1	26,833	1,481	32,980	2,310	.64
	2	28,541	1,708	35,320	2,340	.73
1937	1	29,950	1,409	37,260	1,940	.73
	2	30,320	370	36,790	−470	[b]
1938	1	28,783	−1,537	33,890	−2,900	.53
	2	29,210	427	34,410	520	.81

a. Ratio accurate to only two figures.
b. Ratio negative.

Source: Income data from U. S. Department of Commerce, *Survey of Current Business, National Income Supplement, 1951*, 212–213, Table 48. Consumption data computed from Shelton and Paradiso. All data are seasonally adjusted.

The higher marginal propensities to consume in the third and fourth quarters of 1936 require explanation. Apparently they occurred because income changes in the second and third quarters were dominated by the bonus payment of both June and July 1936. Consumption expenditures accelerated after a lag, following receipt of the bonus payments. From Table 23 it can be observed that the effects of the bonus payments on the marginal propensity to consume appear to have been worked out by October 1936, but the fourth quarter marginal propensity to consume is still markedly affected by the payments.[22]

22. This remains so because income in the fourth quarter is compared with an income figure for the third quarter which was swollen by the bonus payment.

The final calculations relate consumption to income by six-month periods beginning in 1935 (Table 25). Over these time units the marginal propensity to consume apparently increased from 60 to almost 73% in both the second half of 1936 and the first half of 1937. In the second half of 1937 consumption increased slightly even as income declined sharply.

These calculations provide little basis for contending that a failure in consumption led directly to the recession. Only the quarterly marginal propensities to consume show consumption lagging, and even here it accelerated immediately prior to the recession.

The comparisons which have been made between consumption expenditures and adjusted income, personal income, or salary or wage income lead to the cautious conclusion that the data seem inconsistent with the hypothesis that the recession was preceded by a shift downward in the consumption function, or a decline in the marginal propensity to consume.[23] It is not possible, of course, to disprove the underconsumption theory by the data, but the slight changes in the relationship of consumption and income lend little support to an oversavings theory of the recession.[24]

WAS THE RECOVERY OF 1933–37 CONSUMPTION INSPIRED?

A more general question is whether the recovery of 1933–37 was consumption inspired. If investment expenditures were short-termed, dependent upon consumption expenditures, an explanation for the appearance of the recession phase, if not the immediate turning point, may lie in the area of consumption decisions. Hansen has been the principal spokesman for this view although it has also been accepted by a number of other economists, including Villard,[25] Bratt,[26] and Fine.[27] Hansen stated his position as follows:

The recovery was based on an expanding consumer demand fed by (a) a five-billion-dollar expansion in consumer installment credit supporting purchases of automobiles and other durable consumers' goods, and (b) by

23. Of course there may still have been causal effects from the various changes in consumer expenditures and in the production of consumers' goods because of the movements of inventories. For a discussion of the latter see Chapter 12 below.

24. It is suggested below (Chapter 13) that corporate profits were actually among the first series to show a decline, which also seems inconsistent with an oversavings theory of recessions. Professor Abramovitz has suggested to the author that, even so, developments in the consumption area may still have been partly responsible for the recession. The measures which sustained or raised consumption to higher levels may have been at the expense of investment. For a consideration of the problem of wages and profits see Chapters 8 and 13.

25. Villard, *op. cit.,* 339–340.

26. Bratt, *op. cit.,* 170.

27. Fine, *op. cit.,* 107–114.

fourteen billion dollars of federal expenditures on recovery and relief. The recovery vanished when these two stimuli played out.[28]

The recovery experienced in the United States 1935–37 can be characterized as a consumption recovery. By that I mean that the expansion in income, employment and output was based mainly on a rise in consumption. There had occurred to be sure, a very considerable increase in real investment, but investment for the most part followed consumption; it did not, except in limited degree, lead the way.[29]

For our purposes it is not necessary to fill in the entire picture detailing the recovery movement. It is sufficient to press home the point that the recovery was peculiarly one based on a rise in consumption . . . . new investment in plant and equipment was geared rigorously and narrowly, in a quite unusual degree, to the immediate requirements of consumption. Business men avoided as much as possible long-term capital commitments.[30]

The heart of Hansen's thesis is that

a recovery resting almost exclusively on a rising tide of consumption can go forward only so long as the consumption stimulus is applied . . . . as soon as consumption flattens out there is no need for any new investment in plant and equipment. . . . This is the dilemma which confronts a recovery reared on the stimulus to consumption. Such a recovery can proceed no further than it is pushed. It has no momentum of its own. It has no inner power to complete its own development.[31]

It may be conceded that most investment expenditures in the period were based upon short-term commitments. But there remain serious objections to the belief that investment expenditures were short-term because they were induced by consumption expenditures. Fellner has challenged this view primarily on the ground that the statistical data do not support the hypothesis that consumption expenditures led investment expenditures either in the recovery or in the decline. Thus he states: "Factual observation does not suggest any simple relationship between the aggregate flow of investment, on the one hand, and either the marginal propensity to consume or the time rate of increase in aggregate consumption, on the other." [32] Fellner has examined many of the empirical data relating to consumption and investment expenditures in the interwar period and has presented a strong case against this consumption thesis.

He observed that consumption increased at decreasing rates in the 1920's, but net capital formation was "well maintained," experiencing

28. Hansen, *Full Recovery or Stagnation?* 274.
29. *Ibid.*, 276.
30. *Ibid.*, 278.
31. *Ibid.*, 280–282.
32. William J. Fellner, *Monetary Policies and Full Employment* (Berkeley, 1946), 32.

a "slight upward tendency." Although the trend of the rate of increase of consumption appeared linear in the thirties, its rate of increase immediately prior to the downturn of 1937 was greater than in the early stages of the recovery.[33] At first net private capital formation rose at an increasing rate. Later it continued to rise but at a decreasing rate. From these developments Fellner concluded that there appears to be no "simple relationship between the aggregate amount of private investment and the time rate of increase in consumption." [34] He rejected the thesis that investment was "geared to consumption" in the thirties: "Not much meaning can, in these circumstances, be attached to the opinion frequently voiced that in the 1930's, as opposed to the 1920's, investment was 'geared to consumption'." [35] On the contrary, consumption led investment in the upturns following the minor recessions in 1924 and 1927, while all the downturns of the twenties appeared to have been investment led. Consumers' outlay and investment turned together in the upturn of 1921, the 1937 downturn, and the 1938 upturn.

On the basis of his analysis, Fellner rejected simple underconsumption hypotheses:

In conclusion it may be stated that the available factual material does not lend itself to the verification of simple underconsumptionist hypotheses concerning the relationship between consumption and investment. No simple relationship is found between the time rate of change in consumption on the one hand, and the absolute amount of investment, on the other. This does not contradict the Acceleration Principle because "direct demand" and "derived demand" are not coextensive with consumer demand and investment demand, respectively. But the lack of relationship in question contradicts one simple underconsumptionist hypothesis, and another is contradicted by the fact that the marginal propensity to consume does not seem to govern the flow of investment or its turning points.[36]

Fellner's conclusion must be qualified because of the difficulty in dating precisely the turning point in consumption expenditures. Thus the important consumption decisions may have occurred in some areas of the economy a quarter or so before the actual decline in consumption expenditures. But subsequent to these decisions, unintended consumption (consumption which would not occur if expenditures could be adjusted immediately to income) [37] may take place so that an in-

33. It may be questioned whether the crucial relationship between consumption and income was immediately prior to the turning point.
34. Fellner, 34.
35. *Ibid.*, 35.
36. *Ibid.*, 42.
37. The lag between changes in income and consumption may not be sizable, however. Cf. Metzler, "Three Lags in the Circular Flow of Income," 21–22.

crease in consumption may accompany a declining income. Likewise there may be unintended accumulation in inventories even with an expanding consumption.[38]

Hansen's thesis has also been challenged by Samuelson,[39] who argues that there is no significant difference between a recovery stimulated by government deficit spending and one initiated by a burst of private investment expenditures. He criticizes the theory that the 1935–37 recovery was "consumption inspired" on three grounds. First he questions "the significance of the distinction between this 'consumption' recovery and other types."[40] In his opinion the distinction is a doubtful one if based upon the relatively heavier investment in durable consumer goods than in producer plant or residential housing, for the former "partake of the nature of investment goods in general." In general the likenesses rather than differences between consumer durable investment and other types of investment should be stressed. In the second place, consumption spending would respond to either government or private spending: "It is true that government deficit spending stimulated consumption, but by the Multiplier so would have an initiating burst of private investment. Only by not looking upon deficit spending as investment and by skipping to the following time period can the recovery be made to seem a consumption one."[41] Finally, the operation of the acceleration principle provides no basis for distinguishing between this and other recoveries; "a burst of private investment in one isolated section of the economy should induce private investment elsewhere according to the familiar acceleration principle."

In the light of these considerations, Samuelson sees no grounds for differentiating the 1935–37 recovery from other recoveries: "There is a point for point correspondence and isomorphism, therefore, between recoveries initiated by private and governmental investment."

These arguments raise serious doubts that the recovery of 1935–37 may be characterized as consumption inspired. This thesis was advanced to account for the facts that long-term private investment

38. Professor Abramovitz has also expressed the belief to the author that the sharp rise in prices and inventories in 1936 may have left the economy peculiarly sensitive to any weakening in consumer demand. For a discussion of the unplanned nature of inventory accumulation in the recession see Chapter 12 of this study.

39. Paul A. Samuelson, "The Theory of Pump-Priming Reëxamined," *American Economic Review*, 30 (1940), 492–506.

40. *Ibid.* This and the following quotations from 505–506.

41. In the time period following the initial investment, the recovery would seem to be a consumption one, whether initiated by the government or private economy.

failed to revive and that investment expenditures were based upon short-term commitments. It cannot be denied, of course, that much of private investment in producer durable equipment was motivated by short-term commitments. But the hypothesis that the response to recoveries initiated by government spending differs significantly from that attending those initiated by private spending seems untenable. It would appear that the differences between this recovery and, say, the recovery in the twenties, were not pronounced enough to mark the former as "consumption inspired" and the latter as "investment inspired." Instead it may be suggested that the explanation for investment expenditures which were the product of short-term rather than long-term commitments lies in the factors affecting investment decision rather than in the peculiar nature of consumption expenditures.[42] Or, in more general terms: "the downturn in the demand for capital goods is best explained as the result of common causes which affected both consumers' goods and capital goods rather than as a consequence of the drop in the demand for consumers' goods." [43]

Summary of the Relationship of Consumption Factors to the Recession

The problem of this chapter has been to assess the relative importance of consumption factors in the recession. It has been shown that the single development among the consumption factors which may have directly affected the recession was the decline in the rate of increase in consumer installment credit. Even this decline was of slight quantitative importance. The hypotheses that consumers' goods production outstripped consumer income, and that the consumption function shifted or that the marginal propensity to consume declined significantly, appeared to be inconsistent with the data. Finally, the contention that the relative failure of long-term investment commitments and vulnerability of the economy to recession were due to the consumption nature of the recovery has been examined and seems questionable. It is not denied, however, that a substantial shift upward in the consumption function could have assisted in preventing recessive tendencies from developing. Both the acceleration principle and the multiplier would have operated toward that end. The former would have led to an increase in induced investment; the latter would have made what autonomous investment there was more effective in raising income. But from examination of the data on consumption

42. These factors are discussed in Chapters 12, 13, and 14.
43. Slichter, "The Downturn of 1937," 101.

it would appear that the explanation for the recession does not lie in underconsumption hypotheses. The principal causal explanation must be sought elsewhere, perhaps in the factors underlying private investment decision or in the cessation of net government contribution to income.

CHAPTER 11

The Pattern of Investment
Expenditures, 1935–37

IN CHAPTER 2 it was shown that the failure of investment expenditures was widely emphasized as a causal factor in the recession of 1937–38. Several explanations have been given for the weak recovery of investment expenditures. One is that they were based largely upon short-term considerations and were more for replacement than for expansion purposes. Another blames repressive government taxes and other policies. And still another holds that the economy suffered from a condition of secular stagnation.

These factors and any others which might have limited investment expenditures deserve critical examination for their causal significance in the recession. The purpose of this chapter is to provide a background for such analysis by reviewing the changes which occurred in the various components of investment expenditures as well as in the aggregate expenditures.

STATISTICAL EVIDENCE OF THE FAILURE OF INVESTMENT EXPENDITURES

In view of the poor showing by certain of the components, it is surprising that total *gross* private investment recovered to a rate of $4,246 million in the third quarter of 1937, a rate exceeded only by the third quarter of 1923, the first quarter of 1926, and the fourth quarter of 1928. Similarly, net private investment at its peak of $2,109 million in the third quarter of 1937 was exceeded only by the third quarter of 1923 and the first quarter of 1926.[1]

NET CHANGE IN BUSINESS INVENTORIES

However, this recovery of total gross and net private investment was more apparent than real. Investment in business inventories is the key to the surprising performance of investment expenditures in 1937. *Gross* private investment, without inventory change (producers

1. Barger, 114–119. All the quarterly data in this chapter are from this source.

durable equipment, residential and plant construction, and net change in foreign balance), at its peak of $2,759 million in the second quarter of 1937 was 30% less than the peak rate in the twenties of $3,913 million (exclusive of change in inventories) in the fourth quarter of 1928. Again, with inventories excluded, gross private investment was 25% less than the average quarterly rate in 1929 of $3,667 million.

The change in business inventories was even more important in swelling the total of *net* private investment. Exclusive of the change in inventories, net private investment amounted to only $830 million in the second quarter of 1937, or almost 45% less than the peak rate in the twenties of $1,496 million (the fourth quarter of 1928). Net private investment, less inventories, at its peak rate in 1937 was 30% less than the quarterly average of $1,185 million in 1929.

Professor Kuznets recognized the contribution which business inventories made to the total flow of investment expenditures:

Total capital formation for business use, including net flow to inventories, also shows but moderate shortages in 1937, or 1936–37, . . . and in the per capita figures alone do the shortages become significant. But when the flow to inventories is excluded, the conclusion is modified. In the total of producers' durable commodities and business construction the recovery fell appreciably short of pre-depression levels even when not reduced to per capita figures. A similar shortage is still more marked for total private durable investment: the gross totals indicate a shortage of 18 to 25 per cent of pre-depression levels; net totals indicate a somewhat smaller absolute shortage but one that amounts to between 37 and 56 per cent of pre-depression net levels.[2]

In analysis of the components of capital investment, Kuznets again stressed the extent to which business inventories accounted for the recovery in investment expenditures:

One component, net flow of inventories, shows uniformly a much higher level at the end of the recent expansion than the pre-depression level, whether total or per capita. It is this great weight of an increased flow to inventories that serves equally to account for the relatively favorable showing of capital formation and of the first total of capital formation for business use . . .

The differences between inventories as planned or unplanned investment are pointed out in the next chapter. Undoubtedly a large proportion of inventory change in 1937 was unplanned so that the high levels of gross and net private investment were not reliable evidence that capital formation had recovered to the levels of the 1920's.

2. Kuznets, Bulletin No. 74. The three quotations from Kuznets are all from p. 10.

Although the total gross and net investment expenditures, aided by inventory investment, made a good showing, certain kinds of planned investment made a very dismal showing.

RESIDENTIAL AND PLANT CONSTRUCTION

An examination of the performance of the other components of investment expenditures confirms the spotty character of the recovery. If inventory investment contributed most to the recovery of total investment expenditures, it is apparent that residential and plant construction contributed the least:

The most striking failure of recovery is in residential and business construction: total gross value at the end of the recent expansion was still from one-third to one-half short of pre-depression levels. And the net value of residential construction was still negative at the culmination of the recent expansion, as compared with positive values in or before 1929. It is these components that tend to bring down the totals of business or private durable capital formation and account for the unfavorable showing of the recent expansion treated as a recovery to pre-depression levels.

It is quite evident that residential and plant construction, among the components of investment, never fully recovered in the 1930's. Gross private construction expenditures (which includes both residential and plant construction), at their peak of $878 million in the second quarter of 1937, were only roughly one-third of the peak quarterly rate reached in the 1920's.

PRODUCERS' DURABLE EQUIPMENT

The behavior of expenditures on producers' durable equipment throws additional light on the nature of the recovery. A vigorous expansion occurred in these expenditures so that they had recovered to the 1929 level by the fourth quarter of 1936. In the second quarter of 1937 they were almost 20% above the peak in 1929, and for all of 1937 they were 14% greater than in 1929.[3] Kuznets described this sharp recovery as "unusual," and states that, along with the increase in inventories, it "sheds light on the nature of the recent expansion . . ."[4] An investigation of the factors which led to investment in equipment but not in houses and business buildings might well reveal some of the significant causal relationships in the recession.[5]

3. However, in the Department of Commerce data, producer durable equipment expenditures in 1937 were still 15.5% under those in 1929. *Survey of Current Business, National Income Supplement, 1951,* 150.
4. Kuznets, Bulletin No. 74, 10.
5. Cf. Villard, 337–338.

NEW CORPORATE SECURITY ISSUES

The stagnation in the new corporate securities market provided further evidence of the lack of vitality in investment expenditures. The very weak position of new corporate capital issues is revealed in the fact that total new corporate capital issues in 1937 were only 20% of their average from 1927 through 1929. Chapter 13 will consider whether the low level of new corporate issues resulted from an actual shortage of capital or merely reflected a change in the relative contribution of the different sources of funds.

CHAPTER 12

The Role of Inventories in the Recession and Revival

MAGNITUDE OF BUSINESS INVENTORIES

THE IMPORTANCE of inventory accumulation in the recession and revival must now be appraised. As was noted in Chapter 11, among the capital formation components of national income only producer durable equipment expenditures and change in business inventories recovered by 1937 to levels above those of the 1920's. In the fourth quarter of 1936, business inventories increased $937 million, a greater increase than in any quarter of the boom years 1924–29. In the first two quarters of 1937, they rose $306 million and $787 million, respectively. These increases do not seem particularly unreasonable, since the Federal Reserve Board index of industrial production did not reach its peak until May 1937.

However, the same cannot be said of the huge expansion in the third quarter of 1937. This expansion of $1,487 million dwarfed changes in business inventories in any quarter of the 1920's except those of the first quarter of 1921 ($1,548 million) and the third quarter of 1923 ($1,113 million). It should be observed that the substantial accumulation of inventories in the second and third quarters of 1937 comprised almost half of net private investment in the second quarter and over two-thirds in the third quarter.

Because of these data there is little reason to doubt that sizable increases in inventory did occur during the first three quarters of 1937. Nevertheless it should be pointed out that a statistical paradox arises when these data are combined with consumption expenditures, private investment, and industrial production. The increase in inventories in the third quarter of 1937 occurred when industrial production was stable and consumption expenditures had their largest quarterly increase, from $16,124 million to $17,264 million. At the same time net private investment, exclusive of inventory change, declined by only $208 million and public outlay by $914 million. This was a total decline of $1,122 million, or $700 million less than the change in the rate of increase in inventories and in consumption expenditures.[1] The explanation for the inconsistency may be a lack of comparability between the series on industrial production, consumption expenditures, and inventories. Or, quite possibly, the series on inventories is in error because of the great difficulties encountered in determining inventory change. These include the accounting problem of measuring year-end inventories, and the selection of one index to deflate year-end prices and another to obtain inventory change in average prices. Barger emphasized the limitations of this series: "That a considerable margin of uncertainty surrounds inventory calculations, particularly in years of rapid price change, and of rapid inventory accumulation or decumulation, is suggested by the wide variation in results which can be obtained from the use of slightly differing assumptions, and especially by the difficulty of reconciling physical data for commodity stocks with estimates of inventories in 1929 prices derived from accounting measures."[2] Again, when describing the procedure used to obtain quarterly changes in inventories in manufacturing, he said: "The results are not altogether plausible. For example, the series which emerges . . . shows considerable decumulation in the second and third quarter of 1933, at a time when the value of inventories was admittedly rising, and during a period which is usually associated with inventory accumulation rather than the reverse. Similarly the very large increase in inventories in the third quarter of 1937 is difficult to credit."[3] Moreover, his estimates were confined to manufacturing and distribution which in the past have accounted for but 50% of all inventories. With such a wide margin of error in data, it would seem that personal judgment must play an important part in assessment of the position of inventories in the recession.

Other data, however, tend to confirm the direction of change shown in Barger's figures. Elliott found that for his sample of 50 concerns [4] there were large increases in both inventories and production in the latter part of 1936. But inventories, increasing at a phenomenal

---

1. With production constant, the increase in consumption expenditures would reduce the increase in inventories. Therefore, inventories could have increased sharply in the third quarter of 1937 only if there had been a reduction in other investment expenditures and in public outlays to the extent of the change in inventories and in consumption expenditures. The increase in consumption expenditures and in inventories was $1,840 million ($1,140 million plus $700 million), whereas the decrease in investment expenditures and public outlays was only $1,122 million, leaving a $700 million discrepancy.

2. Barger, *op. cit.*, 100–101.

3. *Ibid.*, 312.

4. Selected because they published quarterly reports.

rate in the first nine months of 1937, were 26% higher than at the end of 1929 and 45% higher than on September 30, 1936. Part of the increase was due to higher material and labor costs, but a large part was a physical increase. General Motors estimated that only $32 million of the $53.5 million increase in its inventories in 1937 was caused by the higher cost of materials and labor. For whatever reason, inventories reached a new peak at the end of the third quarter just when the curve of business activity commenced its rapid decline. The 50 concerns, alarmed by heavy inventory positions, restricted their purchases and contributed to almost complete collapse in steel activity: "the rise in manufacturers' inventories was only one of many developments affecting the trend of business during 1937; but it seems reasonably clear that the rapidity of this rise in the first nine months of 1937 was a factor in the rapidity of the business decline in the fourth quarter." [5]

Inventories—Planned or Unplanned Investment?

Before considering to what extent these inventories were excessive or causal, the nature of inventories as business investment must be explored. The function of inventory accumulation during the several phases of business fluctuations varies. The type of planned accumulation which occurs during periods of revival and recovery is similar to other forms of planned investment expenditures. Inventory accumulation which occurs as the result of business collapse is involuntary; it plays a different role and requires special attention. At present there is no means of determining what proportion of the inventory accumulation of the second half of 1937 was planned; it is likely, though, that a large part was unplanned.[6]

In his attempt to show that the recovery of the 1930's was consumption inspired Hansen noted the peculiar nature of inventories as investment. If change in inventories is added to other planned investment, the change in consumption in the 1930's was at a considerably slower rate than in the 1920's.[7] Mack's study also revealed that the nature of inventory accumulation in 1937 differed from that of earlier years: "In 1937 the increase in inventories was accelerated. Certainly a very considerable proportion of the increase was involuntary, unlike the rise of previous years, and was the result of unsold

5. D. C. Elliott, "A Quarterly Series of Manufacturers' Inventories," *Journal of the American Statistical Association, 33* (1938), 352.

6. The speculative inventory accumulations in the early months of 1937 (when prices of raw materials and of some finished goods were still rising) were not involuntary, but these price rises ceased in March 1937.

7. Hansen, *Fiscal Policy and Business Cycles,* 64–65.

goods and retarded production." [8] A similar conclusion was reached by Simpson, who suggested further that the unintended investment in inventories resulting from business collapse should not be considered a part of investment.[9]

It may be contended, therefore, that inventory accumulation is rightfully regarded as planned investment only when the expectations of businessmen as to sustained or rising levels of income and expenditures are fulfilled. Where these expectations are not realized, inventories must be treated separately.

THE RELATIONSHIP OF INVENTORIES TO PRODUCTION, NATIONAL INCOME, AND ORDERS

The changes in inventories, whether planned or unplanned, might appear to be excessive relative to changes in industrial production, national income, or new orders. It would be logical also to compare inventories with sales or consumption expenditures. In Chapter 10 the writer has concluded that no significant change occurred in consumption expenditures relative to adjusted income. Therefore, adjusted income is assumed to be representative of both sales and consumption expenditures.

INVENTORIES NOT EXCESSIVE RELATIVE TO NEW PRODUCTION OR INCOME

Slichter concluded that the change in inventories was not dangerously out of proportion to the change in industrial production. He estimated that in September 1937 inventories were about one-third and production 10% above December 1935.[10] Later data indicate that inventories were more nearly two-fifths above December 1935, but production was increased by approximately 16%, so his comparison remains valid.

Using a comparison of inventory level and net national product, Metzler draws much the same conclusion as did Slichter. In Metzler's opinion, even at the height of the boom inventories were not abnormally large in relation to net national product: "Thus the reduction of stocks which accompanied the collapse of 1937 was probably more a result of fear of inventory losses than of a feeling that inventories were excessive. The painful experience of the early 'thirties was still vividly in the minds of most business men, and the inconvenience of

8. Mack, *op. cit.*, 189.

9. Kemper Simpson, "Securities Markets and the Investment Process," *Papers and Proceedings, American Economic Review, 28* (1938), 41.

10. Slichter, "The Downturn of 1937," 100.

a small volume of stocks was considered preferable to the prospects of inventory losses in a period of declining prices." [11]

It should be observed that neither Slichter nor Metzler developed any tests to determine how great a divergence may occur before the change in inventories is considered "excessive" relative to the change in production. Since adequate data are not available to establish this relationship, their conclusions must be given only the weight normally accorded to the judgments of careful analysts.

A suggestion that the accumulation of inventories was excessive [12] is found in a Brookings Institution study which shows that the rise in inventories in 1937 was considerably greater than the increase in total assets: "At the end of 1937 the amount of inventories was 12 per cent greater than in December 1936—a rise which was proportionally much greater than the increase in total assets." [13]

It would appear that the percentage change in inventories was greater than that in production, national income, or total assets. Even so, it may be suggested that the relationship between change in inventories and any of these variables is not precise, since changes in inventories are based primarily upon expectations about changes in business conditions, which may or may not materialize. Thus, inverse correlations between changes in production and in inventories are not uncommon. For example, from the third quarter of 1934 to the third quarter of 1935, inventories (as measured by the National Industrial Conference Board index) actually declined from 90 to 89, although the Federal Reserve Board index of industrial production was increasing by 14%—from 75 to 85. The fact, then, that inventories in 1937 rose faster than production, income, or sales is not sufficient reason to conclude that they were excessive. A varying relative rate of increase or decrease may be regarded as a normal development. However, it might be presumed that a relatively greater change in inventories than in income or sales toward the end of an expansion would tend to be upsetting for business expectations. Indeed, even if production and sales were growing at approximately equal rates, inventory stocks might be increasing more rapidly than desired by businessmen. [14]

11. Metzler, "Inventory Cycles in the United States, 1921–1938," unpublished paper, 20.

12. Harold G. Moulton and Associates, *Capital Expansion, Employment, and Economic Stability* (Washington, 1940). Moulton does not draw this conclusion however, nor does it necessarily follow from the data quoted. There appears to be no inflexible or normal relationship between inventories and total assets.

13. *Ibid.*, 112.

14. Professor Abramovitz of Stanford University has suggested to the author that stocks might still accumulate "with undesired rapidity," even though production was falling and consumption was rising.

INVENTORIES EXCESSIVE RELATIVE TO NEW ORDERS

Although it cannot be established conclusively that inventories were excessive in relation to the levels of income, production, or consumer expenditures in the summer of 1937, there seems to be no question that they were excessive as compared with new orders, which are a fairly sensitive measure of business expectations. Thus Slichter concluded that the change in inventories was not excessive compared with the change in production, but he believed that: "The crucial question . . . is whether they were large in relation to *new orders*. In September, 1937 they undoubtedly were." [15]

There are only limited data on changes in the value of new orders. The one index, the National Industrial Conference Board index of the value of new orders in manufacturing, confirms the belief, however, that new orders had declined substantially by the summer of 1937. Thus, this index fell by 37.1% from December 1936 (159) to August 1937 (100). From the first quarter of 1937, when the average was 138, new orders fell by 26.8% to 101 in the third quarter. [16]

As early as April 1937 the National City Bank of New York expressed concern over the rapidity of the rise in business activity for fear it might possibly indicate an approaching recession: "It is hardly deniable that the conditions now existing in many markets are those which are more likely to appear toward the end than near the beginning of an upward movement. All business upswings run too fast at times. Speculators push them along, buyers over-estimate their requirements, and interruptions must occur while production and consumption are brought back into line. A very rapid expansion is hardly expected to last as long as a more gradual move." [17] In May the National City Bank was apprehensive about the situation which would result when shipments were completed against orders then on the books, since the flow of new orders was already drying up. [18]

In its June *Monthly Letter* the National City Bank ventured the opinion that no one could tell what the situation would be when manufacturers needed more business: "If buyers have not over-estimated their requirements they will be back in the markets in good time. However, a rapid and prolonged forward movement in trade and prices is admittedly more likely to induce over-buying and accumulation of inventories than the contrary, and this is the uncertain

15. Slichter, "The Downturn of 1937," 100.
16. National Industrial Conference Board, *Supplement to Conference Board Economic Record*, 2 (1940), 7.
17. National City Bank of New York, *op. cit.* (1937), 46.
18. *Ibid.*, 62.

factor." [19] By July it was clear that buyers of foreign merchandise were slow about making large commitments. So much forward ordering had occurred in the spring that more than the usual number of clearance sales were required during the summer to move the goods.[20]

By September 1937, at the beginning of the recession, the steel industry—an important barometer of general business activity—was depending completely on new orders: "By September, bookings had dropped more than sixty per cent below the March level. But production and shipments were maintained at a high level throughout the second and third quarters largely on the basis of the large backlog of orders placed in the winter of 1936–37." [21] It was probably the decline in new orders which first made businessmen aware of the sizable increases in inventories which had already occurred.

Since a precise or invariant relationship between inventories and production is not to be expected, it seems reasonable to conclude that inventories were not excessive from this standpoint. But the available data cited above indicate that they were excessive relative to new orders.[22]

Relationship of Inventories to the Recession and Revival

The investment peculiarities of inventories, when there are involuntary or unplanned accumulations, have been discussed above. In addition it has been suggested that when new orders failed to materialize the level of inventories proved to be excessive. The final question is the significance of inventories as a causal factor in the recession and revival.

Inventories were more resultant than causal to the extent that they accumulated because income and expenditures declined.[23] The *Economist* asserted that they were a "rather minor feature of the recession." [24] But, as Metzler indicated above, they were troublesome because the pressure to reduce them was heightened by the vivid recollection of the losses which businessmen suffered on inventory account from 1929 through 1932. The Bank for International Settlements confirmed the feeling of fear which the business community had over inventory accumulations: "In the latter half of 1937 appre-

19. *Ibid.,* 78.
20. *Ibid.,* 103.
21. Lewis, *op. cit.,* 25.
22. And especially to income and production after their decline.
23. Frederick A. Lutz, of the University of Zurich, has suggested to the author that the decline in incomes and expenditures would explain only a rise in the ratio of inventories to income or sales and not a rise in inventories as such.
24. *Economist, 130* (1938), 339.

hensions regarding future developments began to weigh heavily on the minds of business men and security holders: fears of serious political disturbances, fears of renewed monetary troubles and fears of another depression. And it was perhaps natural, though unfortunate, that the dreaded depression should be thought of in terms of the sinister experiences of 1929–32." [25] According to one writer, businessmen were more apprehensive about the level of inventories in the second quarter of 1938, than in the third quarter of 1937.[26] Although it cannot be demonstrated that overexpansion in inventories was an initiating factor in the recession, their high level re-enforced any recessive tendencies from other causes. Consequently, businessmen regarded the reduction of inventories from September 1937 to June 1938 as one of their most serious problems.

The heavy accumulation of inventory was believed to be a serious impediment to the operation of "natural" forces promoting recovery. One viewpoint stated in the *Economist* was that the sharper the fall in production the better, because inventories would then have to be reduced.[27] The National City Bank believed that the reduction in stocks to the point where current demands had to be met out of current production was the most promising explanation for the revival which occurred in 1938.[28]

As a causal factor, however, inventory accumulation does not rank in importance with net government contribution, Federal Reserve policy, or the other factors which affected the flow of intended investment expenditures. The level of inventories seemed burdensome primarily because national income and expenditures declined; when the reasons for these declines are determined, inventory accumulation takes its place as a secondary factor in the recession. Ohlin has made a good summary of the relationship of commodity price increases, inventory changes, and the recession:

Not only did these prices rise to a disturbingly high level, thereby making real investment less profitable, but the over-speculation which followed led to a set-back. It is a well-known fact, that, when a speculative wave of this character breaks, prices fall heavily during a certain period and that the consequent scare causes people to reduce their inventories rather than make new purchases. Thus, a feeling of uncertainty will be created which is very trying for business in general, and tendencies toward a recession, caused by other circumstances, will be strengthened.[29]

25. Bank for International Settlements, *Eighth Annual Report*, 9.
26. *Economist, 132* (1938), 225.
27. *Ibid., 129* (1937), 471.
28. National City Bank of New York, *op. cit.* (1938), 85.
29. Ohlin, *op. cit.,* 12.

The most reasonable assumption about the relationship of inventories to the recession appears to be that a considerable part of the inventory change was unplanned investment. It resulted when income, expenditures, and production began to decline and when expectations about business conditions failed to be realized. Seen in its proper light, inventory change was an intensifying rather than a causal factor in the recession. Inventory change, however, was probably of some significance in the revival because the reduction of stocks undoubtedly was regarded by businessmen as an encouraging development.

CHAPTER 13

Sources of Capital Funds and the
Profitability of Investment

IT MUST be emphasized again that in terms of the analytic model used
for this study there are only three paths through which any economic
variable may have contributed to the recession: the paths of government fiscal policy, consumption decisions, and investment decisions.
Chapter 5 revealed that the decline in net government contribution to
the flow of income was of importance in the recession but did not
bear primary responsibility for the downturn. Subsequent chapters
have investigated the contributions of various consumption and investment factors to an explanation of the recession.

In Chapters 6 and 7 it appeared that Federal Reserve and Treasury
policies influenced investment decisions and the recession by increasing the costs of funds and generating uncertainty over the future of
business activity. Chapter 8 suggested that changes in price-cost relationships affected the recession through their impact on investment
decisions. Chapter 9 pointed out that changes in the price-cost margin
(change in the degree of monopoly) could affect the flow of income
and production in either the consumption or investment area. Here
again, the rise in costs appears to have been most disruptive for the
investment process.

Chapter 10 examined the relationship of consumption factors to
the recession and concluded that the important causal developments
were not in this area. Thus neither net government contribution nor
consumption factors have seemed adequate to account for the recession. But the analysis of these earlier chapters has pointed toward the
important changes in the area of investment decision. Chapter 12 has
begun the analysis of investment factors. Chapters 13 and 14 must
consider further the extent to which the changes in important economic variables may have affected the level of income and production
through changes in investment. The factors remaining to be discussed
in this chapter are the sources of capital funds and the profitability
of investment. Taxation, government regulations, and psychological
factors will be dealt with in Chapter 14.

Sources of Funds

The three principal sources of funds besides the normal bank credit for short-term investment were public offerings, private placements and term loans, and internal financing. Each of these will be taken up in turn.

PUBLIC OFFERINGS

The low level of new corporate security issues has already been commented upon.[1] In the chapter on Federal Reserve and Treasury policy it was also contended that the cost of funds in the securities markets rose sharply. This would seem to provide an adequate explanation for the turning point in new corporate issues, but not for the virtual stagnation of such issues in the 1930's which appears to have resulted from more fundamental causes. The expansion in private placements and in internal financing may provide a partial explanation for the low level of security issues in the public markets, but an adequate explanation would seem to lie only in the reasons for the failure of long-term investment expenditures.

The increased costs arising out of the new SEC registration requirement would appear relatively unimportant as an explanation for the small volume of new corporate issues in the 1930's. The cost of the preparation and submission of such statements is somewhat higher for small issues than for large, but the absolute cost of registration is an insignificant part of the total cost of flotation. Table 26, on the expenses per $100 of common stocks, shows that registration costs, as a percentage of total flotation costs, varied from 7.59% for issues under $100 thousand to 5.36% on issues of from $1 to $5 million. But the total registration costs ranged only from $1.16 to $.55 on the same classes of issues. It seems unlikely that such increases could have prevented any sizable quantity of new security offerings. Of course even slight increases in costs here may have accelerated the trend which for other reasons was developing toward private placements and term loans. However, as will be shown in the next section, the greatest part of private placements and term loans was for refunding purposes and thus could not have reduced public offerings for new corporate purposes to any appreciable extent.

The funds seeking outlets in investment in the 1930's were large so the primary explanation for the small volume of new corporate issues must lie in the factors affecting the demand for capital funds. In spite of the large supply of capital funds (at a price), it may be argued that the capital market was an imperfect one in the sense that

1. Chapters 3, 11.

TABLE 26: EXPENSES PER $100 OF COMMON STOCK REGISTERED UNDER THE SECURITIES ACT OF 1933, FOR THE YEARS 1938, 1939, AND 1940

Values of Issues (In thousands of dollars)	No. of cases	Amount (In thousands of dollars)	Registry Expenses (Dollars)	Compensation (Dollars)	Cost of Flotation (Dollars)	Percentage of Registry Expenses to Total Cost of Flotation	Percentage of Compensation to Total Cost of Flotation
Under 100	29	1,023	1.16	13.03	14.69	7.59	88.70
100–249	42	6,507	1.07	11.59	14.05	7.65	82.49
250–499	60	21,507	0.91	13.66	15.65	5.80	87.28
500–999	47	31,507	0.81	10.98	12.79	6.29	85.85
Under 1,000	178	60,544	0.92	12.03	13.99	6.56	85.99
1,000–4,999	29	63,481	0.55	8.78	10.21	5.36	85.99

Source: Ganson Purcell's figures in U. S. Congress, House of Representatives, Committee on Interstate and Foreign Commerce, "Proposed Amendments to the Securities Act of 1933 and to the Securities and Exchange Act of 1934," *Hearings* (1942), Pt. 2, 673–674. Secondary Source: Data from John Frederick Weston, "The Economics of Competitive Bidding in the Sale of Securities," *Journal of Business, Studies in Business Administration, 13*, No. 1 (1943), 32.

funds may have been unobtainable for more risky enterprises. This fact, combined with the substantial increases in costs and the more fundamental factors affecting business expectations, provides sufficient explanation for the decline in total new corporate issues. But the explanation for the stagnation in new corporate issues rather than that for the turning point must be found in the factors which restricted investment to short-term expenditures.

PRIVATE PLACEMENTS AND TERM LOANS

The private placements and term lending which began in the middle 1930's increased the imperfections of the capital market on the supply side. They have continued to grow in importance until in recent years private placements alone have amounted to more than 40% of total security offerings. In the period 1935–38, however, they averaged only about 19% of new corporate issues. Table 27 gives the relationship of private placements to total issues for the years 1934–44.[2] Table 28 shows the quantity of corporate bonds purchased privately from issuers, 1932–38, classified by types.

Nature of term loans. The analysis of term loans is taken from the study of Jacoby and Saulnier for the National Bureau of Economic Research.[3] To the extent that both term loans and private placements operate in the same credit market, many of the factors leading to an expansion for one also promote an expansion in the other. Jacoby and Saulnier define the term loan as one: "to a business enterprise that is repayable, according to agreement between borrower and lender, after the lapse of more than one year. Such loans fall within the 'medium-term' credit market, which is defined for purposes of this study to include credits that run for more than one but not more than fifteen years." [4]

Causes of growth of term loans. Term lending grew after 1933 because business demanded medium-term loans rather than short- or long-term credit, or equity capital. Part of the explanation for this increased demand was that there was a relative shift from equity to debt financing [5] apparently because the costs of financing through common stocks were increasing. The increased interest in the medium-term loan, for the purpose of securing additional funds

2. Charles C. Abbott, "Sources of Business Funds," *Review of Economics and Statistics, 28* (1946), Exhibit 3, 140.
3. Neil Jacoby and R. Saulnier, *Term Lending to Business* (New York, 1942).
4. *Ibid.*, 1.
5. However, a comparison of new corporate issues reveals that common stocks were a higher percentage of the total in the period 1936–37 than in 1922–27. See George Eddy, "The Present Status of New Security Issues," *Review of Economics and Statistics, 21* (1939), 118.

TABLE 27: ESTIMATES OF PRIVATE PLACEMENTS, 1934–44, COMPARED WITH TOTAL CORPORATE SECURITY OFFERINGS[a]

Year	Estimates of R. McLean Stewart			Gross Proceeds Estimated by SEC				
	All Issues Placed Directly by Corporation and Foreign[b] Issues with Investors	Total Domestic Corporation and Foreign[b] Issues in All Financing	Per Cent of Direct Purchases to Total Financing	All Private Placements[c] of New Corporate Securities	Total New Corporate Securities Offered for Cash Sale in U.S.	Per Cent of Private Placements to Total New Corporate Securities	Per Cent of All Direct Purchases to Total Bond Issues in All Domestic Corporate and Foreign[b] Financing (Stewart)	Per Cent of Private Placements of New Corporate Bonds, Debentures & Notes to All New Corporate Bonds, Debentures and Notes (SEC)
	(1)	(2)	(3)	(4)	(5)	(6)	(7)	(8)
	(million dollars)	(million dollars)	%	(million dollars)	(million dollars)	%	%	%
1934	96.1	576.2	16.7	....	....	....	17.7	....
1935	391.1	2,551.5	15.3	261.5	895.2	29.2	16.3	29.6
1936	377.3	4,805.3	7.9	412.2	4,207.8	9.8	8.9	10.5
1937	328.2	2,695.4	12.2	327.6	3,705.4	8.8	17.0	11.3
1938	832.4	2,451.1	34.0	357.8	1,289.1	27.8	35.4	34.3
1939	827.9	2,434.8	34.0	749.1	2,445.6	30.6	37.6	33.1
1940	1,556.2	3,570.4	43.6	756.8	2,322.0	32.6	48.0	35.8
1941	1,038.8[d]	2,389.2[d]	43.5[d]	996.4	3,030.6	32.9	47.2[d]	35.6
1942	....	....	....	531.5	1,987.1	26.7	....	31.0
1943	....	....	....	314.8	742.4	42.4	....	46.0
1944	....	....	....	513.7	1,647.5	31.2	....	40.2

a. Calendar year for Cols. 1, 2, 3, 7. Year ending June 30 for Cols. 4, 5, 6, 8. Cols. 1, 2, 3, and 7 compiled from Hearings before the Committee on Interstate and Foreign Commerce, H.R. 4344, 5065, 5832, 77th Cong., 1st Sess., "Proposed Amendments to the Securities Act of 1933 and to the Securities and Exchange Act of 1934," Hearings, Pt. 2, 366, 369. Cols. 4, 5, 6, and 8 based on Securities and Exchange Commission, Tenth Annual Report, Table 3, Pts. 2 and 4, A-9, A-11.

b. Bonds of foreign issuers payable in United States dollars and registered under the Securities Act of 1933.

c. Excludes issues sold by competitive bidding directly to ultimate investors.

d. January 1 to September 15, 1941.

Source: Abbott, op. cit., Exhibit 3, 140.

for modernization or working capital, rather than the traditional short-term loan was influenced by the experience during 1929–33 when banks placed many businesses under severe pressure by calling in short-term loans. The medium-term loan was devised to prevent such a situation from arising again.

TABLE 28: CORPORATE BONDS PURCHASED PRIVATELY FROM ISSUERS, CLASSIFIED AS TO TYPE—FOR EACH YEAR, 1932–38, INCLUSIVE

At Cost Excluding Accrued Interest
(In thousands of dollars)

	1932	*1933*	*1934*	*1935*	*1936*	*1937*	*1938*	*Total*
Rails	0	0	1,560	13,982	21,361	48,457	7,816	93,176
Public utilities	1,133	0	46,890	157,272	188,378	70,016	280,701	744,390
Industrial and miscellaneous	22,287	6,475	32,717	179,913	118,053	249,630	368,980	978,055
Total	23,420	6,475	81,167	351,167	327,792	368,103	657,497	1,815,621

Source: Data collected by the Securities and Exchange Commission and printed in Temporary National Economic Committee, *Hearings,* 76th Cong., 3d Sess., Pt. 10-A (1940), 132.

Advantages of term lending and private placements. The costs of registration under the SEC which are avoided by direct placements have already been indicated. In addition, a large number of other costs are eliminated such as the higher commissions for underwriters, outlays for engraving certificates, transfer taxes, costs of maintaining facilities for transferring securities, costs of listing issues on securities exchanges, and other marketing costs.

Other advantages of the private placements, which are not necessarily cost advantages, include the greater speed in financing and the ready modification of the terms of loan indenture to meet the changing circumstances of the borrower. A final advantage under private placements or term loans is that directors of corporations escape the potential civil liability which is prescribed under the SEC for failure to give adequate public disclosure of their corporate affairs. The avoidance of such liability and the greater flexibility of the investment may be the most compelling reasons for the increases in this type of financing.[6]

Disadvantage of private placements. A major disadvantage which has been claimed for the private placement is its limited marketability. However, it seems likely that in recent years the increased "thinness"

6. Jacoby and Saulnier, 18–19.

of the trading in the stock market is tending to lessen this comparative disadvantage.[7]

Quantitative importance of term lending and private placements as sources of new capital funds. The trend toward financing from these sources appears to have been symptomatic of the developments which led to a low level of new corporate issues in the public market, because the actual volume of funds for new corporate investment from these sources amounts to very little. The statistics on new corporate issues from the *Commercial and Financial Chronicle* already include most of the private placements. The only available estimate of total term loans is for the year 1937, when $1,081.2 million were outstanding. This total included $27.4 million held by Federal Reserve banks, $74.8 million by the Reconstruction Finance Corporation, $152 million by the life insurance companies, and $827 million by commercial banks.[8] Some of these loans are probably already in the *Commercial and Financial Chronicle*'s totals. Moreover, the impact of these loans on the investment process is considerably less than the totals would indicate because not over one-third was money for working capital or new machinery and equipment. Thus it appears unlikely that the addition to the *Commercial and Financial Chronicle* totals for term loans should be greater than $300 million, from 1933 to 1937, and no adjustment would seem necessary for private placements.

Therefore, to repeat, the significance of this trend toward private placements and term lending rests not upon its contribution to the total amount of loanable funds but upon the evidence it gives of the growing imperfection in the supply of funds.[9] The growth of large institutional savers provided the supply of funds which were then made available as private loans to large, well-established businesses. It has been estimated that the life insurance companies alone took from 74 to 99% of the total corporate bonds sold privately during the years 1934–39.[10] In Chapter 7 it has already been pointed out that the $75 million Socony-Vacuum bond issue, the largest single new corporate issue in June 1937, was sold privately to five large life in-

7. *Ibid.*, 19.
8. *Ibid.*, 30.
9. John C. Clendenin of the University of California, Los Angeles, in a private review of this study, has objected to "the characterization of a loan market which supplies good credit risks and refuses poor ones as 'imperfect.'" In his opinion, this situation "is still competitive even if selective re risk-taking." The contention of this chapter is that the developments described have increased the differentiation of the market on the supply side and thus made it more "imperfect," and not that selective risk-taking of itself is noncompetitive.
10. Jacoby and Saulnier, 144. A letter from the Securities and Exchange Commission to the National Bureau of Economic Research.

surance companies. Clearly such sources of funds were *not* available to the unseasoned or even the average borrowers. The growth in private placements and term loans (to a lesser extent) must be viewed as telling evidence of an imperfect market for capital funds.[11]

INTERNAL SOURCES OF FUNDS

Few data are available with which to measure this type of financing. However, inferences may be drawn from estimates which have been made and from certain sample studies, although these are liable to be subject to large errors when used to represent the behavior of internal financing as a whole.

Internal financing has been examined from two standpoints. The first considers its relationship to the secular problems of investment and business expansion. The data on internal financing have been used to bolster the contention that retained earnings of corporations, including depreciation and depletion accruals, and additions to surplus, are sufficient and will continue to be sufficient to finance any necessary increases in equity capital. From this viewpoint the problem of absorbing the community's savings becomes more acute because corporate enterprise reduces its demand for funds from the financial markets. Thus the growth of internal financing is seen to be an important part of the process of secular stagnation in the financial and industrial fields.

The other viewpoint is that the growth in the volume of funds from internal sources, accompanied as it was by extremely low interest rates, precluded the possibility that a shortage of capital funds contributed to the turning point in economic activity.

It seems both inappropriate and unnecessary in a study of short-term fluctuations to consider the relationship of internal financing to secular stagnation. But the extent to which internal funds for capital needs were available in the period preceding the recession must be investigated.

Altman estimated that business enterprises spent $17.4 billion for plant, machinery, and equipment from 1935 to 1937, of which a total of $16 billion or over 92% came from retained earnings, depreciation, and depletion.[12] For 1937 alone he placed business expenditures for plant and equipment at $7.5 billion, of which $5.5 billion came from internal sources. In the preceding two years business enterprises had a net surplus of funds for investment elsewhere to the amount of $600

11. However, it might be argued that the companies which borrowed funds through these new devices merely shifted their demand from one source to another.
12. Oscar L. Altman, Temporary National Economic Committee, *Hearings*, Pt. 9, 3692.

million. Thus the net demand in 1937 for $2 billions from outside sources was a reversal of position. Where business had been a net supplier of funds, it now shifted to the demand side.

Mack made a detailed study of 54 large companies for the period 1932 to 1938 [13] using the sources and application of funds technique. She concluded that in the years 1932 and 1938 there was a flow of funds from corporations to the financial markets. In 1933 and 1937 there was a flow of funds from the financial markets to corporations, and in the years 1934–36 these companies had comparatively little need for funds obtained by borrowing or by reducing their financial assets.[14]

Mack's study also showed that the most common source of capital was retained earnings. Furthermore, apparently only 95% of business receipts were later spent: "The ratio of expenditure to receipts was 95 per cent. In other words, 95 per cent of the dollars temporarily retained, as the result of depreciation and other reserve accruals, operating profits, and non-operating income, was expended on purchase of capital equipment, on expenses charged to reserve accounts, and on dividends, income taxes, interest payments, and non-operating expenses. But this ratio for aggregate data is the resultant of rather different situations in individual years and companies." [15] This last point is a very important one. Whereas the aggregate figures showed that the level of retained earnings was adequate over-all to finance capital expansion, individual companies were not so fortunate. Thus in the 1932–38 period, a number of the companies, among them, Bethlehem Steel, United States Steel, and General Motors, made additions to plant which were greater than their depreciation allowances and profits after dividends.

It may be concluded from this analysis that net retained income exceeded total out payment from 1932 to 1938, but in the crucial year of 1937 there was a net demand for funds from the financial markets, and individual enterprises had a net requirement for outside funds throughout the period. For the period 1936–38 it has also been shown that the losses of companies with no net income exceeded the retained earnings of companies with a net income.[16]

WAS THERE A SHORTAGE OF CAPITAL FUNDS?

Chapter 2 presented the arguments which led Sachs to believe that there was a shortage of capital. From his sample study he concluded

13. Mack, 29–31.
14. *Ibid.*, 321–324.
15. *Ibid.*, 161–162.
16. Abbott, 141.

that the tax structure, particularly the undistributed profits tax, impaired the working capital position and led to a shortage of funds not only for expansion but for maintenance purposes as well. In spite of this argument several analysts doubted that there was actually any shortage of capital funds in 1937. For example, Hansen was inclined to discount any contention that there was a shortage of investment funds because new issues for the better grade companies (not, however, the "cats and dogs" variety of new issues) could be floated in the stock market on very easy terms.[17] Slichter also went so far as to say that there was no shortage of capital except for the more risky ventures.[18] However, the qualitative investigation of new corporate issues in Chapter 7 showed that in the unsettled market of the middle of 1937 even borrowers with the highest credit rating faced increased costs for new funds and the average borrower faced substantial increases in interest costs.

In contrast to the opinions of Hansen and Slichter, a large section of the business population accepted Sachs' conclusions that there was a shortage of funds and that underinvestment precipitated the recession. Ayres offered the following diagnosis: "Financial anemia is the ailment from which American business is suffering. Anemia is a lack of blood. Financial anemia is a deficiency in the flow of new business capital. The capitalistic system requires a continuous flow of new capital, and in our case the flow has become inadequate, and business stagnation has resulted." [19] The same writer reasoned that the capital flow dried up because of the restraints from the undistributed profit taxes, higher wages, SEC regulations, and capital gains and income taxes: "These restraints against capital formation and capital flow have been in effect before the recent business downturn. The handicaps they imposed were largely hidden by the huge outpourings of government borrowed funds. Now the government has curtailed its borrowings because its revenues are supplied from higher taxes and social security income. The result is an acute business relapse caused by under-investment."

Donald B. Woodward of Moody's Investors Service charged that the undistributed profits tax prevented growth of retained earnings and that the unavailability of funds in the capital market led to a decline in business capital expenditures and contributed to the recession:

Experiencing a working capital and cash position which was the poorest in more than a decade and going lower, unable to replenish it in the capital

17. Hansen, *Full Recovery or Stagnation?* 273.
18. Slichter, "The Downturn of 1937," 108.
19. Leonard P. Ayres, "Is America Anemic?" *Bankers Magazine, 136* (1938), 380. The other quotation in this paragraph is from the same source and page.

202   *The Economics of Recession and Revival*

markets, and being pressed against retaining earnings by the undistributed profits tax, business capital expenditures declined violently. . . . This situation is sufficient to explain a decline of importance in business. There were other good reasons why business fell sharply this year as well, but financial developments were certainly a vital part of the cause.[20]

The deterioration in cash position described by Woodward was confirmed in Sachs' study. Mack's analysis demonstrated that the companies studied became large net borrowers in 1937. Lutz's study [21] showed clearly that the liquidity position of the 46 corporations in his sample B declined in 1937 compared with 1936 and with their liquidity position in the twenties. He has distinguished two measurements of normal corporate liquidity, "free cash" and "free liquid" funds.[22] Normal "free cash" is measured by the average ratio of cash to payments during the period 1922–29. Normal "free liquid" funds is measured by the average ratio of cash plus marketable securities to payments during the period 1922–29. It is this latter measure of liquidity which revealed a shortage of funds in 1937: "the year 1937 exhibits a 'shortage' of liquid funds whereas cash alone still shows a slight surplus compared with the average of the twenties." [23] Therefore these studies of Sachs and Lutz support the contention that the liquidity position of corporations was reduced in 1937. Mack's study also reveals that there was a relative increase in the demand for funds from the financial markets. Under such circumstances a substantial increase in public offerings should have been expected, and there was, to be sure, some increase. Yet the volume remained at a very low level. According to Eddy, part of the explanation was that investors had the funds but the prospects for corporate profits and dividends were not sufficiently attractive to justify purchases, particularly of common stocks.[24] The primary explanation in his opinion, however, was that corporations neither wished nor needed to borrow.[25] In view of these studies by Mack, Sachs, and Lutz, this conclusion seems unacceptable for the year 1937. Even the large corporations needed funds at this time. Although Eddy's primary explanation seems inconsistent with the evidence, his suggestion that investors were unwilling to buy common stocks because of uncertainty over future corporate profits and dividends appears to have been a basic reason for the limited response of new corporate issues. It is

20. Donald B. Woodward, "Changes in Capital Financing," *Journal of the American Statistical Association, 33* (1938), 17.
21. Lutz, *op. cit.*, Chart 17, 61.
22. *Ibid.*, 4, 5, 40–41.
23. *Ibid.*, 49.
24. Eddy, 116.
25. *Ibid.*, 120.

important to note not only that the *demand* for funds by corporate enterprise for expansion purposes was limited by considerations of future profitability, but that the *supply* of funds for investment was also limited for the same reason.

It is now possible to draw some conclusions as to the shortage of capital funds. It has been established that the liquidity position of corporate enterprise had been reduced appreciably by 1937, and that there was an increased demand for funds in the securities markets. At the same time, by the middle of 1937 capital funds were available from external sources at moderate increases in costs only to the borrowers with the highest credit. It appears also that throughout the 1930's small companies, although many obtained funds successfully, had considerably more difficulty in borrowing than did the large, prominent companies.[26]

The fundamental problem of capital funds seems to have been that the companies which had access to outside funds had no need for them, while the companies which needed funds were unable to obtain them.[27] The importance of this distinction is that the lack of necessary funds is a sufficient reason for failing to make investment expenditures, but the mere availability of the necessary funds is not even an important reason for making investment purchases.[28]

The conclusion reached here, with the indicated qualifications, is that there was an actual shortage of capital. The growth in retained earnings for total business enterprise was inadequate to supply the new capital needs:

Neither the growth of "private placements" nor the use by corporations of retained earnings has compensated for the decline in public offerings designed to raise new money. Private placements have unquestionably been a major development in the securities markets in the last 10 years, but high percentage of them has been used to refund existing obligations rather than to raise new capital. The fact that their annual amount has been more stable than has the amount of total offerings probably is evidence that large companies, and companies of superior investment merit, can more easily acquire funds in this manner than can other concerns.

Historically, retained earnings have been an exceedingly important type of financing for business in the aggregate. For many companies they have been the chief source of funds. . . . Nevertheless, the conclusion seems warranted that for all business corporations in the aggregate retained earnings have been and presumably will continue to be an inadequate and an extremely uncertain source of funds.[29]

26. *Ibid.*
27. Mack, 293–294.
28. *Ibid.*, 267.
29. Abbott, 145.

It has been traditional to measure the availability of capital by the level of the rate of interest. This appears, however, to have been a very imperfect gauge of the availability of capital funds in 1937. Consequently, two modifications in the theory of interest rates seem necessary. One is to redefine the rate of interest in a fashion somewhat similar to that suggested by Bissell, who believes that the rate of interest should move with the return on equities as well as with bonds if it is to be an index of the supply of capital.[30] Second, it is essential to recognize that the rate of interest, even so defined, provides a measurement only of the terms on which capital funds are available to certain preferred classes of borrowers. The rate of interest is thus only an indication of the cost of capital for those borrowers to whom such sources of capital are available.

It is not necessary to agree that "the recovery collapsed because of a shortage of capital available for industry." [31] But it must be recognized that corporate liquidity was actually impaired, that the effective costs of capital rose substantially in 1937,[32] and that imperfections developed in the capital market. These developments, along with the more fundamental factors which increased uncertainty as to the future and limited business decisions to short-term investment commitments, undoubtedly contributed to the recession.

PROFITABILITY OF INVESTMENT

The remainder of this chapter will consider the profitability of investment expenditure in relationship to the recession.[33]

EARLY DECLINE IN PROFITS

One of the first of the major series to decline was corporate profits. Figure 13, which compares corporate profits to changes in inventories, income, and consumption expenditures (all by quarters), shows the early decline in profits and the time lag in these other series. Barger's data placed the peak in corporate profits in the fourth quarter of 1936. A very slight decline in the first quarter of 1937 was followed by a 5% decline in the second quarter and a sharper decline of 15% in the third quarter. These declines in profits of the first and

30. Richard M. Bissell, Jr., "The Rate of Interest," *Papers and Proceedings, American Economic Review, 28* (1938), 30.

31. *Economist, 129* (1937), 471. One viewpoint expressed in their "Overseas Correspondence."

32. In Chapter 7 the increase in the cost of capital as measured by the yield on all common stocks was shown to have been 33⅓% from March to June 1937.

33. Corporate profits are used as a rough measure of the rate of return on investment.

second quarters of 1937 occurred even as national income (see Figure 13) and production were still rising. To the extent that business decisions are based upon the current levels of profits or upon expectations about the future profitability of investment, these declines must be regarded as of importance in the recession.

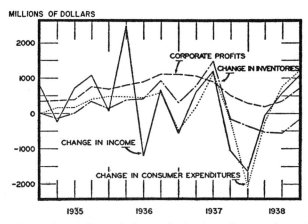

Fig. 13. Corporate profits and change in business inventories, adjusted income, and consumers' expenditures, seasonally adjusted by quarters, 1935–38. Data from Barger, *op. cit.,* 116–119, Table 11 ; 180–183, Table 18; 299, Table 28.

This conclusion, however, is subject to certain qualifying remarks. It has just been suggested that the rate of return on new investment began to decline early in 1937. Moreover, it is this early decline which supports the contention made elsewhere that rises in labor costs were instrumental in reducing investment commitments. It is, therefore, extremely important to establish beyond question that profits began to decline early in 1937. But there is only one series on profits, and it is based on very inadequate data for certain segments of American industry. Nevertheless, in spite of the margin of error in this profits series, it seems probable that the 5% decline in corporate profits in the second quarter of 1937 is significant. Certainly it can be asserted with confidence that profits had declined by the third quarter of 1937, when they were 20% below the fourth quarter of 1936. In spite of imperfect data, such a large percentage decline must mean that the profit situation had seriously deteriorated.

THE LOW LEVEL OF PROFITS

Not only does it appear that there was an early decline in corporate profits, but the profit rate was at an extremely low level throughout the period. At their peak in 1936, corporate profits were still 22%

less than their average for 1926–29. In Crum's study of eight areas in the American economy [34] only two, trade and agriculture, had by 1936 exceeded their average profit rate in 1928–29. By 1936 only trade, agriculture, and manufacturing had exceeded their average profit rate from 1926 to 1929. Even these average figures hide very great differences in the extent to which profits in particular sectors had recovered.

SIGNIFICANCE OF THE LOW PROFITS

The failure of the profit rate to regain the levels of the 1920's has been given different interpretations. The profit rate in the twenties varied from 5 to 7% of stated book values.[35] Taitel, therefore, considers a profit rate of only slightly below 5% in 1936–37 a surprising performance in view of the wide unemployment of resources.[36] He believes, moreover, that factors other than amount or rate of profits have been the major determinants of the level of capital expenditures. The most important of these other factors has been the level of output relative to capacity, and the pressure upon business to introduce new technologies which are available.[37] To Taitel, profits are less incentives for investment expenditure than they are sources of savings which are likely not to be invested. In his opinion, rising profits in 1936–37 had repercussions on income and employment by increasing savings rather than by stimulating investment.[38] It may be inferred that Taitel believes the dangers from excess savings were so great that the lower profit rate in the thirties was actually a desirable development. From this viewpoint, the failure of the profit rate to regain the levels of the twenties was unlikely to affect investment decisions unfavorably.

Slichter, however, drew quite different conclusions about the effects of the profit rate in the thirties on investment expenditures. Thus he attributed the short-term outlook of businessmen to the low level of profits, which was the "crucial element in the situation." [39] He believed that at the height of the boom this was still "dangerously

34. W. L. Crum, "Cyclical Changes in Corporate Profits," *Review of Economics and Statistics, 21* (1939), Table 2, 54.

35. Martin Taitel, *Profits, Productive Activities and New Investment,* Temporary National Economic Committee, Monograph No. 12 (1941), 23.

36. But the value of the marginal product of a capital good would tend to be high where labor was relatively abundant, as in the middle thirties, which may account for as high profits as actually occurred. This figure of 5% profits in 1936–37 is from the Crum data.

37. However, it would seem that these factors would be important only as reflected in the rate of profits.

38. Taitel, 37.

39. Slichter, "The Downturn of 1937," 107.

low": "Far more important, however, than the political relations of business was the dangerously low level of profits throughout the recovery and even at the height of the boom." [40] The principal explanation for the lack of long-term commitments and the limited purchase of capital goods was the low level of profits. The actual turning point in economic activity may well have resulted from the narrowing of the price-cost margin: "fears that costs would in the near future encroach upon profits' may well have restricted the demand for industrial equipment because labor organization was spreading rapidly in the spring and summer of 1937 and wages were rising. Hence, although profits were greater than a year before, their future was uncertain." [41]

Profits in the first and second quarter of 1937 were ahead of the corresponding quarters in 1936, but in the third quarter of 1937 declined below the third quarter of 1936. More important, however, to investment decision and to the turning point itself was the fact that the profit rate began to decline, possibly by the first quarter of 1937 and undoubtedly by the second quarter.

In assessing the importance of profits and profit expectations in the recession, two situations must be compared. On the one hand, if profits are abnormally high, an increase in wages which does not reduce profits below an acceptable level should lead to an expansion in demand for the consumers' goods industries without initiating a corresponding decline in investment. On the other hand, if profits in investment goods are reduced below some normal level, an increase in wages may increase the demand for consumers' goods but may well have severe repercussions on total employment by causing a contraction in the demand for investment goods.

In the case under consideration the level of profits would appear to have been abnormally low. Consequently the adverse effects of the profit reduction on investment expenditures more than counterbalanced any favorable stimulus to consumption expenditures.

The importance of a satisfactory level of profits to the maintenance of production and employment in a free enterprise economy has been clearly recognized by Ohlin. He explains what Slichter meant by insisting that profits were "dangerously low":

The demand for durable goods, i.e. real investment, holds the key position in regard to the business cycle and it is for this reason that the expectation of profits must be watched so carefully. Whether the income derived from profit goes to rich people or not is immaterial from this point of view. One can disapprove of and regret the necessity of opposing certain wage in-

40. *Ibid.*, 106.
41. *Ibid.*, 105.

creases and permitting profits of a certain height but one must respect the construction of the present economic system until some other system has been introduced. Otherwise, retribution is bound to come in the form of low production and unemployment.[42]

Thus it seems beyond question that expected profits were inadequate to stimulate any sizable expansion in long-term investment commitments. Even as the demand for goods was expanding there was a substantial decline in corporate profits. The current profitability of investment influences business expectations as to the future and directly affects business investment decisions. The decline in profitability of investment, by its timing and through its repercussions on investment decision, sheds light on the causal factors operating in the recession.

42. Ohlin, *op. cit.,* 10.

CHAPTER 14

The Relationship of Taxation, Government Regulation, and Business Psychology to Investment Decision in the Recession and Revival

DEVELOPMENTS in the areas of taxation, government regulation, and business psychology were charged by most economists with the greatest responsibility for the recession. This chapter must now assess the impact which these developments may have had upon investment decisions.

THE ROLE OF TAXATION

As noted in Chapter 5, the full effects of fiscal policy cannot be determined solely from the absolute size of the government deficit or surplus. The particular forms of taxation employed, as against the total volume of tax revenues, were themselves regarded as of causal significance in the recession. Most severely criticized were the undistributed profits taxes and the capital gains taxes. Increased individual income taxes were denounced by some authors as a big step toward socialism and praised by others for their effect in redistributing wealth and increasing consumption expenditure. The social security taxes were also criticized for their timing and because they were believed to have restricted consumption expenditures.

It has been noted that Schumpeter believed the capital supply was reduced by the increase in individual income taxes even though this development itself was not held to account for the timing of the turning point. The most serious concern, however, was expressed over the undistributed profits tax. As already pointed out, Sachs blamed the undistributed profits tax for the reduced corporate liquidity which curtailed business investment expenditures. At the other extreme, Wilson viewed it as beneficial because corporate savings were drawn down and consumer spending was stimulated. The undistributed profits tax might have restrained new investment, but "business men were in no frame of mind to launch out on extensive new enterprises" so that the new tax merely tapped savings which would otherwise "have been 'absorbed' in the speculative market." [1]

INDIVIDUAL INCOME TAXES—CAPITAL GAINS TAXES

It is difficult to determine the contribution which increases in individual income taxes and capital gains taxes may have made to the recession. The substantial changes in rates were already in effect by 1934. There were no subsequent changes in these taxes which could have affected the timing of the recession. In a broader sense, however, these taxes may have been a part of the process which was promoting increased uncertainty over future developments. They may have contributed to the unwillingness of investors to undertake extremely risky ventures. The risk of losing everything outweighed the gain after taxes. This was the situation as described by critics of the capital gains tax: "The capital-gains tax undoubtedly has the effect of deterring capital investment. If an investment proves successful, most of the profit goes to the Government. If unsuccessful, the individual bears all the loss; the investor hesitates to wager several to one on a venture attended with such risk." [2]

It is unlikely that these taxes, by themselves, could have curtailed the supply of funds. Where, however, the profitability of investment was declining and where there was growing uncertainty over the future, the level of individual income taxes and capital gains taxes may have assisted in precipitating the recession by limiting profits after taxes.[3]

SOCIAL SECURITY TAXES

While individual income taxes and capital gains taxes may have been a part of the conditioning process which limited long-term investment commitments, the social security and undistributed profits taxes, because of their timing, could have had a direct part in initiating the recession.

Elsewhere it is indicated that the cash budget was balanced for a short time in 1937, partly because expenditures were reduced but primarily because additional funds were collected under the new social

1. Wilson, *op. cit.,* 178. In the last part of this statement he appears to have made the common error of assuming that savings can be lost to enterprise by "absorption" in the stock market.

2. From a statement of Lammot DuPont, president, E. I. DuPont de Nemours and Co., U. S. Congress, Senate, Special Committee, *Hearings, 1, 275.*

3. The best summary of the effects of American tax policy on the flow of capital funds during the period is to be found in Gerhard Colm and Fritz Lehmann, *Economic Consequences of Recent American Tax Policy,* Supplement 1, Social Research (New York, 1938).

security taxes.[4] If the decline in net government contribution was causal in the recession, then the imposition of new social security taxes at this time was unfortunate. Beyond this, the social security taxes affected income and employment directly through their impact on consumption expenditures. The chief criticism of the taxes was that a huge reserve was being accumulated, in a period when unemployment was at a high level, by taxing incomes which probably would have been spent. The funds collected were actually spent by the government for other purposes. The taxes were deflationary even when used by the government for public works or other deficit spending because these expenditures would have occurred had there been no social insurance tax receipts. The government would have had to borrow from individuals or banks, either offsetting savings of individuals or increasing the purchasing power of the community through the creation of new money. Instead, by borrowing from the social security reserves, the government merely spent the funds which would otherwise have been spent by individual income receivers had there been no new taxes.[5]

The attempt to build such a reserve was a mistake in Eccles' opinion: "We have made the mistake, in my judgment, of accumulating a vast reserve in times of large unemployment, taxing it not out of those best able to pay or those whose savings are idle, but out of payrolls mainly of those who otherwise doubtless would have kept the funds moving in the income stream." [6]

The Social Security Board, however, denied that the taxes were deflationary: "Although it is true that at the outset the funds were collected to be used 2 years hence for the payment of benefits, in the interim the funds will be available to retire public debt or to purchase Federal bonds. This will serve to release funds from public into private investment, thereby actually aiding recovery." [7] Clearly the board was in error here. The retirement of debt held by commercial banks would tend to be deflationary since banks would be forced to find new borrowers if the money supply was to be restored to its

4. Cf. Chapter 5.

5. Cf. discussion in Social Security Board, *Social Insurance Financing in Relation to Consumer Incomes and Expenditures,* Bureau Memorandum No. 63 (1946), Pt. 4, 88–105.

6. Eccles, *Economic Balance and a Balanced Budget,* 283. The principal argument for the reserve is that the accumulation of assets in the government trust fund guarantees future benefit payments, whereas with no reserves the maintenance of outpayments is dependent upon the capricious will of Congress.

7. Social Security Board, *Unemployment Compensation, What and Why?* 10–11. In fairness to the board it should be noted that later memoranda accepted a more valid theoretical position on the deflationary nature of social security taxes. Cf. Bureau Memorandum No. 63, Pt. 4, 88.

former level. Whether retiring privately held debt or purchasing federal bonds might be less deflationary would depend upon the uses made of the funds by the new holder compared with what the original taxpayer would have done with them. The collection of social security taxes to retire debt or purchase federal bonds would have a net stimulating effect on income only under the most extreme and unrealistic assumptions.

The social security taxes are still open to criticism for their effect in reducing the net government contribution to income and possibly because the transfer of income from one group of consumers to another may have reduced the propensity to consume. Certainly the taxes were imposed at the wrong time and Eccles' argument against the accumulation of reserves during periods of high unemployment seems sound.[8]

Johnson described the social security tax program as a glaring example of inconsistencies in governmental policies: "The most notable example of inconsistency is the Social Security program, in which a financial procedure was established with alarming deflationary propensities at a time when one can be sure that the Administration had no such objective in view."[9]

UNDISTRIBUTED PROFITS TAX

The undistributed profits tax was supported as a measure to equalize the taxation of corporate and unincorporated business. It was also believed that the expenditures of government from these tax receipts would have a stimulating effect on income and employment providing the payments went to individuals whose marginal propensities to consume were high.[10] The tax was expected to force a greater distribution of profits which would encourage spending and increase income tax collections. These tax receipts would also be paid out to individuals who had higher propensities to consume than did the original profit receivers. The favorable effects on consumption were expected to overbalance any unfavorable effects on investment expenditures. Those who opposed the tax believed it would reduce the capital supply and, by slowing up business expansion and investment, would more than offset any favorable stimulus given to consumption expenditures.

Even without further examination of the background of the tax, it is clear that no other single measure, except possibly public utility

8. It would seem to be equally sound to acclerate accumulation of reserves during periods of threatening inflation such as faced the economy following the war.

9. G. Griffith Johnson, *op. cit.,* 220.

10. It was thought further that the distribution of these earnings would insure that investment decisions were subject to the interplay of competitive market forces.

legislation, was so disapproved of by business: "The reforming zeal of the Roosevelt administration, with its outspoken hostility to corporations, was responsible for much of the resistance to the undistributed profits tax." [11]

Besides the fact that the tax tended to handicap a small concern with limited access to outside funds, the psychological effects were undoubtedly important. Buehler expected these effects would be substantial:

An undistributed profits tax of the type recently adopted, or enacted with a reforming zeal as well as with an eye to revenue, will not only curtail the capital supply but will also dampen the enthusiasm of businessmen and act as a psychological as well as a physical handicap. . . . To the extent that the undistributed profits tax deprived business of funds needed for expansion, it will slow up business improvement, dampen the spirits of businessmen, and tend to reduce the long-run profits of business.[12]

In the Senate hearing on unemployment and relief, business and financial opinion overwhelmingly favored either outright repeal or modification of the undistributed profits tax.[13] Colonel Ayres of the Cleveland Trust Company summarized this attitude: "Rightly or wrongly, businessmen appear to regard the tax on undistributed profits as embodying an attitude of Government toward business, which is unfriendly toward business. Should it be repealed I think it would do more toward wiping out that widespread belief than any other thing of a comparable sort." [14] Senator Byrnes wrote to 100 executives asking them what legislative action they believed should be taken to restore business confidence. Action on the undistributed profits tax was at the top of the list.[15]

There is no doubt that the business and financial community was unanimous in disapproving of the tax and in believing that it bore causal responsibility in the recession.[16] However, it is difficult to

11. Alfred G. Buehler, *The Undistributed Profits Tax* (New York, 1937), 36.
12. *Ibid.,* 90 and 131.
13. Among the men advocating these changes were W. W. Aldrich, chairman of the Board, Chase National Bank; Colby Chester, chairman, Board of Directors, General Foods Corp.; Lammot DuPont, president, E. I. DuPont de Nemours; William J. Kelly, president, Machinery and Allied Products Institute; S. R. Fuller, president, North American Rayon Corp.; R. E. Henry, president, American Cotton Manufacture Assoc.; J. D. A. Morrow, president, Pittsburgh Coal Co.; Robert E. Wood, chairman of the Board, Sears, Roebuck & Co.; and Dr. Claudius T. Murchison, president of the Cotton-Textile Institute, Inc.
14. U. S. Congress, Senate, Special Committee, *Hearings, 1,* 356.
15. *Ibid.,* 509.
16. This unanimity of opinion has been emphasized by one writer: "One of the extraordinary phenomena of the present moment is the violence of public and political reaction to the Undistributed Profits Tax. It is hard to find any other subject in the current political scene on which there seems to be such agreement. Certainly,

determine how much of the opposition arose because of its actual repressive effects.

Schumpeter pointed out that the beginning of the recession was almost perfectly timed to seem a result of the new tax:

No serious economist has, to the writer's knowledge, held that the slump was solely caused by this tax. But if timing of effects carries any weight (the reader knows that we attach but limited importance to time sequences), it is nothing short of ideal in this case. The act went into force in June 1936. Its effects were due to show themselves *urbi et orbi* in the first quarter of 1937. And at the end of the second the first symptoms of impending difficulties appeared.[17]

More important than either the antagonisms which were engendered by the tax or the near coincidence of the tax and the beginning of the recession is the extent to which investment decisions actually were affected unfavorably by the tax. The replies of 360 corporations to a questionnaire of the National Industrial Conference Board provide information on the effects of the tax on investment decisions.[18] Though there is reason to question the validity and usefulness of the replies received under the questionnaire which circulated, it is still desirable to indicate what businessmen said about the effects of the tax upon their planning.[19]

The tax caused a material increase in the cost of preparing returns for 18% of the business. For 61% the tax affected the proportion of earnings paid out as dividends. The average ratio of dividends to earnings was 76.8% for the companies in the sample, which compared with an average of 64.8% for all corporations from 1925 to 1929. Apparently, the capital flow was affected by the tax, for 24% said that they had already relied on banks or other outside sources of working capital to a greater extent, and 213 of the 234 corporations

---

with respect to no other legislative action of the last several years has business presented such a strong and unified front . . ." Willard L. Thorp, "The Undistributed Profits Tax," *Financial Management Series,* No. 53, American Management Association (1938), 11.

17. Schumpeter, *op. cit.,* 1041, n. 1.

18. Lewis H. Kimmel, "Experience under the Undistributed Profits Tax," *Conference Board Bulletin, 11* (1937), 105–115. The best statement on the pros and cons of the theory of the tax itself was that of Willard L. Thorp and Edwin B. George, "An Appraisal of the Undistributed Profits Tax," *Duns' Review, 45* (September 1937), 5–36.

19. A sample of the weighted type of question which reduced greatly the value of the replies is the question on business stability and the tax: "In your judgment, over a period of ten years or more will the tax tend to promote business instability by jeopardizing company reserves, or do you agree with the sponsors of the tax that it will promote business stability because of increased dividend disbursements and the resulting additions to consumer purchasing power?" Kimmel, 111. In reply to this question only 2 out of 322 stated that the tax would promote business stability.

which replied said that the tax would increase their reliance on banks and other outside sources. In 28% of the cases, the tax was a factor causing projects to be curtailed, abandoned, or postponed. In addition, 213 out of 223 thought that the tax would lead to a reduction in such projects over a period of years.

The replies which indicated that 24% relied more heavily on outside sources for working capital and that 28% had reduced projects calling for plant and equipment expenditures are the only ones which show the direct effects of the tax on investment decision. Clearly the sample is too small and too selective to be representative of all American business. Moreover, the questionnaire technique has numerous weaknesses. Nevertheless there seems to have been some ground for the contention of businessmen that the tax contributed to the recession. Some expenditure commitments were reduced. In addition, some corporations were forced to rely more heavily on funds from outside sources. If these funds were available then there was no disturbing effect, but it seems questionable whether outside funds were readily available, at least on favorable terms, to most borrowers.

Besides the objective restraints on investment, the tax had its psychological aspects. The limitations which were placed upon additions to corporate reserves added to the uncertainty and insecurity of the business community. To the extent that the tax was promoted as an instrument of social reform rather than as a source of revenue,[20] it contributed to the belief which business had that the future of long-term private investment expenditures was less secure. It served to reduce the time period of business investment planning.

SUMMARY OF THE EFFECT OF THE TAX PROGRAM

Only the social security and undistributed profits taxes appear to have had a direct influence on the timing and occurrence of the recession. The social security taxes were deflationary and the undistributed profits tax reduced corporate funds for expansion and investment. Colm and Lehmann were convinced that the tax program impeded investment expenditures:

The recent recession was due to inherently unstable conditions of business and to a governmental and credit policy which failed to meet the necessities of the phase which recovery had reached in 1936. In this defective governmental policy the tax measures must be ranked as an important depressive feature. The fiscal policy increased the difficulties by impeding

20. "The undistributed profits tax was adopted not only as an important new tax revenue but also as an instrument of social reform which would permit the government to attack the weighty problems of economic instability, corporate abuses, and inequalities of income taxation." Taken from Buehler, 3.

private investments without stimulating public investments; by increasing consumption when such a stimulus was no longer needed and by accentuating the fluctuations in the security markets.[21]

However, the significance of the tax program appears to lie not so much in its direct effect on investment expenditures as in its effects on business expectations. The tax program was only a part of the larger program in which the businessman's ethics as well as his world were under attack. The tax program played an important role in the political, social, and economic developments, which tended not only to reduce business incentives for investment but to increase the uncertainty concerning the nature of the economic system of the future. More will be said about the reasons for these uncertainties in the section on psychological and expectational factors.

REGULATIONS OF SECURITY MARKETS AND PUBLIC UTILITIES

SECURITIES AND EXCHANGE ACTS

It has already been suggested that the increases in costs from registration of securities with the Securities Exchange Commission were too inconsequential to have been of any great causal significance in the recession. Nevertheless considerable financial opinion blamed the relative stagnation in the security markets on the new regulations.[22] It is possible, of course, that the regulations antagonized the business community so that public corporate financing was restricted: "Both the requirement of registration of new securities and the direct regulation of stock market dealings—whatever their actual effects in the long run may turn out to be—created, at least for a time, mental hazards for business men who might need to float refinancing issues." [23]

Ohlin also believed that the regulations may have had a slight effect on security issues: "in 1936 the issues of new bonds and shares were probably reduced owing to the unwillingness of the financial houses to submit to the conditions imposed by the Commission. Some

21. Colm and Lehmann, 71.
22. The composition of the membership of the Securities and Exchange Commission and its expanded activities may perhaps provide some support for the belief that the business community felt an increased resentment toward the SEC in the period immediately preceding the recession. Thus, W. O. Douglas became the new chairman, 1936–37, and total suits initiated by the commission to enjoin violations of the Securities Exchange Act increased from 41 in 1935–36 to 71 in 1936–37. *Second Annual Report* (1936), 48, and *Third Annual Report* (1937), 46.
23. Albert G. Hart, *Debts and Recovery* (New York, 1937), 183–184.

traces of a general reluctance to make new issues probably survived in 1937." [24]

In spite of the opposition of business to the new measures, the conclusion still stands that the effect of these measures would appear to have been of very minor importance in explaining the stagnation in new issues.

REGULATION OF PUBLIC UTILITY COMPANIES

The regulation of the public utility companies also appears to have had little effect on the recession. Responsible opinion favored regulation of the public utility companies by the government, although there was sharp disagreement with some of the measures adopted.[25] The crucial points of disagreement were over the government's sponsorship of publicly owned utilities and its policies toward those privately owned.

Earlier it was noted that stock prices in public utilities made a relatively poor recovery from 1933 to 1937, and then declined before either industrial or railroad stock prices.[26] Moreover, the recovery from June to December 1938 was at a slower rate than for either of the other major stock groups. The weak stock prices undoubtedly reflected the threat of government competition so that investment was not made and new capital was not sought. The relative depression in the public utility industry meant that, whereas in the 1920's the industry had made large demands for new funds, during the 1930's little new money went into it. It thus seems possible that new investment in the privately owned public utility industry may have been restricted by uncertainty over the extent to which government intended to compete with it.

It was this explanation for the relative stagnation of investment in the public utility industry which was emphasized by Flanders in presenting the report of the Business Advisory Council of the Department of Commerce for the Senate committee investigating unemployment and relief:

So much has been said about the unwise vacillating and threatening policy of the Government with relation to utilities that it is unnecessary to go into the situation in detail here. Suffice it to say that no interest rate, however low, would be of the slightest service to the utilities at the present moment. The risk is so great in view of the undefined yet ever-present threat of Government competition that scarcely any interest rate that in-

---

24. Ohlin, *op. cit.*, 13.
25. Cf. testimony of Aldrich quoted below in this section.
26. Chapter 3.

vestors might demand would be too high to insure against that risk. Truly the utilities situation is the "key log in the investment jam." [27]

In the same hearings, Aldrich was critical of the government competition which generated business uncertainties: "I think that many government policies, such as that which exists or has existed in connection with utilities, where fear has been created of Government competition, *is* most unfortunate."

Later, in replying to a statement by Senator Murray on the desirability of regulating public utilities and holding companies, Aldrich said: "Oh, I wouldn't be in the slightest degree opposed to the regulation of utilities. The thing that I think is disturbing to the investment public is the threat of competition as distinguished from regulation." [28] As his parting suggestion, Aldrich asserted: "Regulation of public utilities does not cause me any fear; it is the Government going into competition with private business that I am afraid of, and it is true not only in utilities but any other kind of private business." [29]

Of course it is impossible to estimate the dollar reduction in investment expenditure which may have resulted from this threat of government competition. Flanders believed that at least a billion dollars was involved.[30] Ayres estimated the curtailed demand at close to one billion per year. Economic evidence to support this contention by business leaders that the public utility industry was "bursting to go forward" is, however, strangely lacking. Dirlam, in an unpublished thesis at Yale University, showed that the industry had a large cash surplus. Moreover, with its conservative rate structure it apparently had no need for physical expansion.[31] Nevertheless it seems reasonable to believe from the testimony of these men that the time horizon for investment in the public utility industry may have been somewhat reduced by this uncertain threat of government competition.

Psychological and Expectational Factors

In the discussion of sources of funds, profitability of investment, tax policy, and the regulation of security markets and public utilities, the objective factors which affect business investment decisions have

27. U. S. Congress, Senate, Special Committee, *Hearings, 2,* 897.
28. *Ibid., 1.* This quotation and the preceding one from 533.
29. *Ibid.,* 538.
30. *Ibid., 2,* 897.
31. Joel Dirlam, "The Regulation of Security Issues under the Public Utility Holding Company Act," unpublished doctoral dissertation, Yale University, 1947, 150–152. Gilbert also denied that government policy restrained investment in public utilities because most of their equipment was modern, and, wearing out gradually, was not yet in need of replacement. *Op. cit.,* 34–35.

been outlined. Even here it has proved almost impossible to discuss internal or external sources of funds, the profit level, the various types of taxation, the Securities Exchange Act, and the Public Utility Holding Company Act, without considering the psychological effects which these factors may have had on the way businessmen felt about the future.

These objective factors which affected investment decision operated in the political, social, and economic environment which has already been described.[32] Their consequences were modified by the sharp division of opinion between government and business representatives over the goals of the American economy. The purpose of this section is to observe and to analyze the interaction of the political, social, and economic environment and the objective factors affecting investment decision. The latter also condition the environment, so that the total expectational context is a complex product of objective and subjective factors mutually affecting each other.

The major problem is to determine the effects which the division of opinion had on investment decisions and which government policies and attitudes had upon business expectations and investment decisions. Consideration must also be given to the relationship of the stock market break to expectations and investment decisions, and to the degree of optimism or pessimism in the recession.

THE STOCK MARKET AND BUSINESS EXPECTATIONS

The sharp break in the stock market which began in the middle of 1937 and which worsened the terms of financing has already been described. Stock prices retreated over 12% from March to June, and then rebounded 8% by August. The precipitous decline of 12% in September was followed by successive declines until in December 1937 the index for all stock prices was almost 32% under that of August.[33]

Such sharp fluctuations in stock prices are likely to have had serious repercussions on business confidence and outlook. Analysis of stock market developments is difficult, however, because it seems impossible to determine whether stock prices merely reflect underlying economic conditions or represent a major factor originating economic change. There is probably an interaction, with the direct influence of stock price fluctuations dependent upon the stage of business activity. Movements in stock prices may "discount" prospective change in business conditions, but changes in stock prices may also reinforce the recovery or decline originated by other major influences.

32. Chapter 4.
33. Percentages computed from Cowles, *op. cit.*, 69.

The stock market decline which began in March 1937 preceded the decline in most major indices of economic activity. Nevertheless income, production, and employment remained high during the period March to June 1937, which may explain the upturn in stock prices from June to August. Even during this period of partial recovery Wall Street continued to generate gloom over the business outlook. This persistent gloom led the *Economist* [34] to observe that some economic significance probably should be attached to the hesitant action of the market: "It would appear that they [indices of stock prices] reflect, and have reflected over the past half year, a profound distrust of the continuity of corporate earnings. This distrust may or may not prove to be justified; but it is not to be dismissed as without economic significance." [35]

An insight into the sobering effects of the stock market decline in business and financial opinion may be had by following American stock market developments as seen through the eyes of the *Economist*. The quotation above suggested that stock market activities might be based upon underlying economic conditions. But when the major break began in September the *Economist,* along with most other market analysts, found little in the state of business and industry to account for the decline: "Whatever the future may hold for American business, nothing in the current state of industry and trade can account for this phenomenon." [36]

At the same time, however, it was impressed by the "pathology of Wall Street": "No amount of analysis of the factors making for resilience in America's domestic economy can obscure the fact that a single scare which causes the market to 'break through the lows' will provoke immediate sales from Dow theorists, chart-readers and speculative holders whose margins have run out." [37]

Because of the irrationality of the market actions, the *Economist* suggested that British investors might retreat from American stocks into U. S. Treasury bonds: "In the meantime, nervous investors who may wish to be near, but not in, Wall Street, may find that although U. S. Treasury Bonds do not yield a handsome income, they do at least provide a secure haven for capital until the snows melt and the trees begin to bud. But whether the oak will precede the ash it is, at present, impossible to say." [38]

34. An excellent source for information on developments in the American stock market.

35. *Economist, 128* (1937), 518.

36. *Ibid.,* 611.

37. *Ibid.,* 570. Or as Hansen put it: "the investing public is regimented into like-mindedness under the influence of the ubiquitous forecasting services—the drill sergeants of the modern speculative community." *Full Recovery or Stagnation?* 286.

38. *Economist, 128* (1937), 571.

While somewhat apprehensive about the future, the *Economist* still expected no general setback in American business: "Last week the markets paid more attention to their fears of a business recession in America, but even granted the possibility of a winter check, there is no new evidence to suggest that this would herald a general setback. Indeed, a great deal of old evidence suggests that this inference would be far from reasonable. There still seems, in fact, an excuse for some dogged optimism about the course of American recovery, despite the rapidly rising trend of costs." [39] This optimism, of course, proved unwarranted and the recession was general and severe.

The course of subsequent events apparently led the *Economist* to conclude finally that the stock market collapse deflated business confidence in 1937, although the market action itself was not based upon any prophetic vision of the impending crisis in business: "It would appear that the stock market collapse in 1937 . . . produced a sort of deflation of confidence or entrepreneurial initiative. It is more than doubtful whether the collapse in 1937 can be interpreted as a demonstration of the uncanny foresight of investors deliberately appraising the extent of a forthcoming business recession."

In the same issue, the *Economist* suggested that stock market developments may have an independent causal relationship to fluctuations in economic activity:

It is difficult to avoid the conclusion that conditions within the market itself may be a positive determinant of economic trends . . . . it may be persuasively argued that, while some sort of recession might otherwise have been looked for in 1937, the severity and depth of the actual depression was in large measure caused by (rather than its anticipation a cause of) the collapse in the market; and that this summer's recovery was to a considerable extent caused by (rather than a cause of) the convulsive market upswing in June. To the extent that this hypothesis is true, it implies that market appraisals are more subjective than formerly; and that even the reduction or virtual elimination of the brokers' loan account has left the market more speculative. [40]

The *Economist's* theory of the relationship of stock market movements to fluctuations in business activity has been presented for two reasons: first, to show how the original decline in stock prices was accompanied by objective developments which portended no serious decline in business activity, and second, to show how there was a gradual realization that stock price movements might exert an independent causal influence on the recession and recovery.

The better data now available on the economic trends reveal that

39. *Ibid.,* 620.
40. *Ibid., 132* (1938), both quotations from 589.

there were weaknesses in the business position some months before the September crash. Yet the signs of weakness were pretty well hidden from most observers at the time. For example, Aldrich testified that his bank saw no signs that business was slowing down until after the stock market dropped: "To tell you the truth, at the time when the stock market first dropped we did not see any signs of a recession of business, and it did not appear in the figures. It did not appear anywhere until well into September, in my opinion. I think some people might, by hindsight, say they had seen some signs of it from the middle of August on. I certainly did not appreciate it myself until well along in September." [41]

While it is possible to overestimate the causal effects of stock market activity, there is no denying that a sharp decline in stock prices may deliver a severe blow to business confidence which may not only impair the ability of the market to float new capital issues but may destroy its willingness to provide risk capital. Sagging stock prices certainly call attention to any existing or potential weakness in the economy. Stock market losses of businessmen, even if paper ones, may intensify any downward movement. Movements in stock prices, even if irrational, are likely to reduce optimistic outlooks and encourage a pessimistic appraisal of the future.

OPTIMISM AND PESSIMISM IN THE 1937–38 RECESSION

In the preceding discussion of stock market fluctuations it was concluded that sharp changes in stock market prices may affect business confidence, though they are, of course, only one of the factors which may determine business optimism or pessimism. Moreover, it is doubtful whether optimism or pessimism can be separated from the general theory of expectations and uncertainty. Nevertheless, a few general comments should be made about the state of business confidence in the 1937–38 recession.

In the first place it should be reiterated that the memory of the great depression conditioned business decisions, and intensified the gloom and pessimism which gathered as production and income declined. As Schumpeter remarked: "The downturn of 1937, following upon that of 1930, impinged upon a business community which for the time being was supernormally 'crisis conscious.' Moreover, many concerns may have harbored vivid recollections of what the 'stand' they had made in 1930 had cost them." [42]

It is probable that the business and financial community has at-

41. U. S. Congress, Senate, Special Committee, *Hearings, 1,* 527.
42. Schumpeter, n. 2, 1032.

tained a greater awareness of trade fluctuations and their consequences partly as the result of the recent experience with the great depression and partly because statistical data have been greatly improved and made more accessible. As a consequence such psychological and perhaps irrational factors as optimism and pessimism have become more important: "The more 'trade-cycle conscious' the world grows the greater becomes the significance of psychological factors and the more incalculable, therefore, the future. In regard to the general, perhaps slightly exaggerated, theorizing on the subject one can see how, the very improvement in conditions having created misgivings, which may have contributed towards conjuring up an incipient decline, people are now trying to mobilize a psychological counter-levy by denying their own fears." [43]

This difficulty of dealing with the increased irrationality which arises out of excessive optimism or pessimism has been pointed out by Mack in a discussion of the effects of psychological factors on the purchase of industrial equipment:

in talking about reasons for not purchasing equipment, it is also necessary to include irrational elements. These things are very hard to isolate and seem to take the form of going further in both restrictive and expansive actions than sensible conservatism or optimism about present and prospective business prospects could possibly warrant. There is, perhaps, something of the manic-depressive in all of us, and it is as optimism becomes manic and pessimism depressive that we must leave the area of reasonable calculation.[44]

Excessive pessimism probably was not an originating factor in the recession of 1937–38, but it doubtless contributed to the rapidity and severity of the decline. It seems probable that the psychological factors which will be discussed in the next section influenced both the recession and the revival. Their importance in the revival has been well described by the *Economist:*

It would be an exaggeration to say that the chief trouble with America today is psychological: a community of 125 millions is run on more than emotions. But it is true that the main cause of the recession is to be found in a stoppage of the channels that connect the savings of the community with the means of their concrete investment in capital goods, and now that the deflationary monetary policy of a year ago has been reversed, the hindrances are mainly those that arise out of the lack of confidence.[45]

43. *Index* (Svenska Handelsbanken),"Economic Survey," *12* (December 1937), 2.
44. Mack, 268. Such is also the position taken by Keynes in his discourse on "Animal Spirits," quoted in Chapter 4.
45. *Economist, 131* (1938), 131.

GOVERNMENT POLICIES, BUSINESS EXPECTATIONS,
AND INVESTMENT DECISIONS

Objective data may provide the background but actual business decisions are still made on the basis of what businessmen expect will happen in the future to profits, prices, taxes, political and social institutions, etc. The degree of uncertainty which surrounds business expectations about developments in any of these areas will determine the time period of investment planning and condition the response of investment expenditures. As businessmen become more uncertain about future profits, the expected profit level must be more highly discounted. The theory of expectations and of production planning will not be analyzed in this study. What is required for the arguments here is only that business decisions must be made on the basis of expectations with varying degrees of certainty of realization.[46]

It has already been emphasized that large-scale, long-term investment commitments failed to materialize in the period 1933–37. In examining the relationship of consumption expenditures to the recovery it was impossible to conclude from the evidence that the concentration on short-term investment expenditures resulted because the recovery was "consumption generated and inspired." The argument in this chapter will be that investment was confined largely to short-term commitments because of the increased uncertainties in the area of business decision which were created by government policies. There were objective changes in the relationship between government and business, but it is the political, social, and economic controversy [47] arising from the impact on business of government social reforms and policies which must bear heavy responsibility for the poor response of long-term investment expenditures. In a political and social environment which was infected with such hatreds and distrusts, the risks and uncertainties of investment decision were seriously increased. The analysis that follows presents both the pros and cons on government policy, because there are sharp differences of opinion over its effects.

Government policies not restrictive on investment commitments. There are few writers who see no causal relationship between government policies and investment expenditures. One observer, however, dissents from the prevailing opinion. There was no "general lack of confidence in the future of investments in this country which may

46. For an extended discussion of production planning, see Hicks, *op. cit.,* chaps. 15–17; and Albert G. Hart, "Anticipations, Uncertainty, and Dynamic Planning," *Journal of Business, Studies in Business Administration, 11,* No. 1 (1940), chaps. 4 and 5.

47. See Chapter 4.

have resulted from egalitarianism or authoritarianism or the financial irresponsibility of the present government or its propensity to harass business." [48]

Hansen was uncertain as to what extent the curtailed investment expenditures of the thirties resulted from government policies. He was convinced, however, that the reduced flow of investment confirmed the emergence of secular stagnation.[49] The Harvard and Tufts economists also insisted that the developments which were leading to a mature economy (declining rate of growth of population, disappearance of geographical and economic frontier, the reduced amount of capital required by new ventures) and not government policies were responsible for the poor response of private investment in the thirties: "It is largely because of these and other similar basic changes in our national life, rather than because the New Deal was 'disturbing to business confidence,' that private industry was unable to continue the recovery movement when the stimulus of government spending had been withdrawn." [50]

Two other points tend to minimize the importance of government policies for business attitudes and decisions. In the first place, although business representatives tended to argue that business confidence was the cause of profits, New Dealers could equally well argue that business confidence resulted from profits. Actually the flow of long-term investment did rise. In this connection it is important to note also that quarterly profits reached their peak in the period which included the bitter election campaign of 1936. In spite of the hatred which businessmen felt toward Roosevelt, business conditions continued to improve.[51]

The other bit of evidence which suggests that government policies may not have been too important for investment decisions concerns some political developments and the turning point in economic activity. If business confidence was so important in investment decisions, and if government policies were depressing business expectations, then it would seem that the political developments of the spring and summer of 1937 should have restored business confidence and optimism. Conservative forces in the nation had every reason to be jubilant over their triumphs in the summer of 1937. The Supreme Court reorganization bill had been defeated, a variety of proposals which the administration had made had been rejected by Congress, and the CIO had been defeated in its attempt to organize steel.[52] But the re-

48. Hardy, *op. cit.*, 171–172.
49. Hansen, *Full Recovery or Stagnation?* 283–285 and 288–299.
50. Gilbert et al., *op. cit.*, 33.
51. *Economist, 131* (1938), 192.
52. *Ibid., 128* (1937), 293.

cession occurred in the midst of these political victories, so that the strategic importance of political developments for investment decision must be somewhat discounted.[53]

Government policies as restrictive on investment expenditures. The majority opinion was that government seriously affected investment decisions. The hesitancy in business investment expenditures appeared to derive from uncertainty as to what sort of an economy the administration was attempting to promote; was the government for or against the private enterprise economy? Much objective evidence seemed to indicate that it was against. It may be argued that the failure of the government to demonstrate convincingly that it did believe in the private enterprise economy provides the key to restricted investment commitments. It is this argument which most deserves serious consideration as a major explanation for the concentration on short-term investment commitments during the period.

The testimony of William J. Kelly, president of the Machinery and Allied Products Institute, provides considerable insight into what business leaders meant when they asserted that long-term commitments were held back largely because of lack of confidence—a lack of faith in the administration's good intentions toward business and the private enterprise economy:

We must have confidence in a favorable long-range view on the part of the man who owns or operates an enterprise, and confidence on the part of the individual investor who ventures forth with the savings with which business is maintained and expanded. . . .

There is nothing about the public statements of certain conspicuous spokesmen [54] for the administration during the last 2 or 3 weeks that would inspire confidence. There is nothing in governmental anti-saving policies— such as the undistributed earnings surtax and suppression of the capital markets—that inspires confidence. . . .

There is nothing in the frequently advocated philosophy of national economic planning, with its essential coercion of free enterprise by Government, which inspires confidence on the part of the operator to seek or the investor to provide capital for new or expanding enterprise.

An operator in the durable goods industries, forced by the nature of his business to make long-range plans, must weigh these conflicting and discouraging factors. He [the small investor] asks himself: "Where are we going?" . . . He knows that no instruction has been voted to Government by the people to take any step toward the abandonment of free com-

53. However, this last argument is not too convincing because, encouraging as may have been a few political victories, Roosevelt with his propensity for experimentation and reform was still president. Many legislative statutes remained to harass the business community.

54. Kelly here refers to the addresses of Ickes and Jackson in which they attacked monopoly and monopoly pricing.

petition or of any other fundamental in our democratic system. But he is wondering what about it all.

The fact that capital is not flowing through investment channels shows that this investor—deliberately or subconsciously—is giving due weight to these important factors. Consequently he is not investing his savings, nor incurring debt. He concludes he cannot risk his capital unless and until he is sure that Government really intends to foster private enterprise, that Government will not interfere or compete with the legitimate operation of private enterprise, that it will not impose unhealthy tax restrictions, that it will insist that labor be fairly treated but resist any demands made by labor or any other group which throw the economic machine out of balance.[55]

Almost without exception business and financial writers indicted government policy for its restrictive effects on investment and for its modifications of established economic procedures:

Clearly, the existing impasse is a reflection of some new factor hitherto not present in our domestic situation. Nor does one have to seek far to determine what that factor is. It is obviously the current political philosophy which in so many ways has gone contrary to accepted economic procedure and by so doing has temporarily arrested the workings of the system of private and competitive capitalism under which this government has always heretofore operated.[56]

In addition to the uncertainties which were created by the impact of the administration's political philosophy on the existing economic system, business leadership suffered loss of prestige and social standing in the community. Business practices and ethics came up for national investigation and condemnation, which undoubtedly helped to reduce business initiative and enterprise:

Recently, however, the question of value placed on profits and growth seems to have been subjected to pressure and some resultant change, which may well be of a highly temporary sort, by some of the recent government policies concerning investigation and regulation of business conduct. When a business man is made to feel apologetic about the fact that he is connected with a large and prosperous business, one set of reasons for wanting to expand and increase profits is qualified and diminished—that having to do with the personal satisfaction and ego boost derived from it. The none too gentle interrogations conducted by "young lawyers" attached to the S.E.C., T.N.E.C., or the F.T.C. tend to make the corporation executive feel more like a martyr than a hero; . . .[57]

55. U. S. Congress, Senate, Special Committee, *Hearings, 1,* 456–457. Material in brackets added to original.

56. T. E. Hough, vice-president, Halsey, Stuart and Co., "The 1937 Bond Market," 60.

57. Mack, 295. Brockie also emphasized the unfavorable psychological repercussions of government policies, "The Rally, Crisis, and Depression, 1935–38," 224.

It would seem that increased uncertainties arose in the absence of general agreement over the extent to which the government might properly intervene in the business economy. Aldrich summarized the relationship of government policies to business uncertainties and investment as viewed by business leadership:

The general uncertainties with respect to the effect of governmental policies on business profits have had the result that business enterprises have preferred to make short-term plans based on their existing capital equipment rather than to initiate long-term plans which involve large expansion of capital equipment. The same uncertainties have had the further result that investors have preferred to buy seasoned and supposedly liquid securities rather than to finance new enterprises.[58]

It is worth noting that not only was the economy confronted with a large number of recovery measures but within a very short period of time it had to assimilate a large dose of social legislation including the Social Security Act, the Public Utility Holding Company Act, the Wagner Labor Relations Act, and so forth. The very pace of the development of social legislation intensified the conflict between government and business.

Government and business opinion on the nature and cause of the recession. The differences in government and business thinking may be illustrated by the appraisals which each made, in the fall of 1937, of the recession. The administration was slow to take action because it believed that the decline was only temporary and was affecting primarily stock market speculation. As a result, its agenda in the special session of Congress, November 1937, included an antilynching measure, an agricultural bill, and wages and hours legislation, in that order of importance and with no mention of tax reform. The business and financial sections of the economy professed to see in the recession, however, a possibility of a serious and widespread decline. Consequently they believed that tax reform should be the primary legislative concern:

This [the conflict over the legislative agenda] mirrors a fundamentally different estimate of the current recession in business. By Washington it has been repeatedly described as a brief recession, disagreeable to stock market speculators, but of no great significance to the country. New York, or at least Wall Street, regards the situation as far more serious, containing at least the germs of a protracted depression. And Wall Street is convinced that taxation is one of the basic causes of the recession.[59]

The controversy between government and business was carried on also at the political level. Thus in December 1937 Jackson and Ickes

58. Aldrich, "Business Recession in Relation to Government Policy," 120.
59. *Economist, 129* (1937), 583. Material in brackets added to original.

renewed their attacks on business, charging that the recession was a great conspiracy by "economic royalists" to discredit the administration.[60] The business community countered this argument by charging that the recession was promoted by a great conspiracy to discredit capitalistic enterprise.[61]

From the beginning of 1938 the administration insisted that the recession had been caused by monopoly pricing, whereas the testimony of businessmen at the Senate hearings indicated an almost universal belief that it was caused by government policies, principally those in the area of taxation.

The relative responsibilities of government and business for the bitter controversy. It should now be possible to assess the relative responsibilities which government and business must bear for the intense conflict between the two. There appears to be no better or more balanced analysis of the responsibility for the ill feeling between the two than that presented by the *Economist* in its April 16, 1938 issue:

For the bitterness of the dissension that now divides the President and virtually the whole business community, blame can be placed on both sides. The President professes to believe in an economic system in which the greater part of industrial enterprise is in private hands, and in any case he has neither the mandate nor the power to substitute for it a system of State control. But many of his actions have certainly had the effect of discouraging the exercise of ordinary business enterprise. He has done this by the wording of his speeches, by his labour policy, by his campaigns against an ill-defined notion of monopoly, by his enmity against the public utilities, above all by his innovations in the field of taxation, which have seemed to discriminate against bigness, wealth and conservative finance as such. Each one of these things in itself is doubtless defensible. Together they have been a frankly deflationary force. But business is also far from blameless. The leaders of industry and finance have resisted needed reforms and criticised the methods of recovery, while offering no consistent and coherent alternative to the New Deal. They have been content to live on contradictions, as when they insist on the removal of taxes and the balancing of the Budget in one and the same breath. Too much of their opposition has been neither responsible nor constructive. Above all, the business community can be criticised for deliberately working itself up into such a lather of hatred (no other word is strong enough) of the President, that its fury is choking the whole industrial and financial machine. . . . Both sides are now in the mood in which each protagonist delights to obstruct the efforts of the other, with the result that American affairs are rapidly moving towards deadlock.[62]

60. P. Einzig went so far as to suggest that big business and capital determined to "sabotage the President's New Deal legislation . . . manufacturers, business men and investors embarked upon a sit-down strike of their own." *Op. cit.,* 35–36.

61. *Economist, 129* (1937), 637.

62. *Ibid., 131* (1938), 131.

The effects of government policies on investment decisions. There is little to be added to the *Economist*'s appraisal of the factors which led to the "American Deadlock." Although some long-term investment expenditures were made, it would seem that the deadlock in American political life helped to dampen the response of long-term investment expenditures. Their failure is thus seen to be a failure of mutual understanding and cooperation between business and government.

It was not enlightened opinion alone that shaped investment decisions. Instead, many of the decisions were conditioned by the bitter division of opinion over Roosevelt and the New Deal. A balanced judgment on the Roosevelt program would lead to a less severe indictment, but the business community placed a most harsh and ungenerous interpretation on the program. Had there been an understanding between government and business, the ill effects of the objective economic changes such as occurred in taxation and government regulation might have been nominal, but in the bitter political atmosphere, long-term investment commitments were restricted.

The analysis of this section also suggests an answer to the question of whether long-term investment expenditures failed to materialize because of secular stagnation. Whatever may be the validity of this argument in the long run, it appears that long-term investment expenditures in the period 1933–37 were limited not by the absence of capital-using innovations or industries but by the uncertainties over the fate of business enterprise in the evolving economy which were generated by government policies. The argument that stagnation was indicated by a shift toward capital-saving innovation would appear to be fallacious, even if it is true, which is questionable, that innovation in the thirties tended to be of this type. Thus Fellner has shown that in the presence of rigid prices or inelastic demands innovation of whatever character eventually has a deflationary impact:

if the cost-saving industries keep their prices rigid or if the demand for their products is inelastic, a continuous flow of subsequent improvements over a period of time must have a continuous deflationary impact, regardless of whether the innovations are or are not of a "deepening" character. . . . The temporary stimulus arising out of the necessity of increasing the stock of capital goods per unit of output must soon give place to the deflationary impact of the cost reduction. . . . On the extremely complex assumptions of the argument it could only be concluded that a flow of "deepening" improvement starts a deflationary process with a slight lag, while a flow of "non-capital-using" improvement leads to deflation without any lag.[63]

63. William Fellner, "The Technological Argument of the Stagnation Thesis," *Quarterly Journal of Economics*, 55 (1940–41), 650.

It should be apparent also that the adverse cost changes, the decline in the profitability of investment, the changes in the availability of credit to business concerns, and the unfriendly government policies were of a different order of magnitude than those envisaged in the gradual emergence of diminishing returns and therefore secular stagnation. It should be added, to avoid misunderstanding, that the argument of this section does not in any way account for the occurrence or the actual timing of the recession. It does suggest some of the reasons for the under employment of resources and for the failure to achieve prosperous or boom conditions.

The criticism made here of the effects of government policies on investment decisions is not necessarily an indictment of the social reforms undertaken by the Roosevelt administration. It is possible to approve of most of Roosevelt's objectives and yet to question the timing and immediate desirability of particular reform measures. Basically it is the problem of reform versus recovery: "If the task of getting a machine going again at normal speed proves very difficult, it would seem unwise to try at the same time to rebuild certain essential parts of the machine. It is safer to leave the construction of the machine alone for some time, until certain friction and difficulties have been overcome and the machine is again running fairly well." [64]

The conclusion from this analysis is that the level of economic activity in the period was conditioned and limited by the uncertainties which arose from the operation of government policies. The response of investment to rising income thus became less marked than it would have been in the absence of these uncertainties. This feeling of increased insecurity arose from and was reflected in a bitter political, social, and economic controversy.

Summary of Relationship of Investment Expenditures to the Recession and Revival

An extended examination has now been completed of the objective and subjective factors which affected investment decision. It has been shown that there appear to have been increased imperfections in the capital supply and possibly capital shortages in certain areas. It has been suggested further that the profitability of investment, already at a "dangerously low level," was reduced early in 1937 and bears no little responsibility for the timing and emergence of the recession.

The importance of the various changes in tax laws and schedules

---

64. Ohlin, 18. A similar position was taken by Hayes: "the downturn of 1937 seems to suggest that when business confidence is unsettled, public reform or control policies (even if they are intrinsically laudable) should be carefully formulated with due consideration to their possible impact on private risk-taking." *Op. cit.,* 240.

also has been emphasized. Corporate and individual income taxes and capital gains taxes had some effect on the incentives and the willingness of business concerns to undertake investment, particularly in risk ventures. In some cases the undistributed profits tax affected the supply of funds and was closely enough related in point of time to have influenced the timing of the turning point in economic activity. The deflationary effects of the social security taxes have again been stressed.[65] The regulatory legislation of the government affected investment decision by opening the way for competition from government sources rather than by restraining investment directly.

Finally, the interrelationship and interaction of these objective factors and the political, social, and economic attitudes of the period were analyzed and evaluated for their impact upon the expectations which shaped business investment decisions. The uncertainties created by government policies as to the nature of the economic system which was evolving undoubtedly reduced the number of long-term investment commitments. It seems probable that the explanation for the low level of investment expenditures rests in these uncertainties rather than in the absence of investment opportunities stressed by the arguments for secular stagnation.

To the extent that bottlenecks arose in production because of actual physical scarcities,[66] some expansion in capacity was necessary. But only long-term investment expenditures would contribute to that end and the will to undertake such investment was notable for its absence. Under these circumstances large-scale unemployment of resources was a natural consequence.

The analysis of Chapters 12, 13, and 14 on the various investment factors makes three essential contributions to an understanding of the recession and revival of 1937–38. First, it suggests that the limited response of long-term investment expenditures to rising income was partly the result of the uncertainties over future economic developments which arose from the conflict between government and business over economic goals and methods. Second, the shortage of funds in some areas, the declining profitability of investment, and the restrictive effects of the undistributed profits and social securities taxes provide additional reasons for the recession. Third, the analysis strengthens the conviction that the primary causal factors for this particular recession operated through the area of private investment expenditures.

65. See in this connection the discussion of net government contribution and the recession in Chapter 5.

66. Colm and Lehmann insist that there were actual scarcities in certain areas such as skilled labor, and capital equipment and materials, 59.

These summary conclusions apply to the problem of the recession. The private investment factors discussed in this chapter were causal in the revival only to the extent that there was some slight reduction in the intensity of the feeling between government and business as a result of the virtual repeal of the undistributed profits tax and modification of the capital gains tax, and in so far as stock market developments had an independent causal position.

CHAPTER 15

The Recession and Revival of 1937–38: The Causal Elements

GOVERNMENT fiscal and monetary policy and consumption and private investment factors have now been investigated and analyzed for their contribution to the recession and revival. In this chapter some judgments will be made as to the relative causal significance of the developments in each of these areas.[1] The cumulative action of the factors making for the recession can best be seen by tying together the different economic elements in a time sequence. First, however, a few general remarks on the world economy as of 1936 will be made.

WORLD ECONOMIC DEVELOPMENTS IN 1936

World industrial production including that of the U.S.S.R., was 10–11% greater in 1936 than in 1929. Excluding the U.S.S.R. world production was 5% less than in 1929, largely because of the failure of production in the United States to regain or to exceed that in 1929. Production in Japan, Finland, Greece, Chile, Denmark, Norway, Estonia, Latvia, and Hungary was at least 15% above that in 1929. It was 382% of the 1929 level in the U.S.S.R., 129% in Sweden, 116% in the United Kingdom, 106% in Germany, but only 88% in the United States. French production, at only 70% of the 1929 level, made a still poorer showing. Production in all other countries for which data are available was 10–30% below the 1929 level.

The recovery in production in both Sweden and the United Kingdom was largely due to the construction boom. In Sweden, buildings completed were 213% of 1929 in 1935, and 171% in 1936. In the United Kingdom, value of permits was 156% of 1929 in 1935, and 160% in 1936. In striking contrast with these figures is the value of permits in the United States, which was 27% of 1929 in 1935 and 41% in 1936.[2]

1. For a discussion of the methodological and statistical limitations of this analysis and an indication of the extent to which these judgments are imperfect and intuitive, see the section below on the limitations of the analysis and portions of Chapter 16.
2. All of the above data are taken from Condliffe, 68–73.

In the manufacturing countries of the world, production as a whole "was rapidly emerging from the depression into the prosperity, if not the boom, stage of the business cycle." [3] Until the end, or at least until the middle, of 1936 the recovery owed little to rearmament expenditures. However, in the first half of 1937 these accentuated the signs of boom conditions in some of the manufacturing countries, particularly England and Germany. The increasing reliance on rearmament programs and the considerable rise in raw material and wholesale prices which began in the middle of 1936 led to some misapprehension over the maintenance of world prosperity.

AMERICAN ECONOMIC DEVELOPMENTS, MAY 1936 THROUGH JUNE 1938

RECOVERY MOVEMENT UNDERWAY, MAY THROUGH DECEMBER 1936

In May 1936, after three full years of recovery, there were still from 8 to 10 million persons unemployed. Real income paid out and industrial production were both 10% less than in 1929, corporate profits almost 50% less, and wholesale prices 18% less. However, though wholesale prices were even less than in the same month of the preceding year, real income, industrial production, and corporate profits were rising. The American economy appeared to be moving toward full recovery.

Prices, production, and income rose rapidly during the remainder of 1936. A stimulating factor was the new peak level in government net contribution to income as a result of the payment of the soldiers' bonus, beginning on June 15, 1936. In the next two months $1,200 million of the $1,700 million total bonus payment were converted into cash. By the end of the year conversions into cash reached a total of $1,400 million. Production increased by 16%; real weekly wage earnings in manufacturing by 6%; and nonagricultural employment by 1.5 million persons. Profits continued to rise, reaching a peak (for the 1933–37 recovery) in the fourth quarter of 1936. New corporate issues revived in response to the marked increase in profits and production.

Expansion in these areas was accompanied by other developments which suggested that trouble loomed ahead. Wholesale prices began to rise rapidly. Prices of semifinished goods increased by 11%, raw materials prices by 13%, and iron and steel prices by 7%. Many businessmen increased forward orders to insure adequate supplies of raw materials, some to anticipate further price rises. When the price rises

3. *Ibid.*, 42.

ceased, disappointments were to be anticipated, particularly if production and income had not increased according to previous expectations.

In August 1936 the Federal Reserve Board had increased reserve ratios by 50% without any apparent effect on business conditions. In December 1936, however, the price of short-term U. S. Government notes weakened, as banks sought to obtain the reserves necessary to comply with a second increase of 50% in reserve requirements.

The undistributed profits tax of June 1936 led to a large outpouring of dividends in December 1936. Although this payment initially stimulated consumption, the reduction in cash position proved to be a real, as well as a psychological, deterrent to business confidence and investment. At the same time, the new social security taxes were collected and served to reduce the income available for consumption expenditures.

WEAK SPOTS APPEAR IN THE ECONOMY, JANUARY
THROUGH MAY 1937

During the first five months of 1937 signs of impending difficulty multiplied. In January production began to decline in both producer and consumer nondurable goods industries. Significantly, there is a suggestion that profits began to decline in the first quarter, as wage and materials costs continued to increase. From December 1936 to April 1937 real weekly wages in manufacturing increased 5.5%. While semifinished goods prices were increasing 9%, raw materials prices increased 6% to their peak in March, followed by a sharp price decline which caused heavy losses to speculators and contributed to a tempering of business optimism. A pronounced weakness was revealed in the securities markets. Corporate bond prices began to decline in January, long-term governments in February, and common stock prices in the middle of March. In March there was also an important downturn in the private construction industry, which was already at a low ebb. Net government contribution to income declined sharply as tax collections rose because of the new social security taxes. The monthly net government contribution was reduced by $300 million from January through March, thus removing one of the basic supports to income and production.

Even as these weak spots appeared, the President, in April 1937, spoke out sharply against high prices in the durable goods industries. Believing that price rises were resulting in excessively high profits, he ordered a shift in public works expenditures away from these industries.

Income and production continued to increase in spite of these depressing developments. The peak in industrial production was attained in May 1937, when income was 4% above the December 1936 level. Private investment expenditures were greater in the second quarter of 1937 than in the fourth quarter of 1936, the previous peak.

FIRST SERIOUS DECLINES IN BUSINESS ACTIVITY, JUNE THROUGH SEPTEMBER 1937

The first serious declines in the major indices of business activity occurred in the summer months. Industrial production, while relatively stable in June, July, and August, fell by 5% in September. Real weekly earnings declined almost 5.5% in the same period, although average hourly earnings increased another 2%. Profits declined by 15%, while wholesale prices were unchanged. Net private investment other than inventories declined 25%, and in many areas new orders fell considerably below current shipments. Stock prices sagged 12% from August to September. The recession was under way.

It should be noted that the outstanding characteristic of the recovery from 1933 to 1937 was the achievement of all-time highs in industrial production. However, this was accompanied by a large volume of unemployment and a failure of national income per capita and in current prices to surpass the peaks of the twenties. In capital formation items, producer equipment expenditures were at new highs, while private construction expenditures were at extremely low levels. In the cost items, hourly wages and real weekly wages reached peak levels. Prices of finished and semifinished goods and raw materials rose sharply through March 1937, although semifinished goods and raw materials prices declined thereafter. Monetary and credit conditions were easy. Government net contribution to income almost ceased, as tax revenues increased and government expenditures remained relatively constant.

THE RECESSION PERIOD, OCTOBER 1937 THROUGH JUNE 1938

In severity, the nine-month decline from September 1937 to June 1938 is without parallel in American economic history.[4] Industrial production declined 33%. Durable goods production declined by more than 50%, national income by 13%, profits by 78%, payrolls by 35%, industrial stock averages by over 50% (with a 35% drop in five months), and manufacturing employment by 23%. At the

---

4. It was certainly the sharpest decline in any period for which there are statistical data.

same time, although raw materials prices fell 21%, most prices and costs resisted the decline.

INTERNATIONAL REPERCUSSIONS OF THE AMERICAN RECESSION

It is quite clear that the causes for the American recession originated in America, and not in world economic developments. It is also apparent that world prosperity was bound up with American economic developments. As the American recession began, Ohlin raised the question whether world prosperity could be maintained. He concluded that since neither the United States nor France, of the industrial nations, had experienced a full recovery, the developments in these two countries would largely determine the course of world economic development.[5]

By March 1938 the world was faced not with the question of whether world prosperity could be maintained but of whether the recession of 1937, now world wide, heralded a depression as severe as in 1929. A French observer insisted that the answer to this question rested almost entirely on the economic developments in America.[6] This world dependence on the United States was even greater in 1938 than it would have been in 1935–36 when production in England and Sweden was booming. The same writer concluded that the world situation in 1938 was much better than in 1929. Stocks of raw materials and commodities had not accumulated so excessively, money and credit conditions were much easier, and the necessity for state intervention to prevent serious deflation was widely accepted.[7]

The recession of 1937 in America provides convincing evidence of how dependent the rest of the world is on American economic developments. The fate of world production and prosperity was inextricably bound up with the rise and fall of American economic activity.

THE CAUSES OF THE RECESSION

In broad outline, the causation may be reduced to a relatively few important elements. In an economy which was still excessively depression conscious and in which business expectations were extremely uncertain,[8] net government contribution to income was drastically reduced in January 1937. Consequently, the responsibility for sustaining and increasing national income and production was shifted to private investment and enterprise.

5. Ohlin, 3–4.
6. E. Wagemann, "Le Problème des prix dans l'économie mondiale," *Revue économique internationale, 30* (1938), 430.
7. *Ibid.*, 434.
8. In part this was because of the serious political conflict between the New Deal and business.

However, at the same time that net government contribution ceased, the Federal Reserve action on excess reserves caused short-term governments to weaken and set up thereby a chain of reactions which resulted in increased costs of capital and the weakening of the securities markets to which business expectations are very sensitive, especially in the United States. The operation of the undistributed profits tax, in addition to its effects on business expectations, also reduced the cash position of even the large companies. The imperfect supply of capital funds and their increased cost made it more difficult for borrowers to obtain capital.

Most important of all, however, was the reduced profitability of investment, beginning in the first quarter of 1937. This resulted from the increased costs, in which labor costs played a prominent part. Given a situation in which businessmen were most unwilling to initiate long-term investment projects which alone could raise income and production to higher levels, the immediate decline in profit ratio, accompanied by the prospect of sharp declines in future profits, is adequate reason for the occurrence and timing of the recession.

In brief, these were the causal elements in the recession. In no sense can it be concluded that any one factor caused the downturn of 1937, since an explanation on the basis of changes in a single variable would ignore the importance of the other causal elements.

Limitations of the Analysis

It should also be observed here that a serious limitation on all the analysis has been the lack of reliability and comparability of certain of the data. This has been true especially of the series on income payments, consumption expenditures, industrial production, inventories, and corporate profits. In spite of the fact that the data in the 1933–38 period are undeniably superior to those in any prior period in American economic history, it is still extremely disconcerting to find that the analysis of economic developments in so many crucial areas is dependent on a single series with serious weakness in derivation, or several series which are quite obviously inconsistent with one another.

Not only are there unexplained inconsistencies in the data, but, what is even more important for a study of turning points in business fluctuations, the direction of change may be uncertain. Generalizations in economic studies are often made on the basis of 2–3% changes in the variables, yet the statistical reliability of the data may not be within 5 to 10% or even more. This is especially important in the study of the recession of 1937–38, since the causal impact of the early decline in profitability of investment has been emphasized. Likewise, observations about the depressive effects of increases in wage costs are valid only if the timing of the decline in the profitability of investment is reasonably accurate. Yet, as already mentioned, there is but one series of profits available, and some of its components are derived from very inadequate data. It does not appear likely, therefore, that the turning point was actually reached until the second quarter of 1937, when this series stood 5% below its level for the fourth quarter of 1936. In fact, only by the third quarter of 1937, when profits had fallen 20% below the fourth quarter of 1936, is it possible to be absolutely confident that profits had declined. Even with imperfect data, such a large percentage decline must be taken to be statistically significant.

In spite of the limitations of the data it seems likely that the recession was originated by the decline in investment expenditures. The point first advanced in Chapter 13 must be made again, that in a free enterprise economy where profits are low enough an increase in costs, rather than stimulating increases in production and income through expanded consumption expenditures, can lead to an almost complete cessation of investment. In retrospect it would appear that something like this occurred in the second and third quarters of 1937 and was followed promptly by the recession.

First Signs of Revival, January through May 1938

Although production and income continued to sag, with income reaching a low in May and production in June 1938, there were signs of an incipient revival some months before. Total and private construction contracts began to increase in March. The President's new "spend-lend" program, based on a reversal of the fiscal and monetary policies of 1936 and 1937, was finally announced in the middle of April. The favorable effects of this expansionary program were undoubtedly anticipated before the program actually got under way. Also, from October 1937 through April 1938, the net export surplus averaged over $100 million per month as imports declined and exports remained relatively constant. Moreover, by June retail sales, department store sales, electric power production, orders for manufactured goods, production of minerals, and several other series had begun to increase.

The Causes of the Revival

The modifications of the undistributed profits and capital gains taxes improved the climate of business opinion. It is also probable that the reduction of inventories and production to the point where they were in balance with current consumption left the economy ripe for revival. But in spite of the tax changes, the improved consumption-production relationship, and the revival of some component economic series before production or income revived, the major if not the exclusive responsibility for stimulating the revival must rest with the new spend-lend program. Only the recovery in the construction series antedated the President's announcement of the new deficit spending program. There is no evidence of substantial changes in any of the other important economic variables which could account for the revival. With the exception of the revival in construction, the turning points in the other series which occurred in May or June could well have resulted from the more favorable anticipations created by the newly announced government spending. The economy may have been ready for revival but the major initiating impulse appears to have come from either the renewed spending itself or anticipation of the favorable effects following from the renewed spending. No other explanation seems consistent with the observed changes in the economic data.

CHAPTER 16

Relationship of the Recession and Revival of 1937–38 to Business Cycle Theory and Implications for Public Policy Formation

PURPOSES OF THE STUDY

This study was conceived in part as an attempt to test business cycle theory by empirical means. The source of much of the disagreement and confusion in the theory appears to have been an unwillingness to examine the economic data in full detail and then evaluate critically the relevance of particular business cycle theories to an explanation of a fluctuation in the real world. It has often been observed that most business cycle explanations are logically coherent. But the crucial test for any theory is its contribution to an understanding of the actual events of the real world.

Much of business cycle theory has been constructed as reasonable hypothesis but has not been tested empirically and impartially. Such a criticism might well be made of some of the theories underlying Keynesian recommendations for public policy and also some of Hansen's prescriptions for policy. The economist develops a theory of business cycles and often tests its relevance by selecting from among the many economic variables those whose behavior best supports his theoretical position. Other variables and data which cast doubt upon its validity may be ignored.

This sort of criticism may be made, to take an example, of Schumpeter's business cycle analysis. No one could accuse Schumpeter of failing to examine the empirical data. But in some cases he apparently selected the economic data which tended to validate his theoretical structure. His study is an outstanding contribution to the understanding of fluctuations, but surely there is reason to question the necessity which he seemed to feel existed for interpreting each ripple and wave of the many economic variables in terms of the three-cycle schema.

It is, of course, true that at various points he specifically denied that the validity of his theoretical model was in any way dependent upon the close time correlation of the three cycles. But having said this he ignored his own counsel, and still found it necessary to advance special reasons for the failure of any of the economic variables to perform in the way expected from his theoretical model.

This criticism of the method of testing business cycle theory which has been employed by many economists who have been among those determining public economic policy should not be interpreted as an attack upon the theoretical approach to a study of business fluctuations. In no sense is an antitheoretical approach, an exclusively inductive procedure, a good or adequate substitute. In fact while the selective empirical approach of Keynes, Hansen, Schumpeter, and others may be criticized, the largely empirical approach of the National Bureau of Economic Research has not been entirely satisfactory either. Its reliance on extensive observation of fact is commendable, and its analysis is not completely lacking in theoretical structure since it arises from Wesley C. Mitchell's theory of business fluctuations. But until recently the Bureau failed to ask many of the relevant questions about causation, and seldom reached the point where judgments were made about the relative causal responsibility of particular variables for business fluctuations. One weakness in the National Bureau approach would seem to have been the overconcentration on a systematic analysis of a multitude of economic series, to the neglect of the collection and analysis of data in certain extremely important areas of the economy. In other words, the most comprehensive observation of empirical data contributes little to an understanding of reality if an attempt is not made to discriminate in some way among the many economic series, preferably on the basis of relative causal importance.[1]

This study of the recession and revival of 1937–38 was undertaken in part as a reaction against the inadequate testing of business cycle theory, and also against excessively inductive analysis of business fluctuations. The method has been to study critically all the major variables for which statistics are available, in order to provide a test of the adequacy of the various business cycle theories to explain a particular fluctuation. The study has reversed the conventional approach to fluctuations which begins with a critical analysis of business cycle theory and then examines empirical data. Instead, it accepts the

---

1. However, this criticism of the National Bureau seems to be losing its sting if more recent publications are evidence of the future direction of Bureau activity. Cf. in this connection, Moses Abramovitz, *Inventories and Business Cycles, with Special Reference to Manufacturers' Inventories* (New York, 1950); Arthur F. Burns, *New Facts on Business Cycles* (New York, 1950); and others.

fact that there are many theories of the business cycle and that each is logically airtight. Instead of refining upon these theories, an attempt was made to study objectively a particular fluctuation in its entirety. The economic variables were examined without a prior acceptance of any theory of the business cycle as more valid than any other, except in the limited degree to which the system of classification of causes resembles a theory.[2] It was necessary first to try to find out *what happened,* and *where,* and insofar as possible *why,* before the special relevance or contribution of a particular business cycle theory to the understanding of the real world could be verified.

In spite of an unwillingness to approach the problem with any preconceived notion as to the relevant cycle theory for the 1937–38 fluctuation, the writer must confess a slight initial bias toward the necessity and desirability of stimulating investment expenditures as a major support to a free enterprise economy, and as a means of obtaining economic progress in the real sense.

Before attempting to relate some of the findings of this study to the verification or invalidation of general business cycle theory, it is necessary to comment briefly upon methodology and the extent to which empirical analysis can be said to prove or disprove any business cycle theory. In the first place, as was stressed in Chapter 10, it is impossible to prove any theory from the data. Therefore, the problem in the use of data is to search for disproof. It is not even possible to prove that one theory is valid by disproving all other theories. It is, of course, possible to suggest that certain data are *not* inconsistent with the given hypothesis. But the mere disproof of all other theories, and the demonstration that the data are consistent with the given hypothesis, is not proof of the validity of the theory. Nevertheless it seems reasonable to believe that the data, with all their weaknesses, disprove the theory that any one cause was responsible for the recession or the revival. Beyond this, preference for one or another set of causal factors must be based partly on intuitive judgment. For this reason the suggestions which follow (as well as all the judgments of the preceding chapter) will necessarily be only *opinions* as to the operation of causal factors in this or any other business fluctuations.

This study suggests that in general the right questions are not yet being raised in the analysis of business fluctuations. Therefore, subject to the qualifications of the preceding paragraph, an attempt will be made to summarize the meaning of the recession and revival of 1937–38 for business cycle theory.

2. See below the discussion under the section on the Usefulness of Tools of National Income Analysis.

Contribution to Business Cycle Theory

First, this study demonstrates the usefulness of classifying and analyzing business fluctuations by concentrating on the components and determinants of the flow of national income. By observing the circulation of income from period to period through the various institutional channels, the forces of restriction, stability, and expansion can be observed directly.

Second, a single or simple causal explanation of any business fluctuation seems inadequate. The causal factors operating in a business fluctuation appear to be complex and multiple.

Third, the term business fluctuation rather than business cycle is used advisedly. Because of the complex, somewhat fortuitous, conjuncture of factors in a fluctuation there would seem to be no such thing as a business cycle, in the sense of a periodic recurrence of business fluctuations in which the same causal factors are present in relatively the same proportion and to the same degree. No useful purpose is served by continuing to think in cyclical terms. In fact, such thinking may prevent intelligent appraisal and attempted control of business fluctuations.

Fourth, if the process of business fluctuations is wrongly described as cyclical, then each fluctuation is unique and must be studied carefully for its own important causal elements.

In the fifth place, the recession of 1937–38 specifically points up the problem of prices, costs, and the profitability of investment in a free enterprise economy.

Sixth, the relative economic stagnation in the thirties, which contributed to the emergence of the recession, was primarily the result of uncertainties created largely by government policies and attitudes, rather than the result of a mature economy. The dramatic effects of the prolonged depression had destroyed the indispensable optimism of private enterprise.

Finally, the methodology used in this study is applicable in the productive analysis of other business fluctuations. Studies of all business fluctuations since the first World War should be made by exhaustive analysis of the economic series. Only by so doing can the theories be confirmed, modified, or rejected. The time has come to verify existing business fluctuation theories not by the "neutral" compilation of data but by their evaluation in terms of causative factors.

THE USEFULNESS OF THE TOOLS OF NATIONAL INCOME ANALYSIS

This analysis has been aided greatly by the use of the formal apparatus (stemming from the Keynesian identities and the analysis of the National Bureau of Economic Research and Department of Commerce) in which three areas of decision, private investment expenditures, consumption expenditures, and the circuit of government finance, are the only paths by which the level of production, income, and employment can be affected. The changes in all economic variables may affect national income, production, or employment only by initiating a change in one of these areas. It must be recognized, of course, that conceiving the problem in these terms still does not reveal the effective causation. What it does do, however, is to concentrate attention on the changes in particular variables which did affect the course of recession and recovery through one of these channels. The formal model in which changes in economic variables impinge on the national economy only through private investment spending, consumption spending, and government spending provides the most effective means of classifying and analyzing the determinants of national income and employment.

This system of classification may be regarded, to a limited degree, as a theory of business fluctuations. In a very formal sense it is probably a theory of causation, just as the Hicksian-Lange tools of general equilibrium analyis imply certain things about causal relationships. Although the classification of causal factors employed in this study cannot establish the relative causal responsibility, it does determine the method of analysis and select the points of emphasis. To this extent it is a theory of causal relationships but not in the generally accepted sense of a theory of business cycles.

A SIMPLE EXPLANATION OF A BUSINESS FLUCTUATION IS WRONG

The causation of the recession of 1937–38 was complex rather than simple. It was impossible to explain why the recession occurred by selecting one variable such as net government contribution as the unique cause. For example, the decline in net government contribution might not have been followed by recession in private investment if it had not taken place so quickly, or if it had not been accompanied by sharp wage increases, or by banking policy which discouraged new financing. The only adequate explanation of the recession lies in the several causal factors which emerged to accelerate the tendencies toward recession. Even in the revival, which was less complex in causation because of the predominant importance of net government contribution, other factors, such as construction expenditures, net export balance, and so forth were also causal.

It seems reasonable to believe further that any sizable fluctuation in business activity must be the product of many forces.[3] No change in any single variable seems adequate to initiate a recession or revival. In 1937–38 the decline in net government contribution gave a severe jolt to the economic system but was insufficient by itself to initiate the recession. It took the developments in other areas as well, such as cost increases, decrease in profitability of investment, banking and government policy, changes in taxes, and so on to precipitate the recession.

If fluctuations are caused by a complex of factors, a theory which relies on changes in a particular variable or the occurrence of a particular event would be an inferior explanation of the fluctuation. An example of the latter is the statement made by Hansen that the recession of 1927 was due to the shutdown of the Ford plant: "The Ford shutdown in 1927 produced a minor recession, . . ."[4] The inconsistency of this statement with the significant movements of the many economic variables which accompany any fluctuation was later recognized by Hansen: "Sometimes special situations are partly responsible for minor recessions, . . . such as the Ford shutdown in 1927."[5]

It seems unrealistic and inconsistent with the economic data to believe that a change in a single factor such as interest rate, capital supply, or inventory accumulation could by itself initiate a recession or revival in an economy as immense, dynamic, and changing as is the American economy.

FLUCTUATIONS RATHER THAN BUSINESS CYCLES

Because there was no single factor responsible for the recession of 1937–38, and because the recession was the product of many causal elements in unique combination, there is reason to question whether there is a business cycle. There are business fluctuations but are there business cycles? There are, of course, recognizable cyclical movements in the major economic variables as, for example, in construction activity and the replacement cycle. There are also causal factors which may be common to more than one fluctuation. Moreover, even if no business fluctuation is exactly like any other this does not mean that there are no fundamental factors in business fluctuations. It does not disprove the existence or the importance of these fundamental fac-

3. The only exception to this statement might be a revival initiated by the huge government expenditures which attend preparation for or the actual prosecution of war, and even this is no exception because of the interaction of a new psychological situation.
4. Hansen, *Full Recovery or Stagnation?* 301.
5. Hansen, *Fiscal Policy and Business Cycles*, 17.

tors. Nevertheless, the uniqueness of the events which precipitated the 1937–38 recession makes it difficult to believe that its causal elements will ever again be combined in the same way to produce a similar recession. The factors which resulted in the 1937–38 recession will inevitably be present in any subsequent recession, but not with the same relative importance, even though a recession may more closely resemble one type of fluctuation than another in structure and character.

There is no reason to believe that the movement of the economic variables makes each business fluctuation a replica of every other business fluctuation. A theory which attempts to explain *all* business fluctuations must take this into account lest it result in abstractions which are far from adequate or realistic as explanations of developments in the real world. Perhaps too much time and effort have been given to determining the length of "business cycles" and their universal characteristics, rather than to examining each fluctuation in terms of the observed economic variables and data. Efforts to isolate a common causal element for all fluctuations, in the belief that they are similar and cyclical, may well do a disservice to a better understanding of such fluctuations.

EACH BUSINESS FLUCTUATION IS UNIQUE

If business fluctuations are caused by a complex of factors which are not necessarily cyclical, then each fluctuation is unique and must be analyzed in terms of its own peculiar causes. In some recessions the more important area of decision may be in the consumption factors. In others, as for example 1937–38, the important decisions may be in the investment area. In still others (the revival of 1938) the major responsibility may rest with the effects of government intervention. It is not possible to predict which area of decision will be the most important.

Because business fluctuations may result from changes in any of these areas, "hand picked" fluctuations may support almost any business cycle theory. It is possible that there are recessions which result primarily from underconsumption. Others undoubtedly stem primarily from underinvestment, although either the underconsumption or underinvestment recessions will be the product of many factors. For example, the changes in the many variables in the area of investment decision (increased costs and taxes, reduced profits), along with government policies, were largely responsible for the 1937–38 recession. But any theory which places exclusive reliance on the change in one variable as the reason for a fluctuation is likely to be in error. Moreover, even when qualified to the extent that the particular factor is said to be only the *more* important variable in a recession, the theory errs if the factor is charged with major responsibility in every fluctuation. There seems to be no theoretical or empirical reason why one variable should be most important in all fluctuations.

If each fluctuation is unique and caused by a combination of factors peculiar to it, the problem of government intervention and policy is made much more difficult. But this does not imply that business fluctuations are "inevitable" or beyond control by business and governmental policies. Discussion of these difficulties will be reserved to the final section. Suffice it to say here that even if each fluctuation is unique there are still certain very sensitive areas in all fluctuations where the crucial decisions made require careful attention and observation. And since there are probably more similarities than dissimilarities between certain types of fluctuations as, for example, inventory fluctuations, it is possible at least to make an imperfect classification.

THE PROBLEM OF PRICES, COSTS, AND THE PROFIT-
ABILITY OF INVESTMENT IN A FREE ENTERPRISE
ECONOMY

Perhaps most significant has been the insistence that in a free enterprise economy adequate investment expenditures are not made when the prospects of profits are too low. In the eagerness to redistribute income and to promote greater equality in the ownership of wealth sight must not be lost of the fact that profits are essential to the operation of a private enterprise economy. Until there is substituted an economic system with different incentives and problems, it would seem that "satisfactory profits" are a price which must be paid if a reasonably full utilization of resources is to be attained under private direction. Most would probably feel that this is not too high a price to pay for a progressive economy. In existing tax laws there are adequate safeguards against an undue accumulation of wealth, or against an increasing inequality in the distribution of wealth. And the acceptance of the necessity for government intervention to maintain employment provides a final safeguard against the widespread ravages of severe depression.

As a point of emphasis, it would seem unwise to accept the belief that the best and only solution to the economic problems is exclusive reliance on redistribution of consumer purchasing power or income, or, in familiar terms, that the surest way to national economic health is to increase money wages without regard for what that does to profits. Raising money wages, as an economic "cure-all" in the face of depression or threatened recession, or even occasionally during booms, has become a faith with labor, many government representatives, and even with some business representatives. But if a choice has to be made between increased wages or increased profits there are numerous occasions when a strong case can be made for the latter. At times an additional emphasis on profits may make possible increases in real wages. Is it too much to say that the fundamental problem is an increased standard of living rather than redistribution? There is great need for expanded investment expenditures and the accumulation of capital equipment so that the general standard of living may be increased and the pressing desire for economic goods, health, recreation, and national well-being may best be met. The experience in the thirties would seem to demonstrate that substantial profits must be obtained to stimulate expanded investment expenditures. The increases in wages in the thirties appear to have been at the expense of increased national income and of employment because profits and investment were depressed. The values secured from the added investment expenditures should far outweigh any unfavorable social consequences of the increased flow of profit income.

Apart from the desirability of an increased flow of investment expenditures which can occur only with the prospects of adequate profits, the point must be made again that decreases in an otherwise low profit rate can lead to a complete cessation of investment expenditures and hence to a recession period.

STAGNATION DUE TO UNCERTAINTIES ARISING FROM GOVERNMENT POLICIES

Examination of the political and social environment revealed the seriousness of the cleavage in government and business opinion during the thirties. While it is possible that in certain areas a relative saturation of investment outlets had occurred, the position taken in this study is that the business feeling of uncertainty, however irrational, was responsible for the failure of long-term investment expenditures. In the character of certain government policies, and with the low rate of profitability on investment, there were reasons to question whether income from long-term investment in the future would be adequate to compensate for the risk involved, and whether such investment would long remain under private direction and in private hands.

Neither in the mature economy doctrine nor in the climate of political opinion is there an adequate explanation for the occurrence of the recession. But it is necessary to understand why resources were not fully employed when the recession occurred. It is also extremely important from a policy standpoint to decide whether the stagnation in the thirties resulted from the emergence of a mature economy or from the business uncertainties generated by government policies. Neither proposition is susceptible of absolute proof, but it would seem unwise to condition or limit analyses of business fluctuations by the special considerations which pertain only to the mature economy thesis. Recommendations on the proper public policy will be made in a later section, but the position held concerning the mature economy doctrine helps to determine the direction and types of public policy recommendations.

ADDITIONAL STUDIES OF RECENT FLUCTUATIONS DESIRABLE

A final suggestion is that similar studies be made of the fluctuations since 1919. It is time to approach these fluctuations as objectively as possible, to examine critically all the major economic variables, and to evaluate the causal elements in terms of business fluctuation theory.

It would be desirable to analyze the recessions of 1920–21, 1924, and 1927 with the methods of this study. Further analysis of the recession of 1920–21 is probably desirable, in spite of the recent work of Wilson and Gordon. The recessions of 1924 and 1927 have particular interest today because they occurred during periods of relatively full utilization of resources and were not preceded by any rise in general prices. The examination of both should provide some understanding of the problems faced in a period of reasonably full employment of resources.

The Great Depression of 1929–32, above all, should have this careful study of the many economic variables. The Great Depression should have more searching analysis than other business fluctuations because of its impact upon recent business cycle theory.

The general recommendation is for comprehensive examination and analysis of the economic data to permit rigorous testing of business cycle theories. Conclusions drawn from these studies will necessarily be tentative and intuitive, but only in such an approach does it seem possible to progress toward the understanding and control of business fluctuations.

WEAKNESSES IN GOVERNMENT POLICIES IN THE 1937 RECESSION

The analyses of Chapters 5 and 7 have shown that both government fiscal and monetary policies contributed to the recession. The untimeliness of certain of the governmental actions shows the great difficulties which beset government policy-makers when determining the areas of potential maladjustment in the economic system and initiating appropriate and effective remedial measures.

The second increase in reserve requirements was clearly an error of judgment. The Federal Reserve authorities assessed wrongly the nature of the new excess reserves of member banks. Not only this, but there were economic developments which should have restrained them from taking restrictive action on reserves. Production of nondurable goods reached its peak in December 1936 and began to sag in January 1937. Also, the Reserve authorities should have known that the stimulating effects of government spending on the economy were ending early in 1937, and as a consequence there would be one less powerful pressure for higher prices and increased production.

There were, of course, the extenuating circumstances surrounding the Reserve action discussed in the earlier chapters, such as the ease of adjustment which accompanied the first change in excess reserves, the almost unanimous public support for the second change in reserve ratios, the surveys by the Reserve authorities of excess reserves which showed them widely distributed, and the persistent belief that the old velocity of circulation of deposits would soon be reasserted. These factors help to explain why it was believed that the action would have no ill effects on the economy. But the action on reserves was unwise in view of the large-scale unemployment of resources. It is difficult to see any danger in excess reserves when 8 to 9 million persons are still unemployed. Under such conditions what meaning can be given to the argument that excess reserves should be eliminated before an unsound expansion of credit occurs? If resources are fully employed, as in 1945 to 1953, and reserves are still excessive, then an additional expansion in deposits may be unwise. But with resources unemployed it would seem desirable to encourage a superstructure of credit on the existing excess reserves.

Had more attention been paid to the over-all problem of the fuller utilization of resources than to the technical fact of excess reserves, it is less likely that the policy error of 1937 would have been made. The experience from this period certainly suggests the danger of formulating policy in the expectation that there will be an early return to normal conditions.

The problem created by the cessation of net government contribution to the flow of income were little understood and very inadequately treated. It should have been self-evident that early in 1937 the Federal Government was to cease being a net supplier of money income to the community. This should have directed the attention of government economists to the problems of promoting adequate private investment expenditures. Yet, in spite of the fact that production of nondurable manufactures by April 1937 was almost 20% above its 1929 peak, whereas production of durable manufactures was 6% less than its 1929 peak, the President attacked the pricing policies in durable goods industries and proposed to withdraw government support and encouragement. He acted in the belief that industrial profits were inflated in the spring of 1937, and that the threat to full recovery lay in rapidly increasing profits and lagging consumer incomes. Apparently no consideration was given by the President and his advisers to the crucial relationship between profits and investment expenditures.

It is possible that some of the difficulties created by government fiscal policies were due to the lack of any central agency charged with responsibility for studying the effects of economic developments in every sector of the economy. The establishment in 1946 of the President's Council of Economic Advisers was expected to remedy any such defect in government planning.[6]

Besides their failure to see the over-all effects of government policies on the economy, it is quite possible that government officials erred in 1937 because they accepted uncritically the theory that every business fluctuation results from underconsumption. Because government economists accepted the underconsumptionist theory of price-cost relationships, little consideration was given to stimulating and encouraging investment expenditures by private enterprise. Yet with the decline in net government contribution to income, the best possibility of increasing income, production, and employment lay in an increased flow of private investment expenditures. But strong commitment on the part of many government economists to the underconsumption theory seems to have precluded objective appraisal of economic developments. As was argued above, it would seem that a doctrinaire commitment to any theory [7] of business fluctuations as *the* explanation of turning points in business activity prevents an objective appraisal of the factors promoting recession or revival as well as an objective prescription for public policy.

THE PROBLEM OF IMPROVING GOVERNMENT POLICIES

Since government policies in 1937 seem to have resulted from a narrow and inadequate appraisal of economic developments, a re-

6. Nevertheless, the record of the Council for short-run forecasting has not been distinguished. The Council was concerned over depression in 1947 and inflation in 1949. See Villard, "The Council of Economic Advisers and Depression Policy," *American Economic Review, 40* (1950), 600–604.

7. In the narrow sense as defined above and not in the sense of a formal classification of causal relationship.

orientation in approach is necessary if government policies are to become more effective.

POLICY MORE DIFFICULT IF EACH FLUCTUATION UNIQUE

If it is recognized, as suggested, that each business fluctuation is unique, the problem of public policy or public control is made more difficult. Economic analysis must not be prejudiced by acceptance of a single theory, such as underconsumption, as the explanation for all business fluctuations. Instead there must be a willingness to examine all the major economic variables with no prior commitment as to what factors are responsible for the particular business fluctuation.

However, many of the recommendations of government officials suggest such a commitment. For example, some of President Truman's statements [8] on the postwar boom and the analyses of his Council [9] seemed to arise from acceptance of the theory that all recessions are the product of underconsumption factors. Yet the recession of 1937–38, for one, was not caused by underconsumption since consumption expenditures apparently did not decline relative to personal income, nor were profit incomes inflated.

THE DANGER OF TOO SIMPLIFIED AN ANALYSIS OF BOTH THE CAUSES OF AND CONTROL OF BUSINESS FLUCTUATIONS

Not only does each business fluctuation appear to be unique with causes peculiar to it, but business fluctuations are the product of complex causes. It is too easy to ignore important changes in economic variables, if a single theory of the fluctuation is accepted. Just as preoccupation with the possible unfavorable effects of inflated profits on the economy could lead to a prescription for policy which might actually accelerate recessive forces, so the concentration upon, say, the relationship between wage income and personal incomes might lead to an incorrect assessment of the relative importance of the factors making for recession. For example, the President's advisers feared the emergence of recession in 1947–48 because the price rises during that period shifted income from wage earners to other groups in the economy. The propensity to consume of wage earners is said to be relatively higher than that of other income groups, and an income shift away from wage earners was expected to reduce total

8. Press conference reported in the *New York Times,* April 11, 1947, and talk before members of Associated Press, from *New York Times,* April 22, 1947.

9. Council of Economic Advisers, *First Annual Report to the President,* December 1946. This same observation has been made recently by Villard. See "The Council of Economic Advisers and Depression Policy," 600.

spending. But the reliability of this conclusion is open to question.

In the first place numerous writers have shown that there may be a substantial difference between the average propensities to consume of two income groups, but the differences between the marginal propensities to consume (and it is only these that are relevant when shifts in income are involved) are likely to be much less marked.[10]

But even more important than the fact that differences between marginal propensities to consume of various income groups may be slight is that it is questionable, and at least remains to be demonstrated, whether the marginal propensity to consume of wage earners is actually greater than that of certain other income groups.[11] Thus a substantial part of the shift away from wage earner income (1945–47) was in favor of unincorporated enterprise and farmers. And it is not at all certain that the marginal spending rates of farmers and small entrepreneurs differ greatly from that of wage earners in manufacturing. It may still be true, but the measurements in this field are extremely inadequate and inconclusive.

In the third place, the effects on investment decisions of either a marked increase or decrease in the flow of profit income are not at all certain. It was suggested in Chapter 14 that there is probably a profit rate beyond which increases in profits have less favorable effects on income through increasing investment expenditures than unfavorable effects through reduction of consumption expenditures. Likewise, it is possible that a decline below some minimum profit rate may lead to a greater contraction in investment expenditures than expansion in consumption expenditures.

Because marginal rather than average propensities to consume must be compared, because consumption expenditures may not be reduced by shifts from wage earners to other income groups, and because the impact of price rises on investment decisions is uncertain, any prescription for public policy based upon only one view of the wage-price relationship comes from too simple an appraisal of economic developments.

The only safeguard against errors which result from too simplified an approach to the problems of causation and control of business fluctuations would seem to be the recognition that each fluctuation is unique, and that developments in all the various segments of the economy must be studied extremely carefully. Acceptance of any particular theory or explanation of business fluctuations may preclude

10. Cf. Hansen, *Economic Policy and Full Employment* (New York, 1947); also, Harold Lubell, "Effects of Redistribution of Income on Consumers' Expenditures," *American Economic Review, 37* (1947), 157–170.

11. I am indebted to Max Millikan of Massachusetts Institute of Technology for this point.

asking the relevant questions and appraising objectively economic developments whatever their implications for the direction of appropriate public policy.

CLIMATE OF POLITICAL OPINION MORE FAVORABLE TODAY FOR BUSINESS DECISION

The above remarks have been critical of some recent diagnoses by government economists of economic conditions. However, since the period 1937–38 there have been some major changes which should make it easier for public policy to maintain reasonably full employment of resources during the next decade.

The unfavorable political and social opinion which was responsible for the sluggish response of investment expenditures to increased demand and investment opportunities in the thirties has been largely replaced by feelings of more general confidence about the future. The social reforms which were undertaken following the protracted and severe depression of 1929–32 have been effected. The social security program has been established and is a part of business decisions. The era of high individual and corporate income taxation has already been entered. There were actually moderate declines in both categories during the immediate postwar years. With the passage of the Taft-Hartley Labor Act in 1947 businessmen could no longer claim, as they have in the past, that labor legislation was unilateral in its support of labor rights. Any future changes in these areas must be at a greatly reduced pace compared with that in the thirties. The tempo of social reform has been slowed if not actually reduced to zero.

Above all, it must have become apparent to businessmen that the pendulum which by 1937–38 had swung far in the direction of anti-business feeling has begun its return movement. Private enterprise is still to be asked, as well as permitted, to carry the major responsibility for providing income and employment in the national economy. There are uncertainties, to be sure (and international instability is undoubtedly more important as a disquieting factor than in the thirties, at least in the United States), but one of these uncertainties is not the type of economy in which business decisions are to be made. There is a qualified but general acceptance in all groups of society that free private enterprise must still be the mainspring of the American economy in the foreseeable future.

RECOMMENDATIONS FOR PUBLIC POLICY

First of all, when public policy is aimed toward the maintenance of the flow of income and production, constant surveillance of certain specific areas is essential. Thus there must be a continual awareness of the extent to which the government is acting in its role of tax collector and public disburser to depress or to stimulate the level of income and production. A current series on net government contribution to income is a necessary tool of government policy.

Because there was no such series in 1937–38, most policy-makers and economists were unaware that the government was acting as a deflationary agent throughout 1937. In fact it was not until almost a year after net government contribution had begun its precipitate decline that professional economists generally learned of this development.[12]

In the second place, not only is a series on the net government financial position necessary in public policy formation but more reliable information is needed on the effects on investment and consumption of redirecting the flow of income from one group of income receivers to another. There appeared to be little appreciation of the problem of profits and the stimulation of investment expenditures in 1937. Instead, public policy was based on the belief that a change in the distribution of income, from wage earners to profits, was certain to reduce the flow of income. But more data and analysis in the area of consumer spending and the distribution and level of income are required before arriving at trustworthy conclusions for public policy.

Thirdly, careful consideration should also be given to various other economic series. Certainly the relationship between the rate of inventory accumulation, new orders, and sales should be intently watched. Additional data on inventories may very well be necessary since it would be desirable to have some way of estimating when the rate of accumulation of inventories is dangerously high in certain areas and may be leading to a serious overinvestment in inventories. Such information was not available in 1937. Some better indication must be had as to where inventories are building up in the production and distribution system and what kind of a relationship they can bear to consumer expenditures and incomes before they are excessive.

A fourth area which must be closely watched is the current profitability of investment and expectations about the future profitability of investment. In a system of free private enterprise adequate profits are the mainspring of the economy. Policy-makers must always be aware of the necessity for adequate profits and must shape policy consciously toward that end. Rising standards of living are obtained only through expanded capital equipment. Adequate profits are the means to that end and represent the least social cost for economic progress.

12. Thus Hansen's statement on "The Consequences of Reducing Expenditures," November 10, 1937, was the first real recognition of the problem. *Proceedings of the Academy of Political Science, 17* (1938), 466–478.

Finally, it is unfortunate that all the data which must be the basis for policy decision are *ex post*. It would be most desirable for policy-makers to know what the *ex ante* decisions are with respect to inventory investment, business expansion expenditures, consumer choices, etc. Government policy-makers are coming to face the necessity of obtaining sample opinion on proposed plans of business enterprises and consumer groups.[13] But lacking that, the careful use of the immediately available data should provide an intelligent guide to the appropriate public policy.

Important national policy decisions have to be made at the governmental level, and the experience in the 1937–38 period shows that very able men can make serious policy errors. However, most policy errors seem to result from a rigid adherence to theoretical or empirical dogmas and a failure to ask the right questions about economic developments. Therefore, a continual and comprehensive study of the movements of economic variables (with policy-makers content to accept whatever policies are appropriate to their findings) offers hope for avoiding many of the errors of the past. It is the way by which government policy-makers may act to promote and sustain a reasonably full employment of national resources.

13. Cf. "A National Survey of Liquid Assets," Pts. 1–3, *Federal Reserve Bulletin*, *32* (1946); "Survey of Consumer Finances," Pts. 1–3, *Federal Reserve Bulletin*, *33* (1947) and similar surveys in later issues. Cf. also regular surveys of planned business investment made by the Department of Commerce and published in the *Survey of Current Business*.

Bibliography

BOOKS

Abramovitz, Moses, *Inventories and Business Cycles, with Special Reference to Manufacturers' Inventories,* New York, National Bureau of Economic Research, 1950.

Angell, James W., *Investment and Business Cycles,* New York, McGraw-Hill, 1941.

Ayres, Leonard P., *Turning Points in Business Cycles,* New York, Macmillan, 1939.

Bank for International Settlements, *Eighth Annual Report,* Basle, 1938; and *Ninth Annual Report,* Basle, 1939.

Barger, Harold, *Outlay and Income in the United States, 1921–1938, Studies in Income and Wealth, 4,* New York, National Bureau of Economic Research, 1942.

Bauer, John, *National Welfare and Business Stability,* New York, Harper, 1940.

Beard, Charles and Mary A., *America in Midpassage, 1,* New York, Macmillan, 1939.

Bratt, Elmer C., *This Unbalanced World,* New York, Harper, 1940.

Brockie, Melvin D., "The Rally, Crisis, and Depression, 1935–38," unpublished doctoral dissertation, University of California, Los Angeles, June 1948.

Buehler, Alfred G., *The Undistributed Profits Tax,* New York, McGraw-Hill, 1937.

Burns, Arthur F., *New Facts on Business Cycles,* 30th Annual Report, New York, National Bureau of Economic Research, 1950.

Burns, Arthur F., and Mitchell, Wesley C., *Measuring Business Cycles,* New York, National Bureau of Economic Research, 1946.

Colm, Gerhard, and Lehmann, Fritz, *Economic Consequences of Recent American Tax Policy,* Supplement 1, Social Research, 1938.

Condliffe, J. B., *World Economic Survey, 1936/37,* Geneva, League of Nations, 1937.

Cowles, Alfred, *Common-Stock Indexes,* Cowles Commission for Research in Economics, Monograph No. 3, Bloomington, Indiana, Principia Press, 1939.

Dirlam, Joel, "The Regulation of Security Issues under the Public Utility Holding Company Act," unpublished doctoral dissertation, Yale University, 1947.

Eccles, Marriner S., *Economic Balance and a Balanced Budget,* a collection of Eccles' public papers, edited by R. L. Weissman, New York, Harper, 1940.

Einzig, Paul, *World Finance, 1938–1939,* New York, Macmillan, 1939.

Faÿ, Bernard, *Roosevelt and His America,* Boston, Little, Brown, 1933.

Federal Reserve Bank of New York, *23rd Annual Report,* 1937.

Fellner, William J., *Monetary Policies and Full Employment,* Berkeley, University of California Press, 1946.

Fine, Sherwood M., *Public Spending and Postwar Economic Policy,* New York, Columbia University Press, 1944.

Gilbert, Richard V., et al., *An Economic Program for American Democracy,* New York, Vanguard Press, 1938.

Gill, Corrington, *Wasted Manpower,* New York, W. W. Norton, 1939.

Goldsmith, R. W., and Salant, Walter, "The Volume and Components of Saving in the United States, 1933–1937," *Studies in Income and Wealth, 3,* Pt. 4, New York, National Bureau of Economic Research, 1939.

Haberler, Gottfried, *Consumer Installment Credit and Economic Fluctuations,* New York, National Bureau of Economic Research, 1942.

Hansen, Alvin H., *Economic Policy and Full Employment,* New York, McGraw-Hill, 1947.

   Fiscal Policy and Business Cycles, New York, W. W. Norton, 1941.

   Full Recovery or Stagnation? New York, W. W. Norton, 1938.

   Monetary Theory and Fiscal Policy, New York, McGraw-Hill, 1949.

Harris, Seymour E., *Economics of Social Security,* New York, McGraw-Hill, 1941.

Hart, Albert G., *Debts and Recovery,* New York, Twentieth Century Fund, 1937.

Hayes, Douglas A., "A Study of the Recession of 1937," unpublished doctoral dissertation, University of Michigan, 1949, later revised and published as *Business Confidence and Business Activity: A Case Study of the Recession of 1937,* Michigan Business Studies, *10,* No. 5, Ann Arbor, University of Michigan Press, 1951.

Hicks, J. R., *Value and Capital,* London, Oxford University Press, 1939.

Hopkins, Harry, *Spending to Save,* New York, W. W. Norton, 1936.

Ickes, Harold L., *Back to Work,* New York, Macmillan, 1935.

   The New Democracy, New York, W. W. Norton, 1934.

Jacoby, Neil, and Saulnier, R., *Term Lending to Business,* New York, National Bureau of Economic Research, 1942.

Johnson, G. Griffith, *The Treasury and Monetary Policy, 1933–1938,* Cambridge, Harvard University Press, 1939.

Kershner, Howard Eldred, *The Menace of Roosevelt and His Policies,* New York, Greenberg, Publisher, 1936.

Keynes, John M., *The General Theory of Employment, Interest and Money,* New York, Harcourt Brace, 1936.

Kuznets, Simon, *Commodity Flow and Capital Formation, 1,* New York, National Bureau of Economic Research, 1938.

Lange, Oscar, *Price Flexibility and Employment,* Cowles Commission for

Research in Economics, Monograph No. 8, Bloomington, Principia Press, 1944.

Lawrence, David, *Beyond the New Deal,* New York, Whittlesey House, 1934.

Ludwig, Emil, *Roosevelt: A Study in Fortune and Power,* New York, Viking, 1938.

Lund, Robert L., Coffin, Howard E., Burkett, Charles W., and Reeves, Earl, *Truth about the New Deal,* New York, Longmans, Green, 1936.

Lutz, Friedrick A., *Corporate Cash Balances,* New York, National Bureau of Economic Research, 1945.

Lynch, David, *The Concentration of Economic Power,* New York, Columbia University Press, 1940.

Machlup, Fritz A., *The Stock Market—Credit and Capital Formation,* New York, Macmillan, 1940.

Mack, Ruth, *The Flow of Business Funds and Consumer Purchasing Power,* New York, Columbia University Press, 1941.

Meade, J. E., *World Economic Survey, 1937/38* and *1938/39,* Geneva, League of Nations, 1938 and 1939.

Metzler, Lloyd A., "Three Lags in the Circular Flow of Income," *Income, Employment and Public Policy* (Essays in Honor of Alvin H. Hansen), New York, W. W. Norton, 1948.

Miller, John P., *Unfair Competition,* Cambridge, Mass., Harvard University Press, 1941.

Pricing of Military Procurements, New Haven, Yale University Press, 1949.

Mills, Frederick C., *Economic Tendencies in the United States,* New York, National Bureau of Economic Research, 1932.

Prices in Recession and Recovery, New York, National Bureau of Economic Research, 1936.

Moody's Industrials, Public Utilities, and Railroads, 1936 and 1937.

Moulton, Harold G., and Associates, *Capital Expansion, Employment, and Economic Stability,* Washington, Brookings Institution, 1940.

National Industrial Conference Board, *Studies in Enterprise and Social Progress,* New York, 1939.

Wages, Hours, and Employment in the United States, 1914–1936, New York, 1936.

Neal, Alfred C., *Industrial Concentration and Price Inflexibility,* Washington, American Council on Public Affairs, 1942.

Neilson, Francis, *Sociocratic Escapades,* New York, Putnam, 1934.

Nugent, Rolf, *Consumer Credit and Economic Stability,* New York, Russell Sage Foundation, 1939.

Nutter, G. Warren, *The Extent of Enterprise Monopoly in the United States, 1899–1939,* Chicago, University of Chicago Press, 1951.

Queeny, Edgar M., *The Spirit of Enterprise,* New York, Scribner's, 1943.

Schumpeter, Joseph A., *Business Cycles, 1* and *2,* New York, McGraw-Hill, 1939.

Silberling, Norman J., *The Dynamics of Business,* New York, McGraw-Hill, 1943.

Sweezy, Allan, Chapter on "Government Contribution," in *Economic Reconstruction,* edited by Seymour E. Harris, New York, McGraw-Hill, 1945.

Terborgh, George, *The Bogey of Economic Maturity,* Chicago, Machinery and Allied Products Institute, 1945.

Utley, S. Wells, *The American System: Shall We Destroy It?* Detroit, Speaker-Hines Press, 1936.

Villard, Henry H., *Deficit Spending and the National Income,* New York, Farrar and Rinehart, 1941.

Wallace, Henry A., *Whose Constitution: An Inquiry into the General Welfare,* New York, Reynal and Hitchcock, 1936.

Wernette, John Philip, *The Control of Business Cycles,* New York, Farrar and Rinehart, 1940.

Wilson, Thomas, *Fluctuations in Income & Employment,* London, Sir Isaac Pitman and Sons, Ltd., 1942.

ARTICLES, SPEECHES, AND MISCELLANEOUS

Abbott, Charles C., "Sources of Business Funds," *Review of Economics and Statistics, 28* (1946), 135–145.

Aldrich, Winthrop W., "Business Recession in Relation to Government Policy," *Bankers Magazine, 136* (1938), 120–121. Condensed from an address.

"Business Recovery and Government Policy," *Bankers Magazine, 134* (1937), 7. Condensed from an address.

American Federationist, "The Federation's Revised Unemployment Estimate," *43* (1936), 64–73; "Employment Gains Continue," *45* (1938), 1342–1345.

Ayres, Leonard P., "Is America Anemic?" *Bankers Magazine, 136* (1938), 380.

Bain, Joseph S., "The Profit Rate as a Measure of Monopoly Power," *Quarterly Journal of Economics, 55* (1940–41), 271–293.

Bankers Magazine, "A Perplexed Situation," *136* (1938), 369–374.

Bell, Philip W., "Federal Reserves Policy and the Recession of 1937–38; a Note," *Review of Economics and Statistics, 33* (1951), 349–350.

Bissell, Richard M., Jr., "The Rate of Interest," *Papers and Proceedings, American Economic Review, 28* (1938), 23–40.

Brockie, Melvin D., "Theories of the 1937–38 Crisis and Depression," *Economic Journal, 60* (1950), 292–310.

Commercial and Financial Chronicle, "The New Capital Flotations in the United States during the Month of December and for the Twelve Months of the Calendar Year 1936," *144,* Pt. 1 (1937), 166–175.

"The New Capital Flotations in the United States during the Month of December and for the First Six Months of the Calendar Year 1937," *145,* Pt. 1 (1937), 183–190.

143, Pt. 1 (1936), 315; *144,* Pt. 1 (1937), 323.

Crum, W. L., "Cyclical Changes in Corporate Profits," *Review of Economics and Statistics, 21* (1939), 49–61.

Crum, W. L., Gordon, R. A., and Wescott, Dorothy, "Review of the Year," *Review of Economics and Statistics, 20* (1938), 43–52.

Cummings, Homer S., "Preserving Democracy," Jackson Day Banquet Address, Stevens Hotel, Chicago (January 8, 1938).

Dunlop, John T., "Price Flexibility and the 'Degree of Monopoly,'" *Quarterly Journal of Economics, 53* (1938–39), 522–534.

Eccles, Marriner S., "Controlling Booms and Depressions," *Fortune* (April 1937), 88a–88d, 178–182.

Economist, 122–132 (1936–38). See especially: "American Deadlock," *131* (1938), 130–131; "Federal Reserve Policy," *129* (1937), 117–118; "The Economic Outlook in America," *129* (1937), 247–249; an editorial, "Priming the Pump Again," *131* (1938), 191–192; and "Wall Street Pathology," *128* (1937), 570–571.

Eddy, George, "The Present Status of New Security Issues," *Review of Economics and Statistics, 21* (1939), 116–121.

Edison Electric Institute, *Statistical Bulletin No. 5* (1937).

Elliott, D. C., "A Quarterly Series of Manufacturers' Inventories," *Journal of the American Statistical Association, 33* (1938), 349–352.

Elliston, H. B., "Blaming the Money Managers," *Atlantic Monthly, 162* (1938), 103–110.

Federal Reserve Bank of New York, Research Department, "Production and Trade Indexes" (June 1944).

Fellner, William, "The Technological Argument of the Stagnation Thesis," *Quarterly Journal of Economics, 55* (1940–41), 638–651.

Gayer, Arthur, "Fiscal Policies," *Papers and Proceedings, American Economic Review, 28* (1938), 90–112.

Gordon, Robert A., "Business Cycles in the Interwar Period: The 'Quantitative-Historical' Approach," *Papers and Proceedings, American Economic Review, 39* (1949), 47–63.

Hansen, Alvin H., "The Consequences of Reducing Expenditures," *Proceedings of the Academy of Political Science, 17* (1938), 446–478.

Hardy, Charles O., "An Appraisal of the Factors ('Natural' and 'Artificial') Which Stopped Short the Recovery Development in the United States," *Papers and Proceedings, American Economic Review, 29* (1939), 170–182.

Hart, Albert G., "Anticipations, Uncertainty, and Dynamic Planning," *Journal of Business, Studies in Business Administration, 11*, No. 1 (1940).

Henderson, Leon, Reports of radio addresses, *New York Times* (April 25, 1937), 19; (January 2, 1938), 2. Quoted in *New York Times* (July 17, 1938), 8.

Hough, T. E., "The 1937 Bond Market," *Bankers Magazine, 136* (1938), 60–63.

Ickes, Harold L., Report of radio address, *New York Times* (December 31, 1937).

Index (Svenska Handelsbanken), "Economic Survey," *12* (December 1937), 2.

Jackson, Robert, Report of radio address, *New York Times* (December 30, 1937), 6.

Johnson, Norris O., "Federal Reserve Bank of New York Indexes of Production and Trade," *Journal of the American Statistical Association, 36* (1941), 423–425.

"New Indexes of Production and Trade," *Journal of the American Statistical Association, 33* (1938), 341–348.

Kimmel, Lewis H. "Experience under the Undistributed Profits Tax," *Conference Board Bulletin, 11* (1937), 105–115.

"Social Security Finance," *Conference Board Bulletin, 11* (1937), 117–120.

Kuznets, Simon, "Commodity Flow and Capital Formation in the Recent Recovery and Decline, 1932–1938," Bulletin No. 74, National Bureau of Economic Research (1939).

Lerner, Abba P., "The Concept of Monopoly and the Measurement of Monopoly Power," *Review of Economic Studies, 1* (1934), 157–175.

Lewis, H. Gregg, *An Analysis of Changes in the Demand for Steel and in Steel Prices, 1936–1939,* United States Steel Corporation, 1939.

Lubell, Harold, "Effects of Redistribution of Income on Consumers' Expenditures," *American Economic Review, 37* (1947), 157–170.

Machlup, Fritz A., "Period Analysis and Multiplier Theory," *Quarterly Journal of Economics, 54* (1939–40), 1–27.

Metzler, Lloyd A., "Inventory Cycles in the United States, 1921–1938," unpublished paper.

Midland Bank Review, "The Slump in America: When Will It End?" (June–July 1938), 1–5.

Morgenthau, Henry, "Federal Spending and the Federal Budget," *Proceedings of the Academy of Political Science, 17* (1938), 534–542.

National City Bank of New York, *Monthly Letter,* 1936–38.

National Industrial Conference Board, "Employment and Unemployment of the Labor Force, 1900–1940," *Conference Board Economic Record, 2* (1940), 77–92.

"Inventories, Shipments, Orders, 1929–1940," *Supplement to Conference Board Economic Record, 2* (1940), 1–12.

Nixon, Russell A., and Samuelson, Paul A., "Estimates of Unemployment in the United States," *Review of Economics and Statistics, 22* (1940), 101–111.

Ohlin, Bertil, "Can World Prosperity be Maintained?" *Supplement to Index* (Svenska Handelsbanken), *12* (October 1937), 1–19.

Railway Age, "Railway Material Costs Up 17 Per Cent in 12 Months," *103* (1937), 791–792.

Review of Economic Statistics, 28 (1946), 197–224.

Roose, Kenneth D., "The Recession of 1937–38," *Journal of Political Economy, 56* (1948) 239–248.

"Federal Reserve Policy and the Recession of 1937–1938," *Review of Economics and Statistics, 32* (1950), 177–183.

"The Role of Net Government Contribution to Income in the Recession and Revival of 1937–38," *Journal of Finance, 6* (1951), 1–18.

Roosevelt, Franklin D., "Madison Square Garden Campaign Address of October 31, 1936," *New York Times* (November 1, 1936), 36.

"Message to Congress Calling for an Investigation of the Concentration of Economic Power" (April 29, 1938), *New York Times* (April 30, 1938), 2.

"Statement on Prices and Wages" (April 24, 1937), *New York Times* (April 25, 1937), 19.

Rothschild, K. W., "The Degree of Monopoly," *Economica, New Series 9* (1942), 24–39.

Sachs, Alexander, "The Financial Dynamics of the Recovery since 1933 and Latest Constriction Phase in Capital Flow," *Financial Management Series,* No. 53, American Management Association, 1938, 13–31.

Samuelson, Paul A., "Fiscal Policy and Income Determination," *Quarterly Journal of Economics, 56* (1941–42), 575–605.

"The Theory of Pump-Priming Reëxamined," *American Economic Review, 30* (1940), 492–506.

Schwellenbach, Lewis B., "Depression or Recession," *Vital Speeches of the Day, 4* (1938), 465–467.

Simpson, Kemper, "Securities Markets and the Investment Process," *Papers and Proceedings, American Economic Review, 28* (1938), 41–55.

Slichter, Sumner H., "The Downturn of 1937," *Review of Economics and Statistics, 20,* (1938), 97–110.

"Corporate Price Policies as a Factor in the Recent Business Recession," *Proceedings of the Academy of Political Science, 18,* No. 2 (1939), 20–33.

"Must We Have Another Boom?" *Atlantic Monthly, 159* (1937), 600–607.

Standard and Poor's Corporation, *Long Term Security Price Index Record.*

Thorp, Willard L., "The Undistributed Profits Tax," *Financial Management Series,* No. 53, American Management Association, 1938, 11–12.

—— and George, Edwin B., "An Appraisal of the Undistributed Profits Tax," *Duns' Review, 45* (September 1937), 5–36.

Villard, Henry H., "The Council of Economic Advisers and Depression Policy," *American Economic Review, 40* (1950), 600–604.

Wagemann, E., "Le Problème des prix dans l'économie mondiale," *Revue économique internationale, 30* (1938), 427–452.

Wall Street Journal, "Yield on U. S. Treasury Notes" (February 26, 1937), 14.

Weston, John Frederick, "The Economics of Competitive Bidding in the Sale of Securities," *Journal of Business, Studies in Business Administration, 13*, No. 1 (1943), 1–51.

Woodward, Donald B., "Changes in Capital Financing," *Journal of the American Statistical Association, 33* (1938), 12–20.

Woolfson, A. Philip, "Our New Depression—What Can We Do about It?" *Bankers Magazine, 136* (1938), 101–112.

U. S. GOVERNMENT PUBLICATIONS

Board of Governors of the Federal Reserve System, *Eighteenth Annual Report* (1931); *Twenty-second Annual Report* (1935); *Twenty-third Annual Report* (1936); and *Twenty-fourth Annual Report* (1937).

Banking and Monetary Statistics, 1943.

Federal Reserve Bulletin, 22–25 (1936–39), *27* (1941), *30* (1944), and *32–39* (1946–53).

"Objectives of Monetary Policy," *23* (1937), 827–828. "A National Survey of Liquid Assets," Pt. 1, *32* (1946), 574–580; Pt. 2, *32* (1946), 716–722; Pt. 3, *32* (1946), 844–855. "Survey of Consumer Finances," Pt. 1, *33* (1947), 647–661; Pt. 2, *33* (1947), 788–802; Pt. 3, *33* (1947), 951–962.

Chawner, Lowell J., *Residential Building,* Housing Monograph Series No. 1, 1939.

Commerce, Department of; Bureau of Foreign and Domestic Commerce, *Survey of Current Business, Supplement, 1932, 1936, 1938, 1940,* and *National Income Supplement, 1951.* Also *Survey of Current Business,* selected monthly issues, 1933 and 1936–42, for various statistical series.

Commerce, Secretary of; *Twenty-seventh Annual Report,* 1939.

Congress; Senate, Special Committee to Investigate Unemployment and Relief, *Hearings,* S. Res. 36, 75th Congress, 3d Session, *1* (January 4–22, 1938) and *2* (February 28–April 8, 1938).

Congress; Temporary National Economic Committee, *Hearings,* 76th Congress, 1st Session, Pt. 9 (1940); 3d Session, Pt. 10-A (1940).

Council of Economic Advisers, *Annual Report to the President* (1946–53).

Holthausen, Duncan McC., "Monthly Estimates of Short-Term Consumer Debt, 1929–42," *Survey of Current Business* (November 1942), 9–25.

Labor, Department of; Bureau of Labor Statistics, *Wholesale Prices 1913 to 1927, Bulletin No. 473.*

Revised Indexes of Factory Employment and Pay Rolls 1919 to 1933, Bulletin No. 610.

Means, Gardiner, "Industrial Prices and Their Relative Inflexibility," Senate Document No. 13, 74th Congress, 1st Session (1935).

National Resources Committee, *The Structure of the American Economy,* Pt. 1 (June 1939), Pt. 2 (May 1940).

Nelson, Saul and Keim, Walter G., *Price Behavior and Business Policy,* Temporary National Economic Committee, Monograph No. 1 (1940).

Painter, Mary S., "Estimates of Gross National Product, 1919–1928," *Federal Reserve Bulletin, 31* (1945), 872–873.

Securities and Exchange Commission, *Security Issues of Electric and Gas Utilities, 1935–1940* (1941) ; *Second Annual Report* (1936) ; *Third Annual Report* (1937).

Shelton, William C., and Paradiso, Louis J., "Monthly Estimates of Total Consumer Expenditures, 1935–42," *Survey of Current Business* (October 1942), 8–14.

Social Security Board, *Social Insurance Financing in Relation to Consumer Incomes and Expenditures,* Bureau Memorandum No. 63 (1946).

  Unemployment Compensation, What and Why? Publication No. 14 (March 1937).

Taitel, Martin, *Profits, Productive Activities and New Investment,* Temporary National Economic Committee, Monograph No. 12 (1941).

Terborgh, George, "Estimated Expenditures for New Durable Goods, 1919–1938," *Federal Reserve Bulletin, 25* (1939), 731–736.

Treasury Department ; *Treasury Bulletin* (March 1944), 58–59.

INDEX OF NAMES

INDEX OF TOPICS AND ORGANIZATION